Al Musalla Prize 2025

Rooted Transience

عابر متجذّر

Edited by Nawaf bin Ayyaf and Faysal Tabbarah

المحـــرران نـوّاف بن عيّاف وفيصَـل طبّـــارة

Diriyah Biennale Foundation 2025

Rooted Transience

This book is published on the occasion of *Rooted Transience,* an exhibition at the Abbazia di San Gregorio, a collateral event at the 19th International Architecture Exhibition – La Biennale di Venezia, titled *Intelligens. Natural. Artificial. Collective.* from May 7–November 26, 2025.

Editors: Nawaf bin Ayyaf and Faysal Tabbarah

Research Assistant: Omar Darwish
English Copyediting and Proofreading: Zeina Assaf
Arabic Translations: Dr Mohamed Ait Mihoub
Arabic Copyediting: Mohammad Hamdan
Color Separation: Nadim Zablit, -scope Atelier

Designer: bytwo
Publisher: Kaph Books

Distribution in Europe:

Les Presses du Réel
35 rue Colson
21000 Dijon
France
www.lespressesdureel.com

Idea Books
Nieuwe Hemweg 6R
1013 BG Amsterdam
The Netherlands
www.ideabooks.nl

Distribution in the Middle-East:

CIEL Book Distribution
3rd Interchange, Al Quoz Industrial I
P.O.Box 282005
Dubai, UAE
www.ciel.me

MuseumShops Company / HAAL
Prince Turki Ibn Abdulaziz Al Awwal Rd,
Al Mohammadiyyah, Dooryard 1st floor
Riyadh, KSA

Distribution in the Americas, Asia and Australia:

ARTBOOK | D.A.P.75 Broad Street,
Suite 630
New York, NY 10004
www.artbook.com

Papers used in this publication are FSC® certified, sourced from responsibly managed forests, recycled materials, and/or controlled sources.

The publisher gratefully acknowledges permission granted to reproduce the copyrighted images in this book. Every effort has been made to contact copyright holders and to obtain their permission for the use of copyrighted images. The publishers apologize for any errors or omissions in the above list and would be grateful if notified of any corrections that should be incorporated in any future reprints or editions of this publication.

Printed by Editoriale Bortolazzi-Stei,
Verona, Italy

ISBN: 978-614-8035-75-3

Foreword
HE Rakan Altouq 6
Aya Al-Bakree 8

Editorial Notes
On the Hajj Terminal 10
On AlMusalla Prize 26

Prologue

Faysal Tabbarah 30
Oscillations, Traces, Entanglements, and Aspirations

Historical Threads

Reflection Nasser Rabbat 45
Musalla: The Spatiality of a Sonic Term

Conversation Farrokh Derakhshani with Sumaya Dabbagh 46
On Reclaiming Heritage, Today

Reflection Khaled Azzam 61
The Primordial Musalla

Material Entanglements

Conversation Ali Malkawi with Elias and Yousef Anastas 64
On the Lightness of Stone

Reflection Wesam Al Asali 77
Grounds, Rituals, Skies

Conversation Azra Akšamija with Sahel AlHiyari 78
On Landscape as Space, Landscape as Material

Reflection Hanif Kara 93
Technology Whispers Quietly

Contemporary Aspirations

Conversation Lina Ghotmeh with Asif Khan 96
On Light and Craft

Reflection Ziad Jamaleddine 109
Without a Drawing, but not Without History

Spotlight On Weaving 111
Winning Proposal

Conversation Nawaf bin Ayyaf *with* Nicolas Fayad and Charles Kettaneh + Rayyane Tabet + Christopher Blust 148
On Intertwined Thinking

Reflection Noura Al Sayeh-Holtrop 169
Beyond the Religious Soundscape

Epilogue

Nawaf bin Ayyaf 170
Juxtapositions, Paradoxes, Dichotomies, and Reclamations

Snapshots of *Al Musalla Prize* 184
Biographies 186
Acknowledgments 192

Foreword

HE Rakan Altouq

The Assistant Minister of Culture, Saudi Arabia
Vice Chairman of the Board of Trustees,
Diriyah Biennale Foundation

The art of architecture and placemaking can best be described as the confluence of tangible structures and intangible human interaction. Islamic civilizations from the Kingdom of Saudi Arabia to the historic Andalus have constructed architectural wonders inspired by and in the service of Islam's teachings. These spaces create community, foster reflection, and transcend time to bind the past with the present. They exist at the intersection of the tangible and the intangible.

The Hajj Terminal, home to the Diriyah Biennale Foundation's Islamic Arts Biennale, is an excellent example of how form and function can converge to create a space that serves and strengthens its community.

As the gateway to Islam's holiest site, Makkah Al Mukarramah, the canopied structure worked with the natural environment to provide pilgrims with a place to gather, worship, and reflect. This interaction between people and place, structure and purpose, is what made the Hajj Terminal the perfect canvas for the Islamic Arts Biennale.

In keeping with this spirit, we launched the *AlMusalla Prize*, inviting artists and architects to reimagine what a prayer space could look like. This architectural competition, grounded in tradition but aimed at innovation, is in line with the ethos of the Islamic Arts Biennale and its central purpose: to celebrate Islamic Art in the most diverse and inclusive way possible, while also creating spaces and opportunities for the medium to innovate and evolve.

Architectural works shape our interactions and mold our communities. They offer a canvas where people can find expression and connection. It is impossible to go to the Hajj Terminal without feeling a sense of peace. Looking out at the canopies that seemingly stretch out endlessly across the horizon, the power of a place to drive a human purpose can be tangibly felt. It is my hope that the *AlMusalla Prize* continues to push the boundaries of how places can best inspire spirituality and reflection, while also bringing us together.

I would like to extend my heartfelt congratulations to the winners of the inaugural competition: EAST Architecture Studio, Rayyane Tabet, and engineering firm AKT II. I would also like to thank the esteemed members of the architectural jury — Farrokh Derakhshani, Lina Ghotmeh, Azra Akšamija, and Ali Malkawi, chaired by Prince Nawaf bin Ayyaf — for their diligence in running the competition and judging the entries.

We hope you will enjoy reading about this unique prize and will look forward to our next edition in 2027.

Foreword

Aya Al-Bakree

CEO, The Diriyah Biennale Foundation

From its inception, the Islamic Arts Biennale has sought to redefine how the lives of Muslims and Islamic culture are represented by interweaving arts and culture with the rich expressions of faith and practice. Spaces for visitors to pray and reflect while at the biennale have been as integral to our planning as our presentation of the contemporary art and historical objects that are featured in the exhibitions.

For this second edition, under the leadership of HE Rakan Altouq, Vice Chairman of the Board of Trustees, the Diriyah Biennale Foundation and the Assistant Minister of Culture of the Kingdom of Saudi Arabia, we have launched an international architecture competition: *AlMusalla Prize*. Through the inauguration of this prize, which will become a regular feature of the Islamic Arts Biennale, we highlight the importance of architecture as an essential aspect of "Islamic Arts" and a contemporary form of cultural expression that we intend to both celebrate and cultivate.

We asked architectural studios competing for this prize to work collaboratively with engineers and artists to develop a practical space for prayer, that also has a compelling design aesthetic given the *musalla's* prominent location in the biennale's landscape.

The Islamic Arts Biennale presents both traditional crafts and artistic expression in the world today, so the *musalla's* design needed to consider both traditional craftsmanship and contemporary fabrication techniques – encouraging manufacturing innovation to deliver a sustainable and reusable pavilion.

I would like to thank the competition jury's chair, Prince Nawaf bin Ayyaf and its members: Azra Akšamija, Farrokh Derakhshani, Lina Ghotmeh, and Ali Malkawi, for their time, insights, and dedication.

The winner of the 2025 *AlMusalla Prize*, EAST Architecture Studio, in collaboration with artist Rayyane Tabet and engineering firm AKT II, developed a design that captured the jury's attention. The proposal focuses on adopting regionally sourced, natural materials to produce the components necessary for their contemporary space, encapsulating a *musalla's* simplicity of spirit and purpose. Such spaces were first created centuries ago, from similar natural resources.

This publication captures a sense of the conversations, concepts, and visions that went into making the first edition of this prize. I hope it will capture your imagination and encourage you to see the winning structure in person in Jeddah.

Editorial Notes

On the *Hajj Terminal*

وَأَذِّن فِي ٱلنَّاسِ بِٱلْحَجِّ يَأْتُوكَ رِجَالًا وَعَلَىٰ كُلِّ ضَامِرٍ يَأْتِينَ مِن كُلِّ فَجٍّ عَمِيقٍ

[سورة الحج : ٢٧]

"And proclaim to mankind the Hajj (pilgrimage). They will come to you on foot and on every lean camel, they will come from every deep and distant (wide) mountain highway (to perform Hajj)." Holy Qu'ran (22:27)

In 2022, over 12 million pilgrims traveled through King Abdulaziz International Airport as they began their Hajj and Umrah journeys. While awaiting their buses, many admired the terminal's tent-shaped roofs, reminiscent of the tents at Mina. However, few knew the remarkable story of the terminal's creation and its architectural significance.

By 1970, the influx of pilgrims into Saudi Arabia was rising dramatically, prompting the government to find ways to accommodate and transport hundreds of thousands arriving by air each year. Hajj requires specific timing and location, presenting unique logistical challenges.

Prince Sultan bin Abdulaziz Al Saud, then Minister of Defense and Aviation, commissioned the development of an airport terminal equipped with the necessary facilities. General Saeed Y. Amin, Director of the International Airports Project, was tasked with overseeing this initiative. The design needed to shield pilgrims from the hot and humid desert climate, and provide essential services such as food, restrooms, banking, immigration, and baggage claim.

The architectural firm Skidmore, Owings & Merrill (SOM) was chosen to lead the design, alongside a consortium of global engineers and contractors led by Gordon Bunshaft. The challenge was distinct: for most of the year, the terminal would be empty, yet it needed to efficiently accommodate a massive influx of people for one month each year. The initial design was impractical due to high energy costs and inefficiencies in processing passengers.

Bunshaft proposed an innovative solution: 210 semi-conical, Teflon-coated fiberglass roof units, each 45 meters wide, designed to resemble a cluster of tents. Unlike traditional tents, these roofs were elevated 20 meters above ground, supported by steel cables and concrete pylons. The realization of this design fell to Fazlur Rahman Khan, SOM's chief engineer. A prominent Bangladeshi-American civil engineer, Khan was known for his pioneering work in high-rise construction. He understood the terminal's unique role as a gateway to Makkah al-Mukarramah, emphasizing a welcoming environment that respected the spiritual journey of the pilgrims. His design prioritized shaded, communal spaces over enclosed, artificially cooled areas, drawing on traditional Arabian shelter forms.

Completed in 1981, the Hajj Terminal became part of King Abdulaziz International Airport, spanning 450,000 square meters with the largest roof of its kind in the world. Two years later, it received the Aga Khan Award for Architecture for its elegant design. Tragically, Falzur Rahman Khan passed away shortly after the terminal opened, unable to witness the recognition of his visionary work.

Hosting the Islamic Arts Biennale and inaugural *AlMusalla Prize* at the HajjTerminal serves as a tribute to its architectural and engineering brilliance. It also offers an opportunity for locals and visitors to engage with this iconic building and appreciate its significance.

Through the Hajj Terminal, Fazlur Rahman Khan puts forward a radical spatial and material practice that mirrors the spirit of *Al Musalla Prize*, as well as the research, reflections, and conversations collated within this book.

Despite the Terminal's many technical complexities, born primarily out of the project's size, Khan's solution developed from a simple conceptual approach to the problem that is deeply rooted in its cultural context. Second, Khan's solution transforms the Terminal into a place that encourages transience: It is a place of prayer and of arrival, but it is also a market, a communal food hall, and a place of waiting. It is all these things at the same time, transforming for the needs of the people it shelters. Another entanglement seen throughout Khan's career in general, but more specifically and intensely in the Hajj Terminal, is the complex and transient entanglement between architect, engineer, and place. In embodying all these entanglements, the Hajj Terminal becomes an apt place to start thinking about the role of *musalla* spaces in our contemporary condition.

Khan's radical spatial and material practice is vividly portrayed in the following set of archival photographs of the Terminal's assembly, infrequently seen when compared with the now iconic silhouette. Thus, these photographs shed light on the Hajj Terminal in a process of becoming a universal place rooted in culture.

CONDOR

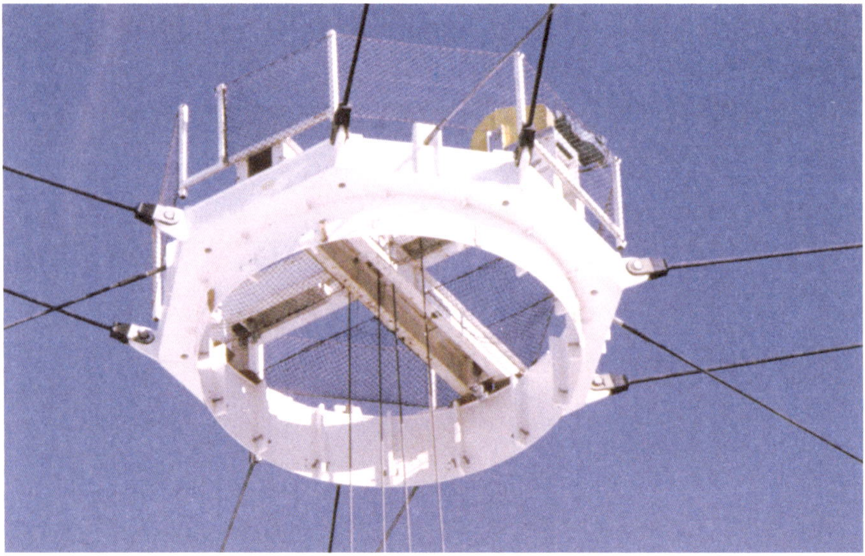

Editorial Notes

On *Al Musalla Prize*

The inaugural *AlMusalla Prize 2025* was awarded for the design of a modular space for prayer and contemplation open to Muslims and non-Muslims alike. Integrating faith, art, and architecture, the *musalla* will form part of the second edition of the Islamic Arts Biennale – the first biennale dedicated to the arts of Islamic civilization.

Inspired by the historical, cultural, and architectural significance of the biennale's iconic site – the SOM-designed and Aga Khan Award-winning Hajj Terminal in Jeddah – the *AlMusalla Prize* celebrates the ideas of diverse architectural teams from different cultures and backgrounds.

For the prize, the Diriyah Biennale Foundation (DBF) wished to curate a diverse longlist of talented architects and designers inspired by, and interested in, making, whether through handcrafting or digital fabrication practices. DBF also sought architects with the cultural sensibility to engage conceptually with the *musalla* building typology, able to balance its dual purpose as a space with a spiritual dimension, as well as an earthly place for cultural and social interaction.

In particular, DBF was able to curate a mix of emerging and established studios and encouraged diversity – a third of the longlisted studios were based in the Arab world, and 38 percent were female-led or female co-led. These considerations resulted in a longlist of over a hundred studios, from thirty-six different countries, across six continents, who were invited to participate in the competition that was managed by Malcolm Reading Consultants. Eighty-three firms expressed initial interest and fifty-six made a submission. Each outlined their proposal for the requested collaborative team, gave relevant project case studies, and presented a dedicated thought piece on the theme of Islamic art and architecture. After a thorough review of these initial submissions, the jury chair and the DBF advisory panel decided on a shortlist of five studios to advance to the competition's design stage. The list of shortlisted architects was comprised of AAU Anastas, Asif Khan, Dabbagh Architects, EAST Architecture Studio, and Office of Sahel AlHiyari for Architecture.

The shortlisted firms were given DBF's detailed brief, which synthesized the strategic vision and programmatic requirements, and had the opportunity to tour Jeddah and visit the Hajj Terminal site early in the nine-week design process. The brief was crafted around four themes: intertwining art and architecture; openness to diverse cultural and artistic expression; integrating traditional artisanship and crafts with contemporary making and expression; and ensuring the *musalla's* long-term sustainability after the biennale.

Competitors were asked to apply a contemporary lens on traditional *musalla* design to create a concept design that was structurally and architecturally innovative, embracing the use of cutting-edge technologies and fast-track construction, all while being sensitive to the historical elements and local contexts. Ideas that would realize the *musalla's* sustainable legacy were a priority of the competition's technical brief. Hence, design proposals were accompanied by a strategy for their post-biennale use: it was left open as to whether it would be relocated permanently, become a touring installation, or have an entirely different use.

Choosing the Winner

The competition's jury brought together an esteemed group of local and international design leaders: Nawaf bin Ayyaf (Jury Chair), Azra Akšamija, Farrokh Derakhshani, Lina Ghotmeh, and Ali Malkawi. Collectively, the group presented vast knowledge on an array of topics related to the core mission of this prize: grounded expertise from the creative arts industry, academic expertise of Islamic arts/architecture, the know-how of an established practicing architect with contextual familiarity, and the fabrication expertise to cover the sustainability and assembly/disassembly component.

The jury convened in June 2024 to interview the shortlisted competitors. After presentations from each team, the jury deliberated on the design quality of all five proposals. They scrutinized and discussed both the merits and concerns against the evaluation criteria: foregrounding the *musalla's* architectural identity, its contribution to Islamic art and architecture, technical and innovative rigor, sustainability, and legacy. After an enthusiastic discussion, a consensus emerged around EAST Architecture Studio's competition submission, entitled *On Weaving*. This proposed an exemplary design concept: presenting the sustainable reuse of date palms as the material for crafting the *musalla's* structure and textile cladding.

The jury members unanimously agreed to recommend EAST Architecture Studio's proposal to His Excellency Rakan Altouq as the winner of the *Al-Musalla Prize 2025*, with a commendation awarded to the runner-up, Asif Khan Studio.

Prologue
Oscillations, Traces, Entanglements, and Aspirations

Faysal Tabbarah

Oscillations

Thinking about the *musalla,*[1] especially through the lens of the built environmont, is a joyfully labyrinthine journey. Does one think about it as a physical space, an object, or a phenomenon? If as a physical space, does one examine it as a solitary space for a single person, or as a celebratory and communal space for many people? Is it a space for arrival, transition, or departure? If it is an object, does one study it as an assemblage of materials, or observe the communal assemblies it enables? Is it built, transformed, or imagined? If it is considered a phenomenon, does one trace its past, search for it in the present, or imagine its future? Oscillating between these very distant edges, it maintains an elusiveness that reveals new worlds for us to explore, making its presence known in the subtle traces it leaves behind in the individuals that occupy it as a space, and object, and a phenomenon.

[1] *Musalla* (pl. *musalla*yaat) is translated from Arabic meaning Islamic prayer space.

In the hadith tradition, the Prophet Muhammed (PBUH) tells us that: "The earth has been made a place of prostration and a means of purification for me, so wherever a man of my Ummah is when the time of prayer comes, let him pray" (Sunan an-Nasa'i 736). *Musalla* spaces sprout whenever and wherever the need for individual or communal prayer arises. By adapting to their immediate physical and temporal environments and reimagining architectures that quite literally dissolve, delineators of *musalla* spaces challenge static spatial and material practices that are foundational to the architectural canon. In the past and present, these practices result in a wide variety of objects and spaces, from a *khumra*, a rug woven from palm fronds and laid on the ground by a traveler pausing momentarily for respite, to repurposed urban conditions transformed into temporary prayer spaces by a few, to the most expansive open fields, such as those used during E'id, typically on the outskirts of urban agglomerations.

Regardless of how one chooses to approach the subject of the *musalla,* it enables us to imagine alternatively built environments by reorienting us toward spatial and material practices rooted in transience.

Traces

Where then, do we uncover the traces of the *musalla's* story to imagine the many possible worlds it wants us to look at? I found this even blurrier than I initially expected, continuing down the misty labyrinthine path. When I started to conceptualize this book, I sat down to do what I usually do when confronted with a project deeply rooted in material histories and cultures – look for hints about its nature in the archives. Almost immediately, I was struck with a realization: How can I find a record for something that is fleeting in nature? While I intuitively understood that *musalla* spaces are transient, shifting, and moving, the archive pointed me toward the *musalla's* quotidian ubiquity. Thus, to try and read its story, I found myself looking not for identifiable objects or spaces, but for images of daily life.

This reminds me of how archaeologists seek to understand the ways in which Bronze Age nomadic pastoralist communities shaped their landscapes for habitation and interaction. One such example is the difference between traces that identify the past existence of semi-subterranean houses and ephemeral structures. Whereas the former is identified through remnants of its stone foundations, ephemeral structures, are identified through the faintest traces they leave behind, such as oval-shaped patches in the grass and barely much else, only to be corroborated by chemical analysis.[2]

[2] Michael D. Frachetti, "Variability and Dynamic Landscapes of Mobile Pastoralism in Ethnography and Prehistory," in *The Archaeology of Mobility: Old World and New World Nomadism*, ed. Hans Barnard (Los Angeles: Cotsen Institute of Archaeology, 2008), 366 - 396. First found in Christiane Gruber, "Islamic Architecture on the Move," in *Islamic Architecture on the Move: Motion and Modernity*, ed. Christiane Gruber (Chicago, IL: Intellect, The University of Chicago Press, 2016): 1-24.

Coupling the *musalla's* quotidian ubiquity – coming into existence through use or rootedness – with transience, enables us to imagine new worlds that run against the grain of the architectural canon, both in theory and practice. Thus, I will try to read these potential new worlds through three traces I was eventually able to glean.

↑ Bahrein: The Tombs, 1918, Photo by Edwin Aubrey Storrs-Fox. Photo Credit: [15-b] (1/1), British Library: India Office Records and Private Papers, Photo 496/6/30, in *Qatar Digital Library.*

↖ Bahrein: The Tombs, 1918, Photo by Edwin Aubrey Storrs-Fox. Photo Credit: [16-a] (1/1), British Library: India Office Records and Private Papers, Photo 496/6/31, in *Qatar Digital Library.*

I found the first traces in a bound photo book, a collection of forty-eight black and white silver gelatin photographs taken by a certain Rev. Edwin Aubrey Storrs-Fox. The collection documents his travels within the Arabian Peninsula between 1916 and 1918, with his trip potentially originating in Karachi. The accidental diptych I am sharing here, presumably taken on the same day in February 1918, is set within the Dilmun Burial Mounds in Bahrain, now a UNESCO World Heritage Site. In the first photo, taken from a relatively high vantage point, possibly from atop one of the mounds, we see an expanse of the burial hills across the horizon. To the left of the photo, within a flat area between the mounds, we see three men and three donkeys (although Storrs-Fox's inscription suggests two donkeys). While it is very difficult to ascertain given the distance from which the photo was taken, it appears that one of the men is in so-called European clothing.

In the second photo, taken from a different location and toward another orientation, we see a thick band of palm groves in the distance, and possibly a human settlement to the left of the photo. Here, the mounds are much closer together, enabling a set of intimate spaces to be occupied by two men and three donkeys. The man in the suit is nowhere within the frame, and Storrs-Fox tells us that "at [the] center a man appears to be kneeling, perhaps praying."[3]

[3] Rev. Edwin Aubrey Storrs-Fox, "Bahrein: The Tombs, 1916-1918," *QDL*, February 8, 2025. https://www.qdl.qa/en/archive/81055/vdc_100023814039.0x000026

↑ "Süssigkeitskrämer" Photographer: Christiaan Snouck Hurgronje, British Library: India Office Records and Private Papers, 1781.b.6/55, in *Qatar Digital Library.*

If Storrs-Fox is accurate in his description, he documented a manifestation of the *musalla,* a space that is simultaneously expansive and intimate, appearing in the moment, leaving no archaeological evidence within a storied archeological site.

At other times, I had to glean the traces of the *musalla* in the things that are associated with prayer, as though they wanted to remind us of their meaning. For example, in one instructive photo by Christiaan Snouck Hurgronje (1857–1936), a Dutch Orientalist with a wide collection of sepia-colored portraits taken during his year-long stay in Jeddah and Makkah, between 1884 and 1885, we see a full-length portrait of a street vendor in Jeddah captioned "Süssigkeitskrämer" meaning "sweets seller."

In this photo, a man leans on a rectangular tray, supported by a stand that is an ad-hoc assembly of what appears to be found tree branches, triangulated and bound together by rope, creating an intuitively rigid structure. Snouck Hurgronje sees "many sticks topped with bird-like and other shapes stand perpendicular from the tray. A pile of wider stalks can be seen on the left of the tray." The entangled pile of "wider stalks" appears to be *miswak*, and Hurgronje suggests the same, if not assertively. *Miswak* is a teeth-cleaning twig of the *Salvadora persica*, or the toothbrush tree, an evergreen native to the Arabian Peninsula, the Indian Subcontinent, and Africa. In Islam, miswak is typically used in the prescribed ablution practices prior to prayer.

Many details in the photo embody the essence of the *musalla* space, even in its physical absence. Materially, the stand itself, put together intuitively out of found material to serve a particular function mimics the ways in which assembled musallayaat appear. Conceptually, the presence of the miswak with a street vendor points to the ubiquity and transience of prayer spaces within this urban landscape.

I picked up the threads of the third trace from a 1964 video showing a train car that was transformed into a prayer space for railway workers in the German town of Helmstedt.[4] In this short video, no longer than 90 seconds, we see a group of six railway workers taking a break to pray inside of a train car. Sharing a single prayer mat, they are positioned behind a man leading the prayers.

This impromptu prayer car has a particularly unique precursor: the dedicated *musalla* car on at least one of the Hejaz Railway trains.[5] The Hejaz Railway, an Ottoman project that began construction in 1900, ran between Damascus and Madinah until its disruption during the First World War. One of its aims was to facilitate the pilgrimage between Istanbul and Makkah for the annual Hajj. Its prayer car was documented by historian Richard Tourret, as follows:

> *"Coach No 13, the famous mosque car specially built at Constantinople Arsenal and fitted with a 6'4ft high collapsible minaret (!) had a large open floor area for kneeling to pray, and a lavatory."* [6]

↓ The Hejaz Railway Musalla Car shown on the cover of a 1907 issue of the Servet-i Fünun. From Gülseren Mungan Yavuztürk Archive. [7]

Another thing that makes the *musalla* car fitting for discussion within our context is its own absence. In photo after photo of the Hejaz Railway trains, across different landscapes and times, from entering a tunnel en route between Amman and Kassir, crossing a bridge in Ma'an, – one of the four purpose-built bridges along the route to avoid flash floods – to arriving in Tabuk on the station's opening day, the *musalla* car is rarely seen.

Given the speed at which we move today between distant places, the prayer car has itself transformed and become more permanent, occupying dedicated, indelible, and enclosed spaces within places such as transit stations, shopping malls, and other institutions. Through the three traces I have described, we can see the entanglements between the historical threads that the *musalla* points us to and its transition into a uniquely contemporary space given social, economic, technological, and material transformations.

Thus, the simple answer to my self-imposed question about where I can uncover the traces of the *musalla's* story has a relatively simple answer: The *musalla* can be traced everywhere, I just had to unlearn some of my acquired methods and look for it through the mist. This is an invitation for you, the reader, to do the same.

[4] AP Archive, "Can 99 Mobile Mosque," YouTube video, 1:30:00, https://www.youtube.com/watch?v=vwnN1EupM_o&ab_channel=APArchive

[5] Richard Tourret uses to the term *mosque* car, but I have chosen the *musalla* car given the distinctions this book draws between both kinds of spaces; For an account of the prayer car see David Simonowitz, "The Mobile Matrix: The Hijaz Railway as Ritual Space and Generator of Space" in *Islamic Architecture on the Move: Motion and Modernity*, ed. Christiane Gruber (Chicago, IL: Intellect, The University of Chicago Press, 2016): 61-100.

[6] Richard Tourret, *Hedjaz Railway* (Abingdon: Tourret Publishing, 1989), 55.

[7] *"First Train to Medina,"* Kent Ve Demiryolu, accessed February 2, 2025, https://kentvedemiryolu.com/medineye-ilk-tren-mo-1908/

Entanglements

This book, entitled *Rooted Transience,* is published as part of the inaugural *Al Musalla Prize 2025,* itself part of the Islamic Arts Biennale, which was awarded to a uniquely multidisciplinary team consisting of EAST Architecture Studio, Rayyane Tabet, and AKT II. Accompanying the book is an exhibition with the same title, taking place at the Abbazia San Gregorio, along with the Venice Architecture Biennale 2025.

Through both the book and the exhibition, *Rooted Transience* highlights the transient nature of *musalla* spaces as flexible sites of assembly and assemblages that transform and mostly disappear over time. Our aim, with both mediums, is to explore the deeply entangled relationships between the following three registers: historical threads, material narratives, and contemporary histories.

Design is collaborative and reflexive, and is rarely successful without both. Thus, my co-editor, Nawaf bin Ayyaf, and I, have conceived of this book as a layered assemblage of conversations, reflections, and visual narratives that expand the story of the *musalla.*

In assembling the enclosed reflections, we approached individuals who would provide diverse yet incisive insights into the *musalla,* nudging them ever so slightly to cast the *musalla* through the dye of its historical threads, its material narratives, or its contemporary histories. The opening reflection by Nasser Rabbat muses on the spatial origins of the word. Following this, Khaled Azzam recollects a personal memory of praying under the open sky, and how a *musalla* can simultaneously anchor and release us. Meanwhile, Hanif Kara implores us to lean forward and listen intentionally to technology when it whispers. Wesam Al Asali describes how *musalla* spaces ask us to oscillate our gaze between the ground and the sky. Ziad Jamaleddine draws out the potential of material and spatial practices which alludes to the architectural record. Finally, Noura Al Sayeh-Holtrop describes the acoustic qualities of prayer spaces within the contemporary built environment. Accompanying these reflections are a series of photographs from Moath Alofi's *The Last Tashahud,* a photographic series in which the Alofi documents *musalla* spaces assembled on roads leading to Madinah. On top of acting as a visual protector for the ephemeral reflections, each photograph was selected specifically to evoke the spirit of the text it accompanies.

To reveal the ways in which many of the participants have engaged with the *musalla,* we have paired one jury member from the *AlMusalla Prize* with one shortlisted designer (or team of designers) in a relatively unstructured conversation taking place under the tents of Fazlur Rahman Khan's Hajj Terminal. In transcribing these conversations, we attempted to bring the reader as close as possible to the human interactions that took place between the participants. Thus, you will find embedded in the text key moments in which we interject to describe the gestures and reflexes that fleetingly appeared throughout the conversations. You will find Azra Akšamija and Sahel AlHiyari discussing the blurring between landscape, object, and space; Lina Ghotmeh and Asif Khan sharing their thoughts about the relationship between personal histories, heritage, and the production of contemporary, yet rooted, work; AAU Anastas and Ali Malkawi thinking through the lightness of stone; and Farrokh Derakhshani and Sumaya Dabbagh reflecting on Jeddah as a place of thresholds through which contemporary architecture can emerge. Finally, Nawaf bin Ayyaf sits with EAST Architecture Studio, Rayyane Tabet, and Christopher Blust of AKT II to reveal the complex ideas and processes that enabled their project to take shape within a multidisciplinary collaborative framework.

The exhibition displays these entangled registers by assembling a set of interventions in the form of at-scale fragments from the winning proposal, and architectural models, images, and drawings by all five participating design teams. Coincidentally, while all the proposals approach the project from different angles, highlighting the malleability of the *musalla*, they are also in conversation with each other. For example, where AAU Anastas' proposal is structured around the idea of a stereotomic *mise en abyme*, creating a multitude of self-similar copies to create a larger, heavier, and porous whole, Asif Khan operates on the other end of the tectonic spectrum, deploying a lightweight architectural line, *ad infinitum*, to create a spectral construct for prayer. Despite this, both projects allude to the meditative nature of repetition.

This dichotomy, between contrasting material attitudes that share a conceptual thread can also be found in the proposals from Dabbagh Architects and Office of Sahel AlHiyari for Architecture. Both proposals have a sense of the archaeological, the first is ephemeral, while the second has visible traces on the ground. Whereas Dabbagh Architects leans on the spatio-temporal idea of the *miqat* – the threshold space that indicates the beginning of the sacred state of *ihram* – and Hajj, proposing a contemporary rereading of lightweight tents seen historically at the proverbial gates of Makkah, the Office of Sahel AlHiyari for Architecture approaches the project minerally, by blurring the ground, space, and sky.

Finally, *On Weaving*, the winning proposal by EAST Architecture Studio, Rayyane Tabet, and AKT II, negotiates between the courtyard spatial typology; weaving as both craft and structure; and the repurposing of waste material. In so doing, their project embraces the historical, material, and contemporary registers through which the exhibition is imagined.

Alongside these objects and drawings are a series of archival images and documents that root contemporary material production with the *musalla's* ongoing story.

Aspirations

By revealing the contemporary relevance of *musalla* spaces, *Rooted Transience* challenges three key misconceptions within the discipline. First, it challenges the lens of permanence through which much of the built environment is conceived, putting forward radical ideas about transformable architectures. Second, it posits that there still exists an abundance of underexplored spatial and material practices within the history of Islamic architecture. Where this history has focused on public and monumental spaces, the *musalla* points us toward the intimate and quotidian within Islamic architecture, expanding the glossary for future researchers and practitioners. Finally, it adds to the voices arguing for the contemporaneity of Islamic architecture.[8] All three provocations suggest that alternative material and spatial practices rooted in transience can transform contemporary built environments.

By tracing the various ways these spaces emerge, function, and dissolve, *Rooted Transience* invites reflection on the adaptable and temporal nature of the *musalla*. In so doing, we aim to reveal the ingenuity and subtle beauty of these transient spaces, celebrating the timeless practice of creating sacred assembly wherever and whenever needed.

[8] Sheila S. Blair and Jonathan Bloom, "The Study of Islamic Architecture: Reflections on an Expanding Field," in *Islamic Architecture Today and Tomorrow: (Re)Defining the Field*, eds. Mohammad Gharipour, and Daniel E. Coslett (Chicago, IL: Intellect, The University of Chicago Press, 2022): 11-28.

XII

↑ This landscape view shows the pilgrims' station, Muzdalifah, situated between Mina and Arafah.

Photo Credit Photographer: al-Sayyid 'Abd al-Ghaffār, British Library: Visual Arts, X463/13, in *Qatar Digital Library*.

Chapter 1

آثــارٌ تاريخيــة

Historical Threads

Nasser Rabbat

Musalla: The Spatiality of a Sonic Term

Musalla (pl. *musallayaat*) is a term with a long (architectural) history that crosses several conceptual spheres from the informal, personal, and intimate to the majestically monumental. It is also a term that stands in dialogue with other Arabic names for worship places, such as *masjid* (mosque), mihrab (prayer room in its original meaning before migrating to designate the prayer niche), and *ma'bad* (temple), each derived from a specific act of worship, but each extending its semantic field into the space of the other terms. Musalla, for instance, stems from the tripartite root sa-ll-aa, which means "to pray," whereas masjid originates from sa-ja-da, which specifically signifies "to prostrate (oneself)," and ma'bad from 'a-ba-da, to worship. Yet, it is masjid that rose to become the primary designation of Islamic worship places, probably because it indicates a worshipping motion that is exclusively Islamic, as formal prayers in other religions do not include the act of prostration.

Musalla in this semantic division embodies the sonic dimension of prayer, which in Islam ranges from the silent prayer, beautifully described as "forming the words in the mouth without sound," to the loudly delivered prayer. This sonic range has historically translated into scaled spaces for prayer from the intimate and transient personal *musalla*, where the prayer is mostly silent, to the large musalla al-'id (holy day) where the prayer is recited out loud, and often magnified by repeaters standing at calculated points, for the total adult male population of a town or a city to hear as they come together for the first prayer of the E'id. In the early days of Islam, these musallayaat were large open spaces outside the city proper with a qibla indication toward Makkah in the form of a mihrab or simply a wall and no roof. They existed in almost every city before the introduction of gigantic congregational mosques, which sometimes appropriated their function. They still exist in a number of locales, where people adhere to the Prophetic practice of holding the 'id prayer in the open air.

The spatial flexibility, and even plasticity, of the historical musalla al-'id is expressed in its open-ended layout and the simplicity of its visual markers. The space was usually animated twice a year on the first days of the 'id by the worshippers gathering in it. Otherwise, it was treated as a public open space the rest of the year with no religious restrictions for its use according to several jurists. This functional pragmatism stems from the higher religious principle of *manfa'a* (public benefit), which undergirded the common Islamic approach in the urban milieu. The polyvalence, however, may have contributed to the disappearance of musalla al-'id from the majority of cities, when the suburban areas became urbanized with the cities' expansion and the land value increased under the pressure of development.

Smaller-scale musallayaat, encompassing the personal-size private variant and the space for a small group of worshippers, fared differently. They responded to change through transience, whether it was the duration of a single prayer or a stopover period for a group of travelers. Ephemerality, however, was not an acquired trait. It was constitutive of the personal space of private worship from the beginning of Islam and was governed by the rhythm of the five required prayers each day from morning to evening. At each prayer time, a Muslim transforms any space—where they can recite their prayer and prostrate themselves in the direction of the Ka'ba—into a personal *musalla*, which dissolves immediately after the completion of the prayer and returns to its usual function.

The mobility of the personal *musalla* is best illustrated by the prayer rug: a foldable and portable human-size surface that is spread for prayer and then stowed away. This simplicity of use can be multiplied when several people spread their prayer rugs next to each other to perform a group prayer, transforming any place into a *musalla*. This transformation can last for the duration of a prayer or several prayers. No wonder then that the prayer rug became a miniature mosque, with the profile of a decorated, arched, or lobed mihrab occupying its center, framed within a band of geometric or floral motifs. Thus, in the prayer rug, the meaning of *salat* (prayer, the present participle of *musalla*) is distilled to its essence.

Written on December 21, 2024

←*Image:* Moath Alofi, *The Last Tashahud*, 2017→

Conversation
On Reclaiming Heritage, Today

Farrokh Derakhshani *with* Sumaya Dabbagh

This conversation took place under the shade of the canopies of the Hajj Terminal, Jeddah, on January 25, 2025. It started at around 12:15 in the afternoon, and ran for about twenty-five minutes. Pairing Farrokh Derakhshani with Sumaya Dabbagh of Dabbagh Architects aimed at revealing the opportunities that emerge when designing through spatial and temporal contexts. In this conversation, Dabbagh Architects' proposal is used to describe the role of architecture in reclaiming heritage, while touching on the unique context of Jeddah in the past and today.

FD: Sumaya, it's great to be here with you.

Knowing you, and your work, and knowing that you are from Jeddah, where this project is situated, I am curious about how you felt when you were asked to submit a proposal, especially knowing that this is a place of exchange.

SD: I felt very honored to be invited. You know, one has an intrinsic understanding of Jeddah from growing up here. Historically, it was known for its fort and a place where pilgrims passed through; there's always an influx of people. But this site is very special.

Glances upwards at the canopy of the Hajj Terminal, while her left palm faces downward in a grounding, expansive way

When I came to visit, I sensed the energy of the many, many pilgrims who have passed through here. I felt that it was really important to capture this sense of the space, especially for a project like a *musalla*. It was an enjoyable journey.

FD: It's the whole concept of Jeddah being a space of transit, a space of transit to another state of mind. In a way, this idea of having a temporary space, such as a *musalla*, is very special to this location. Although buildings are normally built to be permanent, how can we reimagine a building to be temporary?

SD: What you said is exactly right, prayer is a state of mind. It transforms you from your day-to-day into an alternative state, a state of worship, a place of stillness for a short time, until you can go back to your daily life. So, for the pilgrim, there is the *miqat*, the boundary that you cross and enter into your *ihram* (state of being for the pilgrimage with prescribed clothing and cleansing rituals). It's a transformation from a state of worldly concerns to a state of worship, stillness, and the stripping away of all material concerns. This is symbolic, you're telling everybody that I am in this state of mind, preparing for Hajj, but also mentally and spiritually, you're announcing it to yourself. So, it felt like there was an alignment between the notion of miqat, ihram with its clothing, and a design for the *musalla*.

FD: What you're saying about ihram is so important, because this is what makes people equal. In a way, what I saw in your project was a crossing into an inner sanctuary, like a cover within a cover.

Shapes his hands in a cocoon-like motion

Can you elaborate a little bit about the whole notion of miqat in your ideas?

SD: Jeddah has several points where pilgrims could start their ihram. It's a physical border, a physical reminder of that transformation. This is a parallel we wanted to highlight in the form of the *musalla,* through a series of concentric circles.

Uses both her hands to allude to circles contracting into one another

It's a plan where as you move inward toward the middle, you get closer to the sacred space, and you leave the other functions on the outside. Also, when we were looking at the legacy or afterlife of the project, we felt it would be really appropriate to take it to Old Jeddah, where the old port is, which was another place of arrival for the pilgrims, when people used to come by water.

FD: So, the choice of the circle was to describe a space of togetherness, anywhere. Speaking about transience, I remember, in the 1980s, there was a wave of building and infrastructural development in Saudi Arabia. You could find these advertisements in construction magazines about containers which can become offices, sleeping spaces, etc., but they also had a component that was a prayer space, a *musalla*. It was something compact, that was used as needed, and then they would take it away and put it somewhere else. This concept of transience also came up in your proposal through the idea of a kit that you can take with you anywhere. Can you elaborate on that?

SD: Having a *musalla* in a place like this, and in an event such as the Islamic Arts Biennale for four months, makes it important that we think about its transience. It's about using it, packing it in a container, and then taking it somewhere else to erect it again, so it becomes a *musalla* in the future as well, to serve other communities that are on the move. Its legacy is for it to move from place to place.

FD: You touched on something very important. One can say that prayer spaces in Islam are different from the other faiths, because they're a space of gathering, about the coming together of communal life. It's clear in your proposal that you had that in mind, that this is a space that can be used for prayer, but when it's not the time for prayer, it can be used for other functions as well, it's multi-functional.

SD: This is what was unique about the brief – the request for the space to have two or more functions. This brings in another dimension, about designing for multiple scenarios. But again, another thing about a *musalla* is that it's so simple, you don't need all the additional elements that you would have in a mosque. It's another way of really stripping down and stepping away from the material world which is the essence of Islam. You know, you can mark any area and decide to pray on it, and through intention, it becomes a place of worship. It's as simple as that.

I think what is really interesting about this competition and the whole Islamic Arts Biennale is that they ask: What is contemporary Islamic art and architecture? Our interpretation was that simplicity is a real core value and providing it in a place of worship helps create a sense of the sacred. But then, we're using contemporary materials. One of the materials we looked at was a woven carbon fiber mesh to reference the ihram fabric. Historically, Islamic architecture was very innovative, so it doesn't mean that we only look at the past, we can also look to the future and make work that is relevant for us in this day and age.

FD: Relevance is a very important aspect that many don't pay attention to. Here, you have the relevance of the space through having a cover under another cover.

Makes a dome-like shape with his hands

This is very unique, to be able to imagine a space that is already within another contained space. How do you see these layers?

SD: Although we're standing under one of these canopies,

Pauses briefly and looks up at the Hajj Terminal's canopy

the opening in the tent creates a connection to the sky. So, although it's covered - which creates a beautiful quality of light and is cooler with its own microclimate - the connection to the sky is still there. We were able to converse with this by placing our proposal under the centrally located oculus.

FD: Going back to your previous point on innovation in materiality and the role of the architect within these innovations; there are certain functions that do not change, but our ability to interpret and innovate, to create a structure that is relevant today, is very important.

SD: It's a really exciting time for materials. There are a lot of materials being developed that are connected to local places. And I think it's important for us to use those to capture the memory of a place. Materiality can really create a sense of belonging, the story of a place, and its heritage. Think about glue-laminated palm wood in relation to Jeddah, for example.

FD: You mentioned the idea of simplicity earlier, and this also applies to the simplicity of materials and techniques. In a way, you're referencing the concept of *zaher* and *batin*, the outer surface and the inner-working of materials. You're referring to palm frond wood, which is simple on the surface, but at the same time, it's extremely complex at the micro-level. There is always a movement between simplicity and complexity.

SD: Yes, we can look at how the tangible enhances the intangible experience, and to do so, the tangible has to be connected to place, whether it's in the way it's made, or the raw material itself. It's quite elusive, this intangible experience that we try to induce.

FD: In your practice, you've designed a number of mosques which are permanent. And now, you are presented with the challenge of designing a prayer space that is temporary. How did you navigate between these two kinds of time?

SD: If you apply simplicity as a guideline, then they can be quite similar in their approach, as both are about going back to the essence of things. Obviously, they have different aims, but the approach is common.

FD: One aspect about architects is that they're always learning lessons from one project to the other. They do something but then they look at it again and reflect on what could've been different. Was there such a moment here?

SD: This reminds me of Giacometti's work that I saw in Paris once. You just see multiple, multiple, and multiple, long figures.

Makes vertical movements alluding to Giacometti's slender sculptures

It's like he's looking for something, and he's just trying and trying and trying and trying. Architecture, for me, is similar. It's looking for this intangible quality. You find it, but you want to refine it every time you work, to dig into it more, and to uncover something else. It's an endless exploration, really, being an architect. It feels like there's always more, there's always more to do, and there's always more to dig into, but, it's very enjoyable and rewarding.

Pauses and tilts her gaze while thinking

In addition, it's important for the region, because what we're trying to do with our work is to reclaim our heritage. I think for a long time in our region, we've imported a lot, we've imported materials, and we've imported architecture. It's time, and the renaissance is already happening, to sort of pause and say: we want to tell our own story to the world, rather than going somewhere else to hear our story.

FD acknowledges and repeats: our story

So, in the same way, through architecture, we want to create this sense of belonging. We want to create this sense of connection to place in a contemporary language. I'm not saying that we want to go back to recreate the past, but we really want to create something that is relevant, contemporary, and innovative. It's starting to happen, but we would like to see more of it in the region.

FD: You bring up a very important issue about continuity. Some see continuity as a repetition of the past instead of being inspired by the past. Unfortunately, as you said, this might be a reaction to rapid development, new techniques, and new materials that people find appealing.

But now, we are more confident, and we are using our resources, as you said, to tell our own story. It's important to learn from all these processes and technologies, because in reality, when you look at history, the world has never been disconnected. Maybe the means were less, but it was always interconnected in a way. Especially if we come back to Jeddah, because this is a place where, for many, many years, people of different regions have come and settled, bringing their ideas, and together we were able to create an identity for the place.

Layers his palms on top of each other

SD: This multi-culturalism – you see it in the food here – is a real influence from all those pilgrims who settled here over the years. It does create a unique mix. I was speaking to someone recently and he said his word for Jeddah was "stew,"

As she smiles

which is a mix of things, but it's a very tasty mix,

They both erupt in laughter

and you can't pinpoint exactly where the stew comes from.

FD: Coming back to the idea of East and West. In the Western way of thinking, you compartmentalize every issue, so art, architecture, painting, and I don't know, food, they're all very separate, but in our tradition, they're all the same, exactly as you said, you have to feel and breathe the building. It's not only the smell of the building, it's the smell of the sky, it's everything altogether. This is what makes a sense of place, and a sense of place is the sense of belonging. And most importantly, if the architect can sense it, the users will have a sense of belonging as well.

SD: This is a lifelong mission for us.

Memory of Place

The competition design of Dabbagh Architects was deeply connected to the Hajj Terminal's position as *Miqat* – the boundary line on one's journey to Makkah where pilgrims must enter *Ihram*. Their musalla design sought to harness the memory of the hundreds of thousands of pilgrims who have inhabited this particular space over many years, at this significant moment of their transformative spiritual journey.

Ihram – the sacred state pilgrims must enter to perform Hajj – is an inner and outer declaration of their commitment to purification and detachment from material distractions. Any expression of wealth and status is stripped away from the body is covered in a simple, unstitched white cloth.

Dabbagh brings a sacred dimension to their musalla by referencing the white cloth of Ihram.

Their musalla design was a central cylinder made up of low earthen walls and i-mesh privacy screens woven from fiberglass threads, topped with a circular, geometric steel and i-mesh canopy. A highly flexible, exterior of mesh panels could be lowered and raised to provide multiple configurations and entry points, including an open central space for public events such as exhibitions. A contemporary adaptation of sacred Islamic geometry across the musalla's canopy would create a dialogue between the past and present, amplifying the site's history and honoring its memory.

Historically, pilgrims traveling by land and by sea started their ihram upon arrival in Jeddah, south of the city at the port near Al Balad, the suitable permanent home for Dabbagh Architects's musalla, bringing the memory of the pilgrims' point of entry to Jeddah back to its original location.

Khaled Azzam

The Primordial Musalla

The human state exists between two fundamental dimensions. One is our actual physical state that is experienced through our body, which defines itself within time and space. The other is our eternal soul which seeks its fulfillment in eternity. The act of prayer brings these two dimensions together.

When we pray, we address and symbolically face, eternity through the aspiration of our soul. Yet, we communicate this through the physical realm that our bodies occupy and cannot transcend. Through the intention of prayer, we anchor ourselves to a particular place by stepping out of the worldly realm's distraction and fragmentation that rules our daily lives. Then, the act of prayer starts, and we deepen this anchor to the core of our consciousness to find our center. This center exists as a unity of being, which sits without serene independence from the world of distraction, fragmentation, and multiplicity that rules our daily lives. By connecting to our center through prayer, this center marks the vertical axis to the heavenly realm and the start of the journey of the soul toward eternity. It is by connecting to our center, through prayer, that we get a taste of our eternal soul.

Just as each Muslim makes the journey of orientation toward their center to embark on their spiritual journey, the collective community orientates itself to its communal center. The Ka'ba is the center of the world for the Muslim community, but it is also the point where heaven and earth meet, marked by the descent of the heavenly stone in Makkah. By extension, the Ka'ba marks the start of the vertical axis that connects heaven and earth, and therefore, the orientation of the Muslim community is not just toward a geographical location, but also toward the spiritual axis of the heavens.

The Ka'ba is not located in a mosque as such, but rather a sanctuary, Al Haram. Although physical structures have been built surrounding the Ka'ba, and have somewhat encroached on its presence, it still remains, in essence, what it was in the days of the Prophet Muhammad (PBUH) – a heavenly object placed in an earthly sanctuary. The Ka'ba has always stood on its own in an open space surrounded by what we recognize as the principle and most important musalla, the *sahn* (courtyard) which, in essence, extends throughout the world as a continuous space where Muslims, wherever they are, find their place to connect in prayer.

From this point, one can begin to appreciate how a variety of prayer spaces find their context in our world. The Prophet (PBUH) instructs us that the world was created as a sanctuary for prayer: *"The earth has been made a place of prostration and a means of purification for me, so wherever a man of my Ummah is when the time of prayer comes, let him pray."* This, in a way, confirms the expansion of the musalla around the Ka'ba to cover the whole world. It is also illuminating to note that in the Qur'an, the term masjid, referring to both the Masjid al-Haram in Makkah and the Masjid Al-Aqsa in Jerusalem, was not referring to a physical building or structure, but to a blessed place of sanctuary in this world – *"the neighbourhood whereof We have blessed"* (Surah Al-Isra, verse 1).

From this, we understand that the natural world is the reflection of heaven on earth and is, therefore, the most primordial environment through which we experience the manifestation of the sacred – nature is the primordial musalla. By extension, there would be no need to build a mosque, as a space for prayer, in the context of pure nature. The need to build mosque structures arises when we have to create a contemplative prayer space in a fragmented environment that has lost the primordial beauty of the natural world.

Prayer is about entering into a contemplative state, this entails a movement away from the fragmented context of our daily lives and an orientation toward the realm of our spiritual essence. This intention needs to start, and be supported by, locating ourselves in the right physical environment - a contemplative space that helps to calm the agitation of the mind and which sets the true rhythm which our hearts will follow.

If we are to build mosques as congregational places for prayer, then we have to build structures that recreate the serene and inspiring experience of the natural world. The decoration of mosques and other prayer spaces with geometric patterns and biomorphic forms – that have come to represent the character of Islamic architecture – is often misunderstood as a cosmetic exercise simply focused on surface decoration. In fact, it is much more profound than that and is cosmetic in the root form of the word: to make cosmic-like, interpreting the physical forms of the natural world and its underlying creative order, and placing them onto the buildings dedicated to prayer. This was a means to allow worshipers to resonate with the forms and rhythms of the divine order of the natural world which is also at the core of our being, and which we experience instinctively through our *fitra*, recognizing the oneness of God.

The musalla, on the other hand, simply marks a prayer space within the context of the natural world. It is directly connected to the earth, as a space where Prophet Muhammad (PBUH) declared its totality as a sacred place of prayer. Possibly ephemeral in nature, the musalla simply marks a place where an individual or community has decided to pray. This space does not necessitate the extension of the order of nature into the prayer space, through an architectural interpretation, since it is already directly connected to nature.

The narrative of these thoughts was confirmed to me directly through a personal experience I had while traveling in the Atlas Mountains outside Fez. I was visiting a small village where a pious man was buried whose writings had inspired me to make this journey. During my stay, the call to prayer was made, and not knowing where I should go, I simply followed the streams of people heading in a certain direction that I assumed was to the local mosque. Eventually, we arrived at a large open space where the locals lined up to start praying. We took our places in rows under the open sky overlooking the mountains and valleys, surrounded by the cork trees from which a layer of cork was flattened to create a comfortable surface to pray on. I realized that in this beautiful environment, there was no need to build a mosque structure. It was just enough to demarcate a space that was dedicated to prayer. The natural world was our musalla and we were engaging in prayer through our primordial nature, our fitra, as part of the divinely created order of nature.

This simple but profound experience brought the realization that virgin nature is the true setting for our souls. We resonate with its essence which is our true essence and there is no separation or duality between our primordial nature and the natural world – both are created as an integral part of the divine order of being, manifesting the heavenly realm in the human context.

When we make the intention to pray in a certain location, we anchor ourselves in that context and engage with our center – which is fundamentally the center of all being. This engagement is facilitated through the formless musalla, the blessed potential of prayer, that we carry within us wherever we may be. By bringing this center to connect with a place, through prayer, we enable the musalla to come into physical form. This particular prayer space becomes our personal extension of the principle musalla, the sahn around the Ka'ba, but also a connection to the Ka'ba itself as the symbol of the center of our being and the spiritual orientation toward the eternal.

Written on February 2, 2025

←*Image:* Moath Alofi, *The Last Tashahud*, 2017→

Chapter 2

تشَابكات مادِّية

Material Entanglements

Conversation
On the Lightness of Stone

Ali Malkawi *with* Elias and Yousef Anastas

This conversation took place as a digital call on February 11, 2025. It started at around 16:30 in the afternoon (KSA), and ran for about thirty minutes. Pairing Ali Malkawi with Elias and Yousef Anastas of AAU Anastas aimed at revealing the relationship between physical and cultural performance of materials can challenge perceived contradictions, such as the lightness of stone, and transform them into generative spatial and material conditions. In this conversation, you will read about AAU Anastas' ongoing project, Stone Matters, and how it was adapted to the context of Jeddah, revealing a throughline in their complex body of work.

AM: This exhibition and publication explore the *musalla* as a fluid and adaptive typology emerging organically in response to the need for individual or communal prayer space. So, these spaces embody culturally resonant design principles, seamlessly integrating spirituality with architectural expression. My question is, how do you see the *musalla* typology, which is a flexible prayer-oriented space, contributing to or aligning with your broader vision of creating architecture that is both sustainable and culturally meaningful?

EA: One way to respond to that would be to look at the work that our practice has focused on for the last twelve to thirteen years, especially the research on stone as a material and how stone was central to the construction of the Palestinian city in the early 1900s. And finally, how the evolution of the material throughout the last hundred years has totally shifted. One of the main elements of stone construction that has been of interest to us is how to desacralize its use and how to make it more accessible as a material. In this way, it is not only reserved for noble typologies, but it can reverberate with the climatic and social conditions that we're going through here and globally.

In this context, we are looking at the historical typology of the *musalla* and the contemporary use of massive stone structures, especially through stereotomy – the way you cut stones in order to create self-standing structures – as a way to reposition stone into a more democratic and open lexicon or vocabulary of architectural production. So, from one end, the *musalla* is a very sacred and noble form of architecture, but at the same time, it's a form of architecture that is supposed to be open to the widest spectrum of the population. Trying to balance between these two conditions is a way to desacralize stone.

AM: So, then, let me just follow up with a question in relation to stone. In your proposal for the *musalla*, and your work in general, you talk about stone lightness. Can you elaborate on how you introduce this question of stone lightness in your design and how it challenges the traditional perception of stone as a heavy solid material? And, what role does it play in shaping the spatial and atmospheric qualities of your project?

YA: Maybe to start with something kind of significant, stone, in general, has similar density to glass. So, if you take an equal volume of glass and an equal volume of stone, they will have a similar weight. Usually, these two materials are seen as opposed to each other, because one is transparent and the other is completely opaque.

If we go back to Robert Hooke, a well-known engineer from the seventeenth century, he worked to solve the riddle of the ideal shape of an arch, the results of which were revealed after his passing. His solution for the ideal shape of an arch was derived from the shape of an inverted flexible line, which takes on a catenary curve.

Draws a parabolic shape with his hands

This results in a compression-only structure, where there is no tension, and since then, we have considered stone to be a compression-only material.

This is not completely true, and while his theory has brought many advancements and developments to stone construction, it has reduced the possibilities of building with stone. If you look at architecture made out of stone that is more than five thousand years old, stone lintels were used as well as slabs of stone that behave in tension, too. We used to have a lexicon of architectural elements made out of stone that functioned with both tension and compression. When stone starts resisting tension, its lightness emerges and suddenly this opens up many possibilities.

AM: In addition to the materiality itself, there is also the construction method that you used, which is corbelling. Can you discuss how the corbelled arch in your proposal works in relation to stone, lightness, and spirituality?

YA: When we first visited the Old City of Jeddah, we saw structures built out of coral stones. Within these structures, you'll find, along the lengths of the walls, horizontal timber members that work with temporary buttresses installed during maintenance periods. Sometimes they need to replace or repair a coral stone, and it cannot be done when they are load-bearing, so they put up buttresses that support the horizontal timber members, allowing the coral stone some relief. Then, they take out the damaged stone, repair it, and replace it. Once the buttresses are removed, the walls are fully loaded again.

To us, this challenges the question of formwork and stone structures. The carbon footprint of stone structures is significantly lower than that of concrete, steel, and even timber structures, especially if there is a nearby source of stone. That being said, we started looking at references to build with stone using minimal formwork, such as the dome of Santa Maria del Fiore in Florence, which was built without formwork using a spiraling structure. Other examples can be found in Mamluk structures, that integrated traditional vaulting with corbeling.

A corbel structure is made by cantilevering every layer of stone further into space, compared to the layer below requiring no formwork because each layer is stabilized.

Makes decreasing sizes of rings with his hands

We used similar principles of corbelling in the *musalla* proposal, while also being influenced by what we saw in Jeddah, because the project needed to be assembled and disassembled several times.

EA: I'll just add one more thing in direct relation to your work, Dr. Ali. One question that constantly comes back to the studio is whether we should continue making buildings or if we should focus more on their preservation by investigating new formats of restoration. So, for us as well, our thinking about the *musalla* was inscribed in a logic where we were trying to conceive of a building with a long lifespan, while at the same time, imagining how it could be brought back to nature and become an artifact or archaeological remnant. So, the construction method was very much based on that, along with the idea of the buttress.

AM: I can see that the environmental concept is very important to you in relation to the use of the material itself, in terms of its rigor, durability, and embodied carbon lifecycle, as well as the refurbishment of the building. It also seems to me, in addition to all these fundamental principles, the other principle that you've held is the meaning of the materiality and method of construction.

This brings me to another concept that you've introduced in your proposal, what you refer to as duality between the courtyard and the prayer area. Can you describe its significance in shaping the concept of the *musalla*?

EA: One of the things that we really wanted to push is the idea of the threshold, a form of architecture that links many places in the Global South, where architecture becomes more and more permeable. So, in the *musalla*, we wanted to look at the very traditional forms and typologies of prayer spaces and try to formalize a new interpretation, as well as conversing with the infrastructural scale of the Hajj Terminal canopies and how they can lead to an introverted space which is much more at the scale of the human being. This was formalized through a duality between a space that focuses on the light penetrating it and another that embodies the idea of nature, leading visitors inward to seclude themselves and reconnect to their own spirituality.

AM: It seems to me, then, that the garden has a lot of significance in the *musalla*. Can you elaborate on how it contributes to the spatial experience that you alluded to and the spiritual atmosphere created by nature and contemplation within the prayer space?

YA: I think the project, as Elias was saying, is a series of thresholds. When seen from far away, you can call it an organic form. As you approach it, some details start to be revealed. So, this is the first threshold in the project. Once we approach it, we enter into a space and we find ourselves in a courtyard or the garden. Then we enter through another threshold into the prayer space. This series of thresholds connects the architecture of the proposal to the typological, which is an essential component of Islamic architecture. At the beginning of this project, we asked, a little provocatively, if there is such a thing as Islamic architecture. This is because there are typologies attached to architecture in Islam that can be transformed and adapted.

This relates a bit to the work we've been doing in Palestine, where there is no iconic architecture, if you look at the historic Palestinian city. Architecture here relates to typology and climate, and a way of living through the proportions of space, of windows, and of thresholds; creating shared spaces between the outdoor and indoor, spaces that are neither public nor private. They're not really public. They're not really private. This makes for architecture that is rich but also very adaptable.

AM: It seems to me that the relationship between typology and environmental issues is fundamental to the project. This results in the threshold, which is very much linked to the idea of layers, the layers of the structure, as well as the layered spatial approach as a transition from one space to the other. Although you have stone, which is fixed, you try to balance that with other variables that would allow a transition from the outside to the inside through the introduction of light and the garden. You bring together multiple things from construction, to meaning, tradition, and a sense of space and place.

This leads me to ask you a question about fundamentals, specifically, about your broader Stone Matters project, which advances the use of structural stone in contemporary architecture. How does it contribute to the discourse on environmental issues related to carbon impact, resilience, and responsible quarry extraction? More broadly, how do you see its role in shaping more sustainable architecture practices?

EA: That's a very big question, but maybe it's important to trace the history of Stone Matters.

Smiles

We were born into a family of architects and our grandfather was an architect that built bridges with massive stones. In Palestine, we inherited a law that dates back over a hundred years to the Ottoman Empire mandating the use of stone in buildings. Gradually, during the last century, the use of the material evolved and moved away from being a structural and thermal component to only being used as ornamental cladding for concrete structures, especially after the 1950s and 1960s, when there was a global tendency and expanded use of reinforced concrete.

In Palestine, this resulted in a transformation of urban morphologies, which was linked to the way stone was quarried, where each construction had a quarry in the backyard, resulting in a very limited carbon footprint. So, we wanted to explore - given the climate crisis and the way our cities are transforming, and with the help of both technology and the very rich know-how of our stone masons - how we can reposition the use of stone in a contemporary language while trying to address environmental issues.

The project began as an experimental approach to the use of stone and we started developing different elements of architecture such as vaults, flat ceilings, columns, slabs, lintels, etc. as standalone elements. Up until today, the project has approximately ten different iterations at various scales, and now, we are reaching a moment where we have the opportunity to put together structures and buildings based on these principles.

AM: The multi-layered approach to your thinking about stone as a material that can be contemporary but is also linked to a sense of space and place is wonderful to hear. Thank you for telling the story of your *musalla* proposal and your larger body of work.

Mise en Abyme

AAU Anastas interpreted the *musalla* project as a series of intertwining scales and thresholds, from entering the gates to the monumental, infinite infrastructure of the Hajj Terminal to the smaller scale *musalla*, usually found in waystations or places of transit, underpinned by a reference to Jeddah's role as a transitional threshold to Makkah.

These scales unfold further as one would approach AAU Anastas's *musalla*. The small domestic object would become a stone building, its shape slowly unveiling details of its architecture. During the day, night, and different seasons, the lighting conditions vary and the shifts in stone layering would unveil an ever-changing appearance. Thresholds are not only space-based but determined through light and time. The architecture of the *musalla* would become a witness of its immediate entourage.

AAU Anastas's approach to the *musalla's* construction was deeply anchored in global and local traditional stone building techniques. The firm brought together a key principle of stone building, the corbel – a method of load distribution – with a practice abundant in Jeddah, *takaleel* – where timber is used to distribute weight. In this approach, heavy stone structures are liberated and become versatile. Reinforcing this idea of impermanence, the 476 ashlars of locally sourced coral stone that would form the *musalla's* structure could fit into a single loading vehicle.

Wesam Al Asali

Grounds, Rituals, Skies

"In the name of God, the Most Gracious, the Most Merciful. This mosque was built by Ahmad ibn Hadidi from his own wealth in pursuit of God's reward. It was completed with God's help by the hand of Musa ibn Ali, the builder, and was finished in Muharram of the year 309 AH."

At the entrance of Bab Al Mardum, I pause for a moment to contemplate and perceive the space: a miniature forest of columns and inscriptions, with just enough light for the eye to acclimate to the scene. As my vision adjusts, I find myself thinking about the light once more, before shifting my gaze back to the mosque's niches, carved from stone and brick. This mosque follows a unique architectural approach, three distinct structural compositions condensed within the constraints of a small space, measuring no more than 36 square meters.

Earth Assembly

The first structural composition of this mosque lies in its floor plan: a square divided into nine smaller squares, each supporting a dome. Three interwoven aisles create a harmonious and dense rhythm, a feature deeply admired by architects, including modernists. This architectural model gained popularity across the Islamic world between the eighth and tenth centuries, appearing from Mosul to Toledo and from Aswan to Kairouan. Islamic architecture historians refer to this distinctive formation as the "nine-dome" style, named after the Haj Bida Mosque in Karkh, the earliest known example of this layout.

I recall how K. A. C. Creswell, an English architecture historian, attributed this design to funerary architecture, C. Ewert, another historian, traced its origins of early Islamic architecture in Qasr Khirbat al-Mafjar, while other sites to Byzantine cisterns. This open-ended origin of the architectural style of Bab Al Mardum marks one of the earliest attempts at developing a non-monumental form of religious architecture – experimental in nature and diverse in its materials and applications, resembling a flexible architectural model adaptable to both religious and secular contexts.

Quotidian Assembly

I read in the guidebook that Bab Al Mardum was one of several nine-domed mosques that once dotted the neighborhood, although only a few remain. Built by rulers and prominent figures of Andalusian society, these mosques have left historians debating whether they were private places of worship for elite families or open to the public. Gazing at the mosque's solid walls, I try to imagine how they might have once appeared – open arcades crowned with brick lattice screens. This vision leads me to consider Bab Al Mardum as an urban oratory, similar to a present-day small prayer space or *musalla*. It was part of Toledo's network of oratories, forming a religious landscape interwoven within the city's fabric, blending seamlessly into daily life. Unlike grand congregational mosques, which were closely tied to politics and governance, these smaller spaces were more fluid and integrated into their surroundings. However, Bab Al Mardum is an architectural oasis, a 6 x 6-meter space that utilizes dense architectural elements to set itself apart from the surrounding city, the world, and their shifting realities.

Sky Assembly

In the urban oratory, there is a fascinating structural experiment, as each of its nine domes is distinct, unlike most nine-domed mosques. The space resembles a three-dimensional collage of various intersecting arch formations beneath the domes. In my hotel room, I read about these ribbed domes in Andalusian architecture and learned that their first documented appearance was in the expansion of the Great Mosque of Cordoba under Caliph Al Hakam II, just thirty years before Bab Al Mardum was built. I imagine how this innovative technique must have captivated its builder and architect, Musa ibn Ali. I picture him immersed in exploring the possibilities of these forms – adjusting the arches at different angles, and experimenting with square, octagonal, and hexagonal configurations to create new spatial compositions. Over time, he would have realized that some of these formations were fractal variations of Cordoban domes, such as the central dome, which rises above the others in the oratory. The domes here seem to serve as a laboratory for architectural experimentation on a smaller scale. While they may lack the refined ornamentation of Cordoba's earlier ribbed domes, they offer a greater variety of structural solutions. It is as if they form a dynamic interplay of design solutions, shaping the evolution of intersecting dome architecture in Al Andalus – from the Taifa period through Gothic architecture to modern Spain.

The architectural compositions of Bab Al Mardum offer valuable lessons on how a musalla can serve as a site for architectural, urban, and social experimentation. Its scale allows for innovation, while its compact form enables a concentrated architectural expression. I see in this tenth-century prayer hall an experiment akin to a competition, a race in the evolution of musalla architecture. It represents a historical continuum of the architects' efforts in this book to advance religious architecture, both conceptually and practically, toward greater complexity and freedom.

Written on February 4, 2025

←*Image:* Moath Alofi, *The Last Tashahud*, 2017→

Conversation
On Landscape as Space, Landscape as Material

Azra Akšamija *with*
Sahel AlHiyari

This conversation took place under the shade of the canopies of the Hajj Terminal, Jeddah, on January 25, 2025. It started at around 13:00 in the afternoon, and ran for about 25 minutes. Pairing Azra Akšamija with Sahel AlHiyari aimed to highlight the different ways in which both their practices approach ideas of transience. Here, you will find them challenging the concept of transient structures by oscillating between the nomadic and the archeological, and the role of geometry as a bridge between the past, the present, and the future.

AA: I have admired your work for a long time, and it's really nice to see the innovations that came through in your proposal for *AlMusalla Prize 2025*. Could you elaborate a little bit on the initial thoughts that led you to the concept?

SA: Well, to begin with, I started to look at the function of the *musalla*, which is a prayer space, and the nature of prayer in Islam, which is not necessarily connected to a consecrated space. So, the idea was to make a space or create a space that is an intersection between: the land, an object, and the *musalla* space. It stems from the fact that the *musalla* can emerge anywhere, really. It could be on the side of a road, out in the desert, or in a room within a building. And so, there is that ambiguity that is carried into the design of the proposal: to create an object that is partially landscape, partially an object, and has this very distinct spatial experience within it.

AA: Yes, your work is often very site-specific, and here we are in this amazing, hypostyle structure of the Hajj Terminal.
In what way does your project go into and respond to this site? Maybe it's about replicability,

Uses her right hand in a circular repeating motion

and the idea of extending into the landscape.

Separates both her hands to emphasize the notion of expansion?

SA: If you look at the structure and scale of the hypostyle hall, it starts to have an impact on the horizon, almost like an atmosphere that encompasses the horizon. So, it's really at the scale of the landscape

Leans forward ever so slightly to emphasize the word "landscape"

rather than an object, or a building, or a space. So, the landscape itself becomes an important compositional part, The *musalla* becomes a gesture so the ground actually transforms in terms of topography. It rises up, and then there's another transformation which is the body of the *musalla* itself. If you want to translate it to musical terms, it's almost like a mezzo-staccato where you have one movement that transforms into another. The movements are not entirely distinct from one another, one is a geometric transformation of the other.

In short, sand in my proposal begins to have a geometric expression. The texture and the color of the body of the *musalla* are the same, but it has two different aspects. It transforms from the topography into the niche-like faceted muqarnas. A muqarnas is normally a decorative transitional area between a wall and a dome. Considering that we have a dome here.

Glances backward to allude to the terminal's tent above

The *musalla* itself becomes the muqarnas, the transitional space that connects you to the sky, to the oculus.

AA: That aspect is really interesting. Also, there is an architectural innovation around the muqarnas itself, which is not necessarily meant to be a structural part of the building, right? Here you have taken something from the realm of decoration and craftmanship and turned it into a structural ornament.

SA: Absolutely. The way the muqarnas is constructed in segments was inspirational in terms of

creating parts that can be assembled and attached together and then dismantled, because that was part of the brief.

AA: So, it is a modular system in that case.

SA: Yes, it's a modular system and the muqarnas itself is a modular system, but in this case, it also becomes structural and spatial. The whole space becomes a muqarnas.

AA: That's brilliant. In that sense, you could endlessly multiply it.

SA: Indeed, you can.

AA: Horizontally and maybe vertically as well?

SA: Yes, absolutely. It's possible, by adding other pieces, to create a completely different section, height, or even scale. It has that potential.

AA: That, I think, makes it uniquely contemporary, but, also, it is truly Islamic. We can say that, if anything, muqarnas is an element that is unique to Islamic architecture. Whereas everything else is developed in dialogue with pre-existing architectural forms.

SA: Exactly. I think that the engagement with geometry in Islamic architecture has been quite distinct, historically. It's the geometry of these elements, how they manifest, and how they start to create and sculpt space, right? So, there is this connection to the project, and of course, because the *musalla* structure was placed under the oculus. Then you have the canopy of the existing terminal,

Outlines the sweeping sectional quality of the canopy using his hands

and finally there's an oculus through which you see a patch of blue sky.

AA: Inside the structure is a hollow square. It is like a footprint of the K‘aba in a way. It reminded me of an almost presence of the K‘aba, or its absence. Was this an intentional reference?

SA: It wasn’t really an intentional reference. But when I look at it, it could be interpreted as the absence of an object, obviously, or a courtyard as well. And, yes, the earliest mosques in Islam were constructed in courtyards and gardens and so on, in Madinah. So that can become a connection.

AA: Tell me about the blue lines. Throughout the design, there is this gorgeous blue line in terracotta, reminding us of decorative elements from historic Islamic forms.

SA: Yes, absolutely. The blue line comes as a direct referencee from Islamic scripts that you can find on Islamic buildings across the world. And the idea is that the geometry is reiterated through lines, right?

AA nods in agreement

Usually, a muqarnas is quite heavy when you look at it in its unadorned form. It’s very sculpted and if it has decorative lines it tends to be more delicate. So in my proposal, I tried to play with the idea of the weight of the elements of the muqarnas through the lines. So I brought in a very delicate line that also relates to the patch of blue in the sky, and to the ribbing of the canopy. By having these lines, there is a direct connection between the ground, the ceiling, the canopy, and the sky beyond.

AA: That delicate interplay between weight and lightness in your design is really compelling. The way the blue line ties together different spatial elements – from the ground to the sky – creates a beautiful continuity that enhances the ephemeral quality of the *musalla*. Now let's talk a little bit about the material. There are some really innovative aspects in your work. There are the sandbags, which allow for this type of project to be replicated in any other place, and specifically in climates where sand is plentiful.

SA: Yes. There are two ways of building and creating structures that become like landscapes. One is simpler than the other, which basically uses sandbags to stabilize the topography, and have a solid periphery on which there is a layer of stabilized sand. So, this is one idea. Then the inside of the segments themselves are made from reinforced concrete, using the material of the ground itself, the aggregate of the ground, the soil of the ground, creating a contuity with the sand itself. And the segments basically create a continuity with the sand. The Hajj Terminal itself has walls that are plastered in the same material. So there was also the idea to replicate what is already there, and to replicate the most fundamental building techniques or one could say, rudimentary building techniques, that you find locally, which is reinforced concrete.

SA indicates the tile size with his thumb and index finger

Then, the interior is finished with terracotta tiles and the blue lines are inlaid terracotta on concrete. So, it's, in a sense, multiple materials that are working harmoniously together, although created and functioning in different ways. The idea was to place it, once the biennale is finished, in any landscape.

AA: That's so fascinating about your design. It's a massive structure and works with materials like concrete, but it's completely deployable in various locations. It's mobile and it has this nice aspect of sustainability, which can be replicated with locally available materials in many other sites.

SA: This is true and it also does not require a lot of maintenance. It is essentially a project that can be given back to nature and it would survive the elements here in Saudi Arabia.

AA nods in agreement

AA: So, let's talk about some of the larger lessons that we can learn from your project, but also from this competition, about the idea and the conceptual framework of the *musalla*.

In my previous research on mosque architecture, I have theorized the mosque in terms of generative design principles – its essence is shaped by the volume of the body, the performance of the ritual act of prayer, its inherent directionality, and the purity and ritual cleanliness that define it. This perspective builds on the Prophet Muhammad's, (PBUH), characterization of the mosque as a space of prostration, emphasizing that wherever one prays, the mosque is present. In that sense, architecture is not a necessity for prayer – it can take place in the desert, on a street, or simply with a prayer rug. Why and how, then, do we use architecture to create a mosque? What parameters guide your approach when designing a *musalla* or a mosque? How do you navigate the balance between a structured space and the fundamental simplicity of prayer, which can happen anywhere, even in a mass gathering on a carpet or in an open context?

SA: That is a very interesting question. Indeed, it is true that prayer can occur anywhere, and a prayer mat can do the job, basically. But I do believe in this

term called *khoushou'*, which is the state of presence in prayer that allows you to be present and in the moment, while in the presence of God. And that is the fundamental aspect of prayer. I believe that space or architecture can provide the setting for that moment, the tranquillity and the peace that allows the worshipper to immerse themselves in this state. For me it's light, it's proportion and systems, even geometry when you see the muqarnas for example, or when you see Islamic patterns surrounding you, your mind does not focus on one aspect, but it's sort of dispersed. It's almost as if, the ego is dispersed. And, this has a very interesting psychological effect on the mind. In that sense, I think prayer spaces or prayer halls can perform an additional function which is to provide that atmosphere or feeling.

AA: And to enhance that spirituality.

SA Mimics AA's hand motion in agreement

SA: To enhance the feeling. It's also not done in one way, it can be done in multiple ways, and that's the beauty of it, its plurality.

AA: That is very interesting. You know, in my own work I have done a lot of research on the representation of Islam in the West as well as with Muslim diasporic communities and groups. Muslims who live in non-Muslim majority countries are seeking formal ways in which they can visualize their identity. In that context, the *musalla* is also about culture and presence. And in those contexts, what I noticed was, it was very important for these communities to draw from specific historical and cultural precedents to signal their identity. But because when you build Islamic prayer spaces in places with a non-Muslim majority, there's this question of negotiating with the pre-existing or dominant culture and how that comes into dialogue, right? And here it's always this negotiation of historical forms. Which one do we select? You might have, especially in the West, many Muslims coming from different backgrounds, right? So, you have Egyptians and maybe someone from Central Asia or China, and they are all praying in the same mosque. So even for their identity, there would be different historical precedents to draw inspiration from. So, these questions for me are also interesting in the sense of: what is generic and what is culturally specific or locally specific about mosques?

SA: What you're asking is a thorny thing, I think, because if you start to say, I am only going to do a project that's specific to the culture of India and that's it, or wherever, which time period do you choose your inspiration from? I mean there is a plethora of references that can be used, but I do believe that the way it can emerge is through a much more organic and intuitive way. A way that actually comes from or emerges from the site itself, as a conversation with a sense of place. In my case, it was the faceting or the idea for the muqarnas came because of the ceiling and the ground. It wasn't necessarily to make a particular reference. It came intuitively like an essence, but an essence that works with the context itself, an essence that converses with the context. And I think this, at least in my work, is how I like to think of history, that it's something that emerges from kind of a direct involvement with the context. But your question is very interesting because I don't think there's an answer. For instance, where do you draw the line between what is generic and what is not generic. I often think that when we try to insist on certain references it's because we want to make a certain statement; it becomes too forced.

AA: In the case of your design, it's so beautiful that there's this reference again to the archaeological site. A kind of digging into the landscape and learning from its history which unfolds in the design. It corresponds to the site and works with local materials, but then also innovates on that history.

SA: It explains a certain ambiguity, right? Ambiguity, because ambiguity allows people to interpret, to create their own meaning, or assign the space a certain meaning

AA nods in agreement

I don't want to force a definition. You know, I feel like this is something that emerges through use, emerging through the people using the space. I mean, somebody from one country can look at it in one way and another person can interpret it in an entirely different, polar opposite way. And so, the concept of defining specific messages and forcing meaning to me is like painting oneself in a corner.

AA: Finally, what is something that you are taking from this project, what was enriching for you?

SA: You know, what has been very enriching in the particular context of this project was that we never really think of creating architecture within a much larger architectural space, within a massive system, a massive shelter, and so on. And for me, it was particularly meaningful because I went to the Hajj Terminal when it was functioning as a terminal. I've seen it filled with pilgrims, and that was something absolutely stunning. And now, I'm seeing it in a completely different light. When architecture is powerful enough and when it's done in a certain way that can promote its own longevity, or maybe when it inherently has ability to transform and have different meanings and different functions across time, it just goes to show how important architecture can be.

An Intersection Between Landscape, Space, and Object

Office of Sahel AlHiyari for Architecture (OSAA) approached the musalla as an embodiment of the essence of Islamic tradition, where prayer transcends physical boundaries and adapts to various contexts. It emerges from its surroundings, embodying both public and private, interior, and exterior realms. Therefore, a musalla is not necessarily linked to a specific typology with clear formal characteristics; rather, it emerges as a function (prayer) taking place within a setting.

Central to the musalla's function is facilitating an atmosphere conducive to worship and the attainment of khoushou', a state of presence, awe, and humility intrinsic to Islamic prayer rituals. The nature of the space where prayer takes place should enhance this state without distraction.

OSAA''s competition proposal sought to define an infinite space within the expanded Hajj Terminal, without losing the presence of either. The ground plane – the location for prayer – was key to their concept. The musalla takes the form of a mound, a topographic layer of stabilized sand which encloses the space. The musalla would appear as constructed by the site itself, becoming both object and landscape.

The geometric forms that make up the mound reflect the association of Islamic arts and architecture with nature and cosmology through a geological mineral expression. The glazed terracotta interior of OSAA''s musalla continues the geometric arrangements of its exterior but at an intimate scale. The space connects to the sky through an oculus, which would allow light to filter through the gaps of the interior structure, adding another geometric dimension.

Hanif Kara

Technology Whispers Quietly

The appropriation of architectural traditions that embody the spirit of Islam is a pertinent lens through which we can see that technology has long coexisted with the working philosophies of adaptability and responsiveness. I would also posit that this can connect with meaningful interpretations of Islam, the diversity of the Islamic peoples, and Islamic precepts of living. The duality – between the imposing and the understated – is poignant when thinking about functional spaces shaped by cultural and spiritual practices as in the case with the prayer space of the *musalla* (pl. *musallayaat*).

In my experience, musalla spaces, whether grand or humble, often share a core principle: they are rarely rigid, fixed structures but fluid environments, expanding and contracting in response to the needs of the people who use them. For context, they can be public and private spaces, the slightest essence of their ambiance is drawn out using sound, texture, pattern, light, and smell, constructed artificially to impact their environment minimally. I find this to be an important reflection of how technology, even in its simplest form, can shape space in ways that prioritize human experience over permanence.

That said, material practice as technology feels too slippery, vast, and elusive to write about in this short reflection. In design, the relationship with technology (as a method for inventive production rather than elevating it to a quasi-religious status) can manifest in many ways both subtle and monumental. Sometimes, it is the sheer presence of a "structure" that reveals technological prowess or progress like the tallest skyscrapers or the longest bridge. Other times, technology whispers quietly through spaces that respond not with grandeur alone, but with flexibility, grace, and harmony, retaining context and particular use.

It's within this frame that I see Fazlur Rahman Khan's work – not as a singular achievement but as part of a larger continuum of technological exploration. In the specific case of the Hajj Terminal at King Abdulaziz International Airport in Jeddah, his design is a rare example that simultaneously takes fabric structures a giant leap forward while depicting historical continuity and unique purpose. And at a certain level of pioneering, it aligns with ideas of adaptability. Its vast tensile structured roof offers what many describe as a soft monumentality – that doesn't impose – and at a distance, it even appears to *levitate*, emulating the *experience of flight*, and echoing the lightness and impermanence of the rituals and journeys of the pilgrims in transit. It was conceived for eighty-thousand air travelers, many from non-industrialized countries, voyaging for up to thirty-six hours. The Hajj Terminal is a huge space used only for two months every year, leading up to and following the Hajj.

As another temporal space of assembly, musallayaat are much smaller, in comparison, and appear when the function of prayer arises. Used in frequent short durations, by small groups or individuals, they can be set up and dismantled easily in many shapes and sizes. Technology, in this case, is used to enhance adaptability and impermanence rather than dictating rigid forms.

The technology behind the Hajj Terminal is complex and sophisticated. The design development and structural modeling used advanced calculation processes that we follow to this day. Yet, the result is simple – uncontrived, unambiguous, and relevant to its context – standing the test of time as intended. Having spent much of 1976 studying Islamic heritage, Khan was also a great collaborator working with his colleagues at Skidmore, Owings & Merrill to steward familiar geometries that combine the circle and sphere (signifying the world of the spirit) and the square and cube (referring to earth and stability) as a basic module that aggregates almost infinitely to create the terminal.

This project is a reminder that the technology we apply to architecture is never neutral or innocent. It carries the weight of the context it serves. In Khan's case, technology became a way to mediate between environment, culture, and the demands of modern infrastructure. What resonates with me is the absence of excess. There's a clarity in how the terminal reflects the essentials – movement, rest, and shelter – rather than attempting to impose unnecessary permanence on a space inherently shaped by transition and a transient community.

What I find compelling is the idea that technological progress does not have to contradict tradition thus allowing us to slacken the tension between innovation and heritage, as if the two exist in opposition. Many of the most enduring architectural forms, particularly within Islamic and other cultural traditions, reveal that technology has always been part of history – not as an external force, but as an organic extension of how humans solve problems and interact with their environment.

As a structural engineer who cannot separate design, research, making, construction, and teaching, from quality of life; I am careful to maintain a balance in the engagement with projects and ideas that embrace impermanence and fluidity as well as the impulse to create fixed, monolithic structures. The temptations of originality and novelty thus become a by-product of this practice.

I want to also avoid an obstinate gaze, given the accelerated impact of climate change. The boundaries between temporary and permanent structures (new and existing) are adopting new profiles at an unprecedented pace, the *playground* between permanent and temporary structures is not the same and is in constant flux. This territory has a fascinating capacity to surprise and turn new concerns into new opportunities just as Khan once did when he designed the Hajj Terminal.

Undoubtedly, there is something powerful in designing spaces that can shift and breathe. The power of technology, in this sense, becomes a tool not for control but for responsiveness – a way to let architecture move with life rather than stand apart from it. Reflecting on this,

I realize that what draws me to technology isn't its capacity for spectacle but its ability to disappear into the background, creating conditions that feel natural, intuitive, and aligned with how people inhabit space. The most interesting innovations, to me, are the ones that blur the line between the artificial and the natural, where materials and systems work quietly to create environments that feel effortless yet deeply considered, it requires an interdisciplinary approach not constrained by traditional professions and isolated disciplinary thinking.

This, I think, is where the real power of technology lies not just in what it builds, but in how it adapts, responds, and ultimately becomes part of the rhythms of human experience. Whether through prayer spaces, transport hubs, or temporary structures, the technology that endures is the kind that listens first, shaping itself to fit the world it inhabits in harmony.

Written on January 4, 2025

←*Image:* Moath Alofi, *The Last Tashahud*, 2017→

Chapter 3

تطلُّعات مُعاصِــرة

Contemporary Aspirations

Conversation
On Light and Craft

Lina Ghotmeh *with* Asif Khan

This conversation took place under the shade of the canopies of the Hajj Terminal, Jeddah, on January 25, 2025. It started at around 13:00 in the afternoon, and ran for about 45 minutes. Pairing Lina Ghotmeh with Asif Khan aimed to allow the space for two practicing architects to put forth ideas about their shared commitments for unearthing narratives of continuities between the past, the present, and the future. Here, you will find them collaboratively discussing personal and professional origins, actively blurring the disciplinary boundaries of their practices, glass as a mediator of light and ideas, and aspirations for a better future.

LG: It's wonderful to see you, Asif, I had the pleasure to be on the jury of *AlMusalla Prize* and I was really fascinated by the process of your research and how the idea of your *musalla* proposal came about. It was quite magical, especially this fascination with light, enlightenment, and Surah An-Nur that was part of your narrative.

I want you to tell me more about it. As an architect, I'm always intrigued and passionate about this kind of discourse that leads to projects.

AK: For me, the project was the coming together of personal history complemented by research. As someone who was born in the UK as a Muslim from both the Indian subcontinent and East Africa, my heritage is twice removed. So, when a project like this comes along, and more so in my life now, as I am over forty years old and getting older, the need to reconnect and strengthen those roots becomes more important as the tree gets taller.

Pointing his finger upward

So, when I found myself being given the chance to work in this extraordinary context, so close to the holy cities, and on this path that leads pilgrims on the once-in-a-lifetime Hajj, I felt the need to reach deep within, not just within my practice, but also into my past or my DNA.

LG interjects quietly: Yourself

Exactly, and to use the project as a magnifying lens to explore some of that. I was lucky to have my foundations, after I finished school, at the King's Foundation, where they gave us an education that drew upon traditional arts, geometry, and the classical understanding of esthetics and construction from the Islamic

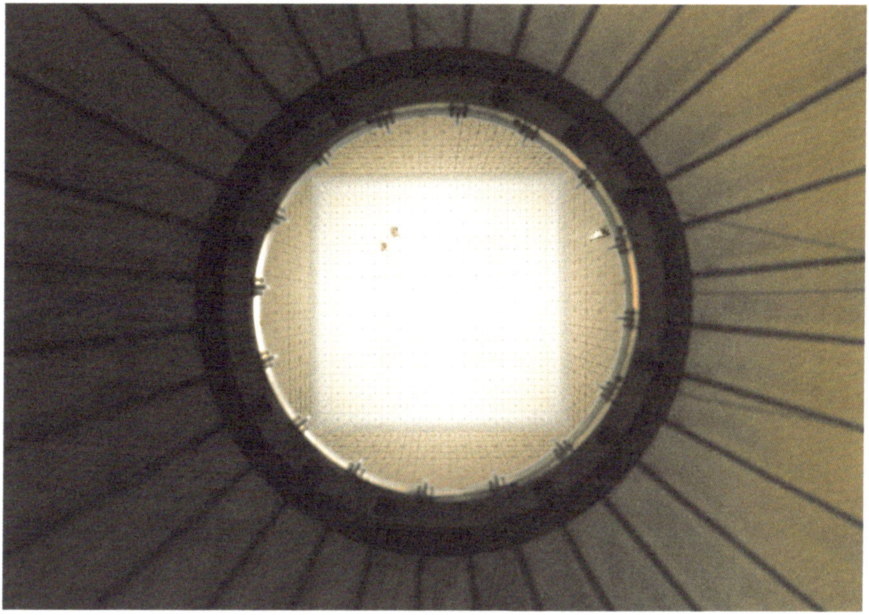

world, ancient Greece, and ancient Rome. They were trying to create a fusion of those things to help us become better architects. I put it aside for many years, and when this brief came out, everything I learned twenty years ago started to come back. Very simply, there's a kind of thought process from Keith Critchlow, who is a great sacred geometer and Islamic arts professor, who based his thinking on Plato. These sorts of fundamentals were the origin of my understanding of architecture and also my journey into the project.

LG: That's beautiful. And I think this relationship to origin is something that echoes so much in the way I perceive architecture and in the way that we work in the region. There is a sense of belonging that emerges, that is really deep inside of you, and then it suddenly comes out, when you're working in this context, especially when while living in distant places. You know, I practice in Paris, I grew up in Beirut, Lebanon, so even the Arabic language emerges again.

The spirituality of your *musalla* proposal really echoes your roots in a way and brings up something very magical. I'm also interested to know about your artistic endeavor when developing the project. As architects, we're always between being architects and artists, we're somehow making or creating built spaces that are inhabited, but they are also forms of art that are also inhabited and experienced, and they can allow for this kind of emotion that unfolds in space. I felt there was a sense of art that was performed in your project. Is this something that you uncovered during this project? Or is it something that is also very much present in every project?

AK: Absolutely. I think this question between art and architecture is an important one. Architecture has been called the mother of all arts, so sculpture, poetry, dance, theater, these art forms, calligraphy, all of these forms unify in architecture. We find a way of working as an artistic practice rather than as a service, because it's about being yourself and finding yourself in the project, and the project finding itself through you. So, you are a conduit for the project.

↗ *Image:* Marco Cappelletti, 2025

I tried to embody both myself and the opportunity presented within it. For example, what is a *musalla?* What is the relationship between a person and that space? Moreover, for me, what was interesting, was the relationship between the Qur'an and the architecture. Even though, I've been here several times before, this time I was looking to see whether I could find a correlation between the Qur'an, which the Islamic faith is predicated upon, and the architecture that unfolds from it.
LG: True, and it's really fascinating, because if you go back to the words in the Qur'an, they can unravel a whole space, a feeling of space and time, a very intense one, and this can open up

the door to a strong spatial experience. I feel that in your interest in the Surah An-Nur, there was this kind of spatial realm that opened up that was so beautiful, that was so delicate as well. It's the space in between the physical realm and the intangible, and it gave way to an expression in your *musalla* that was invisible, very fine, and very delicate. Actually, it echoes the idea about being in between; in between the heavenly and the terrestrial.

When you're talking about art and architecture, I think one of the common threads between both is the question of the hand, you know, craft and making. When we look at all the historical artifacts that we see exhibited at the Islamic Arts Biennale, there's a sense of craft that really transcends categories as well as time and space. You explore this very nicely in the artwork that you are also exhibiting, the book of glass, where the text is scripted and done by hand. I would love to know more about how you reveal space within that artifact itself. And this idea of craft, how does it play a role in generating a new realm?

AK: This is an amazing question. Islam, in my opinion, is like the birth of conceptual art. It moves from abstraction to logic, science, esthetics, art, and ritual. It compounds and amalgamates... My feeling is that Islam is the highest art... It's what art was all about after all. It started with a faith in something beyond; it was a means to understand something beyond what we can comprehend. It was a tool, how to unravel, and how to understand.

LG: Yes, without fully understanding, and that's what's beautiful. So, you're in that state, right? You're always in this kind of abstract state of being, which is really magical in a way, right?

AK: That's right, and you said it's the in-between, which is exactly right. So, in-between means that some will understand more, and some will understand less.

LG nods in agreement

The whole of a community will have this state of mind, which is like a cloud of feelings, it's like a shared...

LG: It's a shared metaphysical existence, and maybe we can say the invisible really binds us together in a way, and that it's power that is much more present than our own presence. And I really love how this was embodied in the way you presented your project as this kind of cloud that we could experience, even if it's a virtual experience. I think, as architects, we always do competitions; sometimes we win and sometimes we don't, but I think the thoughts and the processes of making continue with us, from one project to the other. Your project ended up with artwork here, but maybe it will be continued in different art forms as well.

AK: I don't know whether you've had this experience before, but one project can be a gateway to something else you know,

LG interjects: Of course, yes

the purpose of it from the beginning may have not been where you ended up, but it was just a matter of following the current.

LG: It's part of the journey.

AK: That's right

Sometimes you don't see the link immediately, but then you realize it at some point. It's part of this kind of continuous journey that we're endeavoring.

AK: Let's go back to the study of Surah An-Nur. I love this verse because it is the most universal verse, in my opinion. A Muslim or non-Muslim can find meaning in it because it tries to, in human terms, convey something inconceivable and like light itself, it is an analogy for... the magnitude of God. So, the idea of a pavilion of light is devotional; if we can find it and design it, it can be seen as an act of devotion. So, this was the exploration and why glass was a medium because glass is an ancient material. It's beneath the earth but it has these cosmic qualities; it's a transmitter and emanator of light; and reflection and refraction. It's mentioned in the Holy Qur'an a multitude of times, along with lanterns and light. These two thoughts, and you mentioned the second just now, the hand, become very important. The hand is disappearing from our world of production, and craft is isolated from the user. We buy things in shops, but we don't have any relationship with how they are produced.

LG: Maybe another hand that we are not able to understand yet emerges. Maybe it is less tactile.

AK: We have a kind of digital world emerging and we come to museums and extraordinary events like this to remind ourselves of the human-made world and our relationship with it, but often our architecture is very far away from that. At the scale of the *musalla*, you can bring craft back. And so, this act of making through repetition, which is a meditative act, it's like the repetition of a verse. This is something that I feel is important, which is why it's a pavilion of linework, of repetition. Every point is connected to other points which convey meaning through their geometric relationships, but they are also conductors of light, emanating around us and creating this cloud-like feeling. You could think of it as micro-architecture, as a building, and then the building fell away because we didn't win the competition. Now all these ideas are contained within the artwork we are displaying.

LG: When you were describing this question of linking the lines, I was thinking about threading and weaving. I think that moment of threading, of weaving things together, and the process of it, is an experience that is very profound. Sometimes we explore this in architecture, or in the process of thinking about a project, even in the artwork that you're presenting, and now we can see this within the current pavilion as well.

She motions toward the winning proposal nearby

I'm thinking about: how can we, as architects, actually push that, in the making of our built space? How does it perform? Today, I mean, it could perform using craft in the way we build, whether crafted by hand or crafted using a machine. How do you actually see that in

your work? Do you still work with craft as part of your architecture and projects? Are you able to move from the crafted object to architecture?

AK: I think this is the question of the era. First of all, my perspective on it is to be true to myself. As a person, if you can realize and center yourself, you can discover deep foundations, which is, basically, ancestral knowledge.

Humans haven't changed for a long time, right? We've remained the same. We still like weaving, we still like threads, and we still like handwork because it nourishes us. We still like planting things. We like dancing, we like music, we like the softness and silkiness of things and the roughness and we like cutting things and shaping them. The malleability of the world around us nourishes us. We have a lot of tools in the world now which take us further away from the earth, clay, rivers, the tastes in our mouth, and all of these things. When you pick up a hand-brewed Arabic coffee and you can taste the cardamom, of course, it's better than regular coffee. I think in my practice I'm always trying to find my way back to this... Taste. You tend to come back to these same things, like scratches in the earth, and like textures that give you goosebumps, and the pleasure of your hand running through hair, and this is...

LG: And the light hitting it.

AK: The light hitting it, the sunbeams, and all those basics, they're not contrivances, they're the essence of what it is to be conscious and that's what human beings are, and we need to reinforce that today more than ever and it will be even harder as we go on. So, I search to find what is our common ground.

LG : Who we are.

AK: Who we are, yes exactly, and then the architecture is going to be easy, we just need to be a conduit for who we are.

LG: I wonder how AI will affect these things.

AK: I think this is a...

Hesitates

potential future. The question that arises is: What is the value of things? What does it mean when we start to value the work of a computer as equal or better than the work of a person? With all of the messiness, of what it is to be human, and we know how difficult it is to be human: to live and to survive biologically, but also to become a master of something. If other people start valuing the work of a computer, with none of those difficulties of life, it starts to ask what value is there in anything that human beings do. And, what kind of society is that?

LG: It's true. You know, as humans, we're always struggling, or working to build an understanding of the world. We're describing architecture as a way of constantly building knowledge, but also to understand the world.

Architecture is a profession that allows you to constantly question, to build, to reconfigure the environment in a different way and allow that dream to constantly be present in our lives.

AK: This is the real moment, the new Industrial Revolution, but I think that it's more fragile than we assume. Let's look at this extraordinary building,

Looks backward, with arms wide open, to emphasize the expansiveness of the Hajj Terminal

this will never be made again. No one will have the belief or the take the risk to try to make an open-air airport again. This is the most extraordinary work, and it is because of a belief in something.

LG: There's an embodiment of that belief and the space that it creates which makes it so precious.

This is why, to wrap up our conversation, I think AlMusalla and similar initiatives, somehow, bring back the belief

AK: Exactly, exactly that the meaning of architecture is not just a functional, consumerist manifestation, but that it is also about the experience between here and the beyond. AK: The *AlMusalla Prize* is about planting a seed for others and for ourselves, and hopefully, this seed finds fertile ground to change a little bit the direction we're going in.

Space, Line, and Number

As the competition's runner-up, Asif Khan Studio was awarded a commendation for their design which draws from the idea of Tawhid – oneness – a concept which underpins aspects of Islamic art, architecture, space and ritual. This concept is embodied most in the Ka'aba, the center of the earth and towards which every qibla in each of the 3.6 million mosques and musallas around the world points. During this shared practice of prayer some 1.8 billion lines could be drawn in one direction, revealing a singularity and constant that has held for over 1400 years.

Asif Khan Studio's musalla is a four-sided open weave structure with a roof supported on each of its four corners. The walls form eight pivoting sections which could be opened into a number of different configurations. At the center of the space within a display case would sit a glass Qur'an. As in nature at all scales, geometry leads to structure and to reconciliation in forces. Asif Khan's design proposal posits that if structural order at all scales of nature embody a divine expression, structures and art created by humanity in keeping with these geometries are themselves acts of worship.

Ziad Jamaleddine

Without a Drawing, but not Without History

How can we design a *musalla*, when the historical record lacks drawings of its past manifestations?

One might think to look toward other religious structures' records such as the survey drawing by K.A.C. Creswell of al-Azhar Mosque which played a critical role in defining disciplinary knowledge of Islamic architecture. Historically and through their inclusion in architectural survey books, planimetric drawings contributed to the formation of a fixed classificatory system of Islamic spaces of worship. The musalla, a transitory space for prostration, was absent from this strictly scripted visual history. This representational lacuna is an affordance that allows us to speculate on the spatial, material, and programmatic possibilities that open up when this space of worship is freed from the pictorial weight of the canon, and consequently, begins to question the established typological history of the mosque.

Since the late nineteenth century, the production of planimetric drawings in survey books of Islamic architecture history has followed scientific methods of representation, which evolved to facilitate the increasingly accurate capture of the plans of complex historical buildings. Through these techniques, the multiple layers of buildings' expansions, accretions, and renovations over time were depicted for study. Planimetric drawings were instrumental in the comparative analysis of diverse buildings and, thus, in the typological classification of mosques from across the vast geography of the Islamic world.

Reproduced in *The Muslim Architecture of Egypt* (1952–1959), Creswell's canonical survey drawing of the al-Azhar Mosque epitomizes this representational method and the disciplinary knowledge it produced (Figure 1). The large 70 x 85 cm elaborate folio drawing is scaled at 1:300 and uses color-coded poché walls to delimit the building's various periods of construction from 1130 to 1894. Centerlines cross over the mosque's form seeking to identify compositional symmetry and alignments between its entrances and other parts. Thoroughly measured dimensions further enforce arguments about underlying geometric compositions, proportions, and rhythms. In addition, a north sign indicates orientation toward Makkah.

Creswell's painstakingly accurate depiction of the edifice both captured the state in which he found it and opened an inquiry into the reconstruction of its historical past. Through his exhaustive identification of construction periods and meticulous dimensions, Creswell graphically argued that he had uncovered traces of the building's supposed origin, hypothesizing that it must have been a rectangle. Like his scholarly contemporaries, Creswell believed the mosques he studied had "true" original forms that reflected clear typological models.

Creswell also omitted al-Azhar's urban context from his drawing, unmooring the mosque from its ground to be read as an autonomous object. A subsequent idealized drawing titled "Proposed reconstruction of original mosque" emphasized this interpretation and allowed the building to be analyzed against the plans of other mosques (Figure 2). Paradoxically, the precision of the survey drawing facilitated the eventual abstraction of the mosque. As it was reproduced and disseminated through twentieth-century history books, these drawings were progressively simplified into diagrams, reducing histories of dynamic building practices into fixed forms.

The survey drawing excels in the static representation of knowledge, fixing dimensions, periods of construction, and uses. The overly simplified drawing of al-Azhar reverted its manifold eras, directionalities, and programs into a clearly oriented, single-use, Fatimid-era building. In contrast to the fixity of the mosque survey drawing, the musalla, a malleable religious space – that continues to escape such rigid metrics – offers a critical lens through which to reexamine mosques represented in survey books. Historically through its temporal spatial practices, the musalla has no graphic presence in survey books. As such, it has no pre-determined geometric composition, no strict alignment of parts that create a unified whole, and no poché walls to define space or reveal origins. While it is oriented toward Makkah, its temporary general directionality (*jiha*) is permissive and approximate. When it physically shapes a space for prostration, it leaves no identifiable traces to map, analyze, or classify after it is gone. The musalla, thus, exists outside of typology.

If the survey drawing claims to capture the multiple temporalities of historical structures only to erase them, the musalla's lack of systematic representation leaves us only with its temporalities. The musalla's resistance to being captured by the survey calls for the development of alternate forms of historical knowledge for Islamic spaces of worship – including the Friday mosque – and of new practices through which to represent them. The cumulative spatial practices embodied by the musalla – both persistent and reimagined – and the community benefits they provide to worshipers offer a rich source on which to build this expanded knowledge. Freed from the fixity of the survey and the compositional typological diagram, Islamic spaces of worship can be recomposed in relationship with their social milieus, and urban and environmental contexts. By understanding these connections anew, the mosque can be disentangled from the functionalist typological tradition disseminated through the planimetric drawing. Renewed programmatic flexibility and spatial layering will unlock these buildings to a diverse array of users, allowing them to respond to a variety of needs. As we move away from a focus on the purity of the drawing, we can finally stop looking for the "origin" of the mosque's typology. Instead, we can start to mine its entangled, aggregated architectural histories, learning from its more permissive, if fragmented, pasts, and opening previously foreclosed futures.

A mosque without its survey drawing, is not a mosque without history. On the contrary, it is a mosque that seeks to uncover histories obscured by the survey drawing. That history is waiting to be rewritten and undrawn, beginning with musalla design explorations.

Written on January 23, 2025

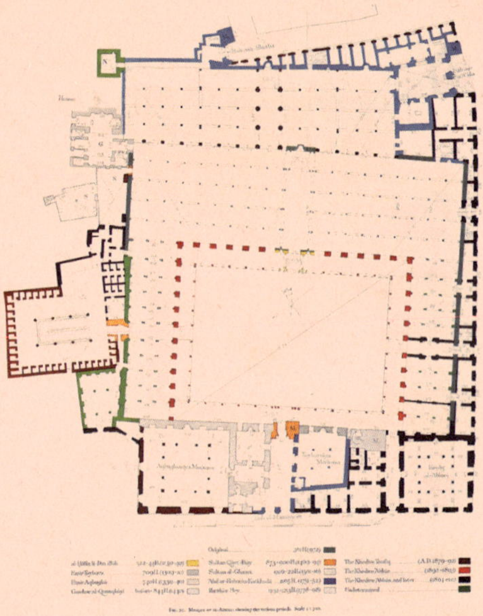

Figure 1. K. A. C. Creswell, Mosque of al-Azhar: Showing the various periods, from *Muslim Architecture of Egypt*, Source: Creswell (1952). Avery Classics, Avery Architectural and Fine Arts Library, Columbia University

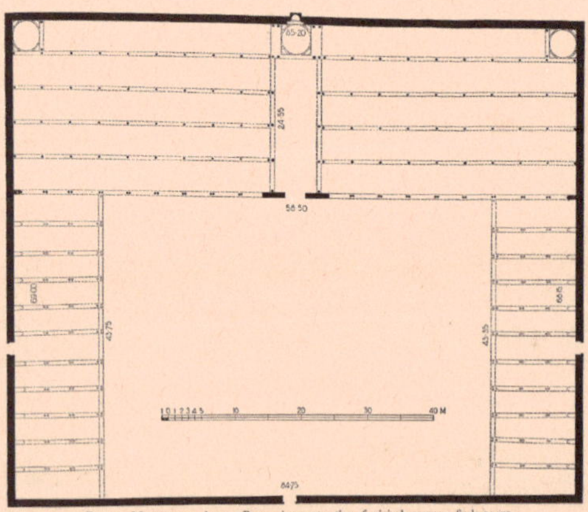

Fig. 21. Mosque of al-Azhar: Proposed reconstruction of original mosque. Scale 1:400.

Figure 2. K. A. C. Creswell, Mosque of al-Azhar: Proposed reconstruction of original mosque, from *Muslim Architecture of Egypt*, Source: Creswell (1952). Avery Classics, Avery Architectural and Fine Arts Library, Columbia University

←*Image:* Moath Alofi, *The Last Tashahud,* 2017→

On Weaving
عن النسيـج

EAST Architecture Studio
Rayyane Tabet
AKT II / Christopher Blust

On Weaving, the competition winning proposal, by EAST Architecture Studio in collaboration with Rayyane Tabet and AKT II, takes inspiration from a book of the same name by prominent textile artist, Anni Albers. Their design reflects on theoretical approaches to craft and its inherent potential to create spaces of coexistence, where weaving becomes a multi-scalar act of making. The concept for the first edition of the *Al Musalla Prize* approaches the idea of making as an immersive process of abstraction: form, shades and shadows, program and authorial intent are articulated using the same line-making procedure.

In their research, the team identified that Saudi Arabia is the second-largest producer of date palms in the world. They discovered that once the plant has passed its productive life, trees are typically felled, burned, or sent to the landfill. The team recognized an opportunity to transform the fronds and fibers left by these neglected local trees into a sustainable material for crafting the musalla's structure and textile cladding. This decision also revives the practice of using date palms in everyday life, once widespread in Saudi Arabia before the ease of access to hardwoods and plastics from abroad.

↗ *Image:* Marco Cappelletti, 2025

On Weaving's design process reorients the narrative of woven textile as both an art and a functional discipline, and seeks to identify the tangible and intangible cultural heritage of weaving – one of the oldest crafts in the region – in particular, its structural performance and the repetitive, ephemeral qualities of its making which introduces an infinite dimension. This reference to infinity deeply echoes the circular ritual of *Tawaf* around the Ka'aba, the holiest of references. Also drawing from weaving, the design examines grids at multiple scales. At the macro scale of palm tree plantation, the field's guiding principle followed a 6x6m grid.

The final design is a double-sided pedestal staggering in its ascent and thinning out as it as it soars upwards towards the canopy of the Hajj Terminal. Its appearance resembles the form of a loom, paying homage to weaving traditions and craftsmanship. It is autonomous, but also modular to suggest its multiple uses, simultaneously acting as a structure, function, and

ornament. The musalla's open courtyard invites visitors to sit, gather or pray, communally or individually. The earthy colors that make up the musalla's exterior are energized with color within the structure's interior, where natural dyes made from local and regional plants are used to illuminate the space with bright reds, blues, greens and yellows.

The fragmented nature of the musalla opens it up to interpretation and reinterpretation, imagination and reimagination. Each fragment comes with a public offering – a prayer space, an arts and crafts platform, an exhibition space, and a public garden. Together they become seeds for collaborations beyond the structure's short life in the Hajj Terminal.

All photos in this section by Mansour Alsofi unless otherwise indicated.

1

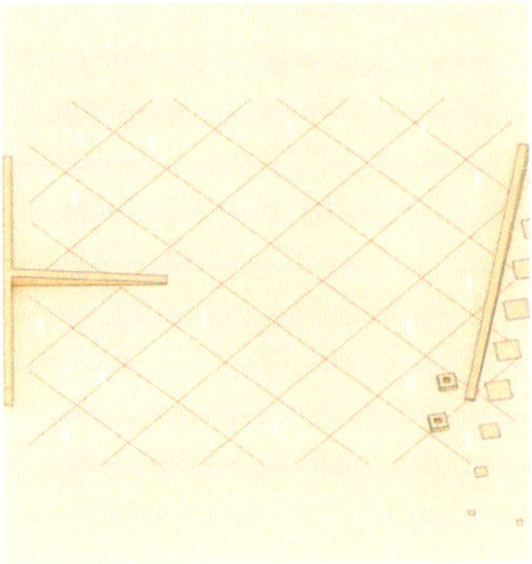

2

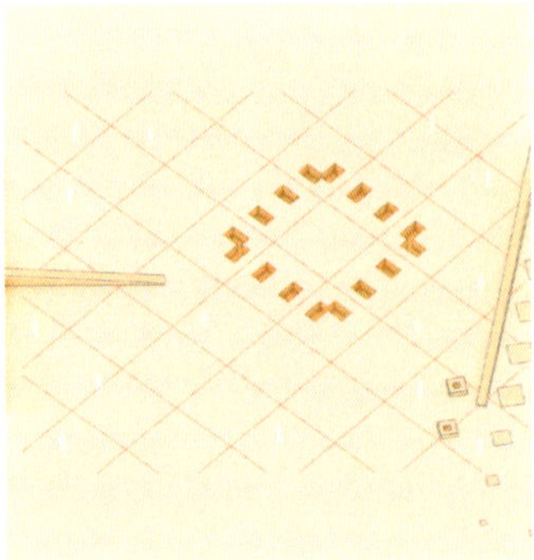

3

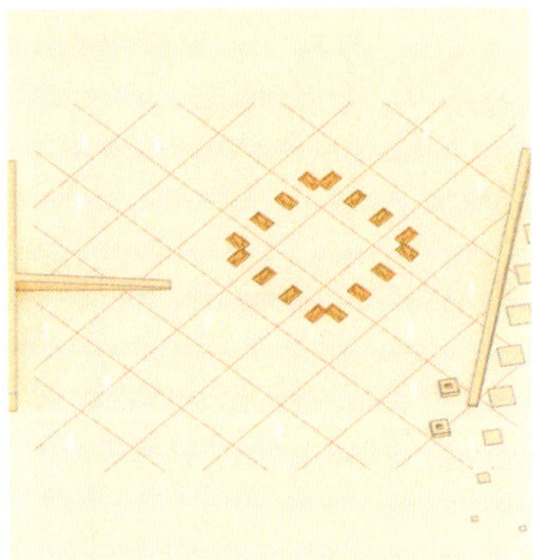

4

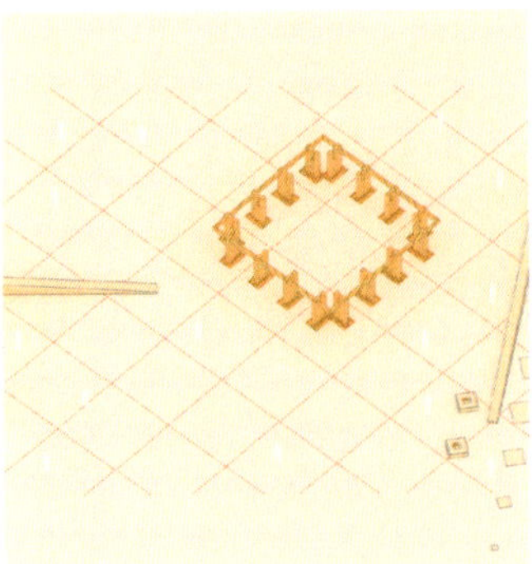

5

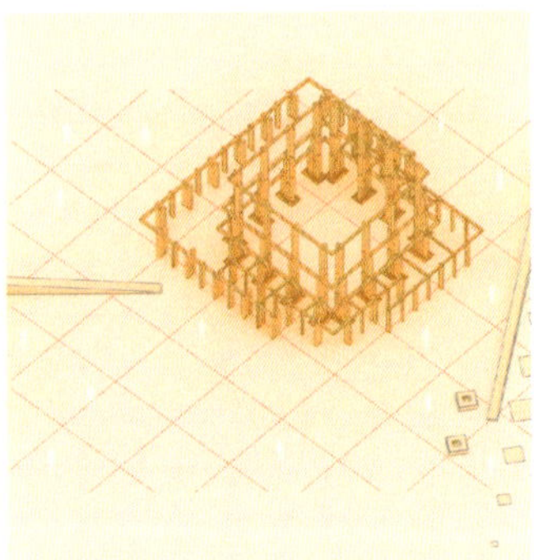

6

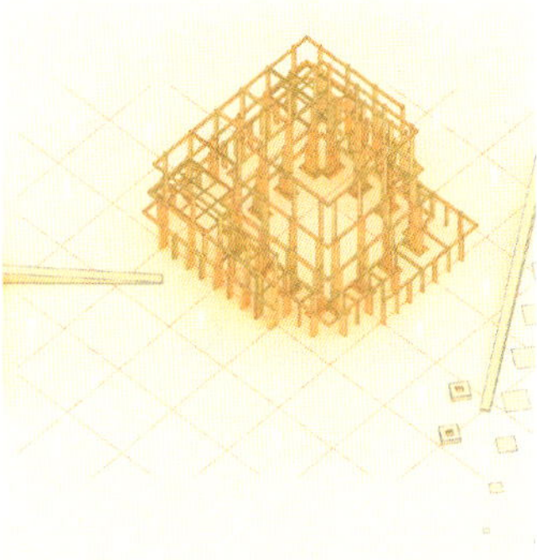

7

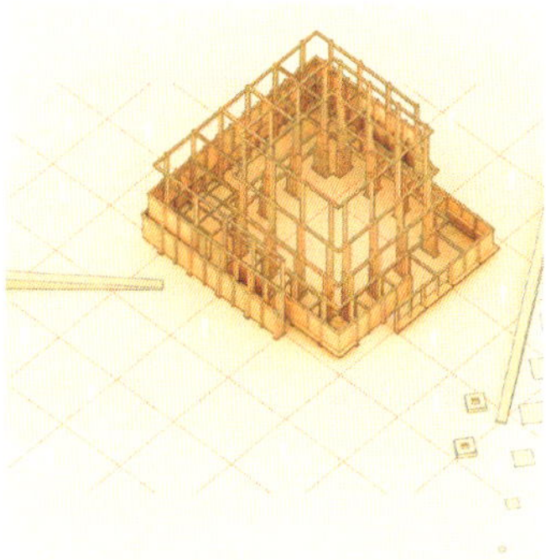

8

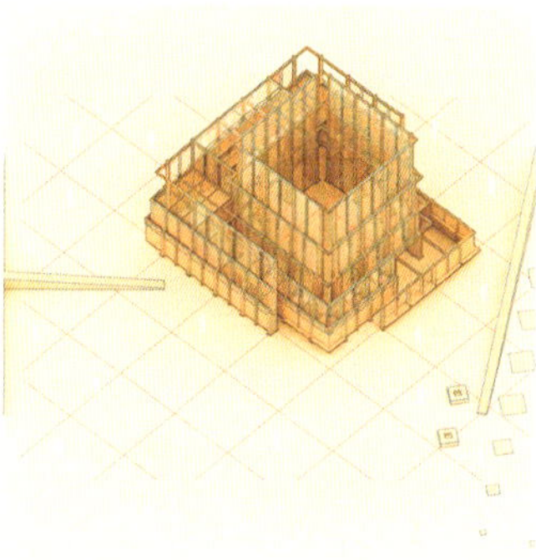

9

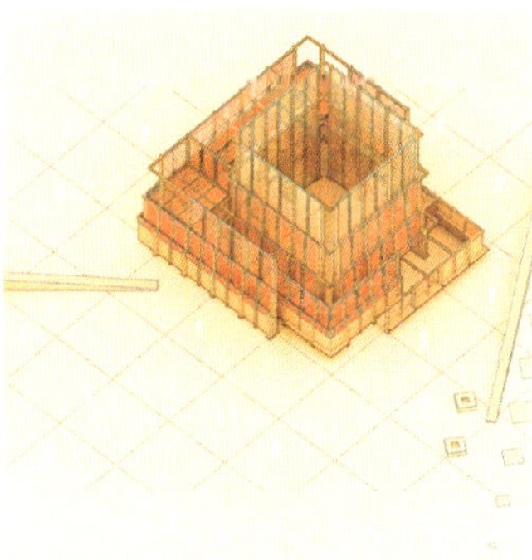

Serving as a protective shell that encloses communal spaces while mediating interactions with the Hajj Terminal's environment, the structure connects exterior and interior realms. The wire frame that embraces and retreats from its surroundings to cultivate serenity, allowing for new meditative possibilities.

1

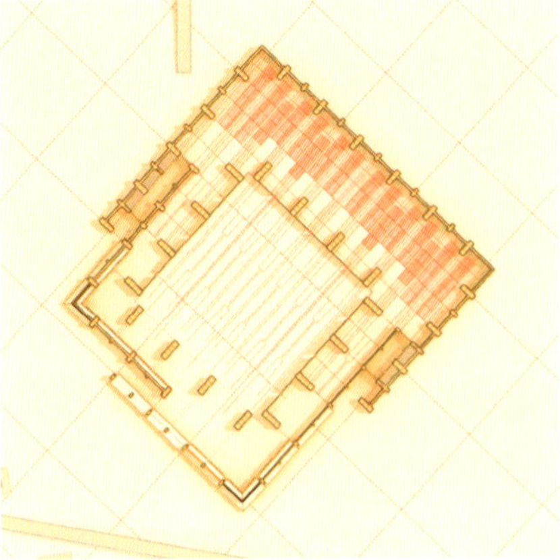

2

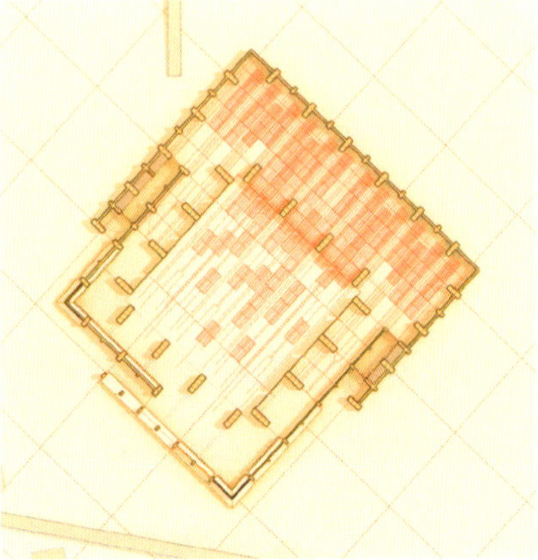

3

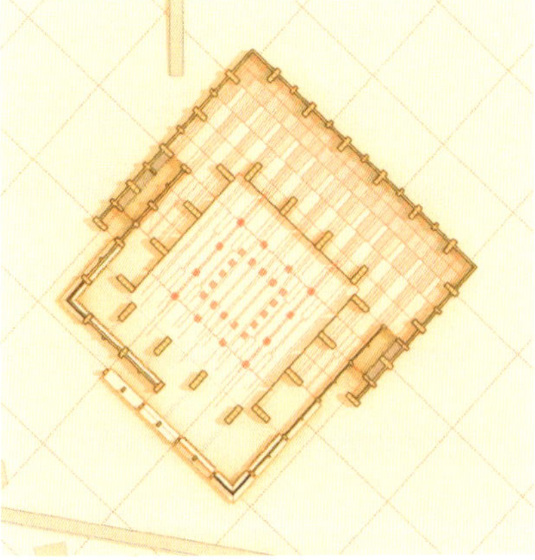

4

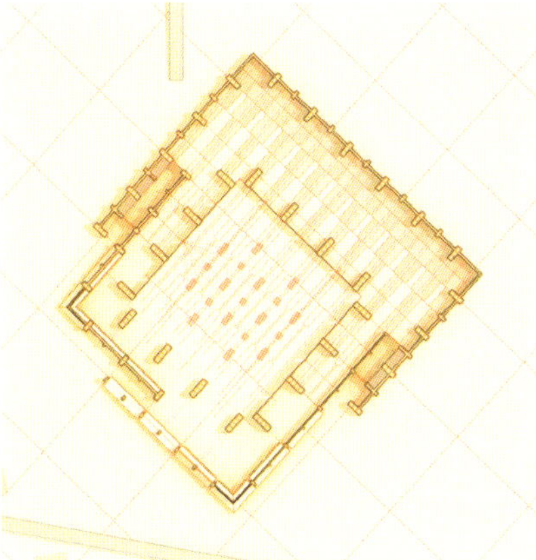

Weaving becomes a model for creativity. In the plan, spaces of different sizes overlap and intertwine. Together, they allow for an experiential quality that calls for continuity, repetition, and order.

5

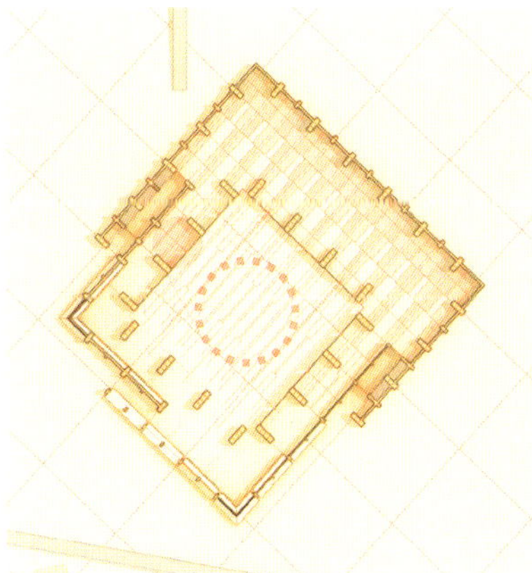

The design approach to materials was guided by a sustainability principle: to source natural and local. This was amplified by the principles of lightweight, scalability, and simplicity. Local palm trees were identified as an underutilized low-carbon material.

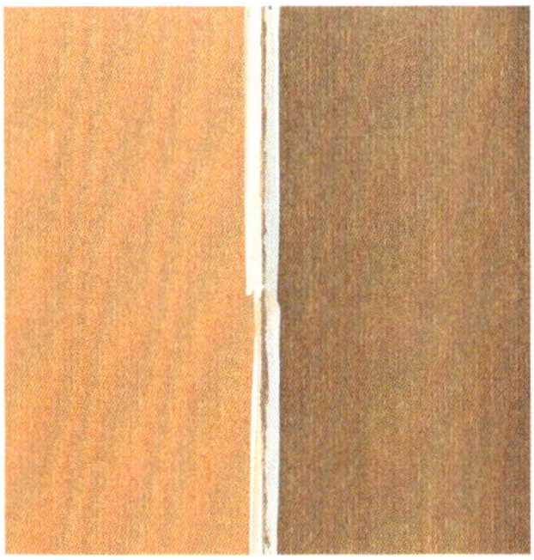

On Weaving *references abstraction in architecture, defined by process rather than style. Affect and ornament are the byproducts of processes of making. Layers, transparencies, and the acts of composing/decomposing come together to form an architectural assemblage that speaks the language of weaving.*

Dayim

On Weaving *is both grand and intimate, offering visitors an experience that is simultaneously shared and deeply personal, echoing the space within the Hajj Terminal. By centering the structure under the canopy's oculus, the structure mitigates the relationship between the ground and the sky, offering a framed view of what lies in between.*

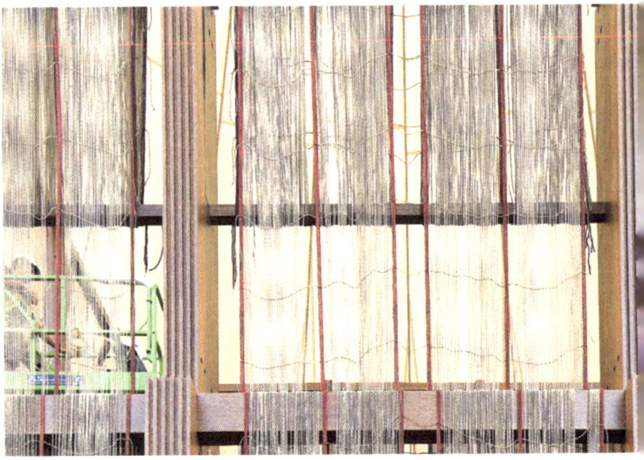

Envisioned as an abstract painting, activating the interior courtyard, the palm-fiber woven screens are partially dyed with a series of colors that have both decorative and narrative dimensions. Native local and regional plants such as henna, pomegranate, indigo, buckthorn, and marigold were the base for colors. Used in regional weaving practices, these dyes are a reflection of the elements found in nature like soil, water, trees, and sunlight. As such, the project inscribes itself within the continuum of traditional crafts that remains alive to this day.

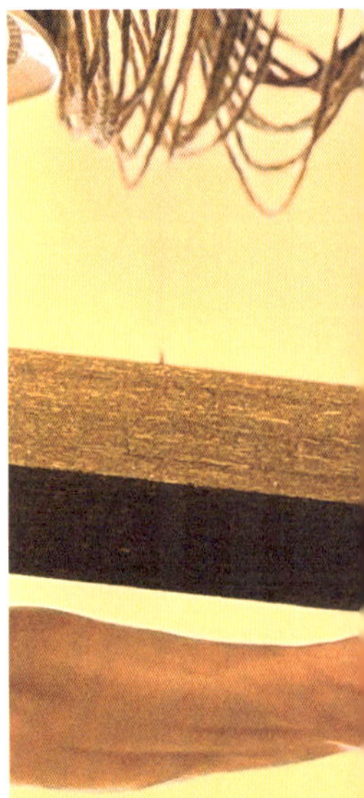

On Weaving *comes to life as a modular and demountable system, capable of having several lives beyond the Islamic Arts Biennale, challenging ideas of material waste – which was also an inspiration.*

Simultaneously concealing and revealing space, the surface for On Weaving *brings together 200 linear km of date palm fiber, handwoven and stretched. The length of the rope is equal to the distance that links Jeddah to Makkah, thus, the enveloping membrane is a reflection of the pilgrimage.*

The assembly system and its material derivation all come from the same natural element, date palm-frond waste that would have otherwise been burned. These are fully engineered into a series of structural elements, stacked and intertwined, framing areas and composing space. What we deem as waste is a reflection of the limits we place on our vision. This is a message to the world: nothing is truly waste - it is merely a material only waiting to be reborn.

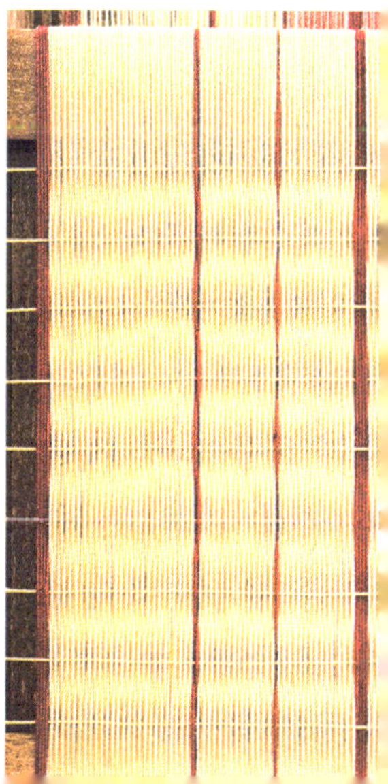

1

2

We imagine the future of On Weaving *as a cultural scaffold, both present and transient, taking root across time and place to situate programs from different realms into the same platform becoming a conduit for fragments of the past, while planting the seeds for further research and collaboration in the future.*

3

4

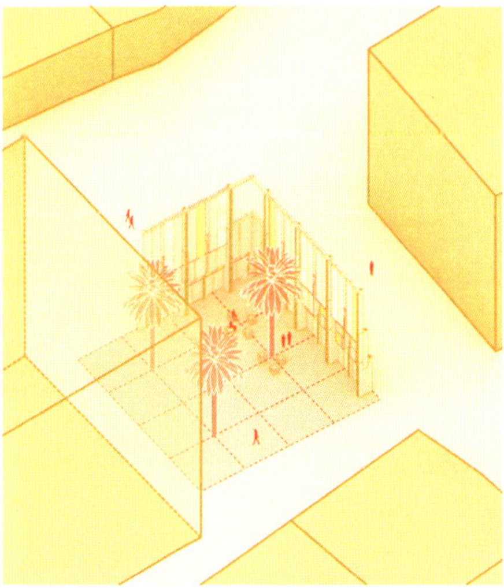

Conversation
On Intertwined Thinking

Nawaf bin Ayyaf *with* Nicolas Fayyad & Charles Kettaneh + Rayyane Tabet + Christopher Blust

This conversation took place under the shade of the canopies of the Hajj Terminal, Jeddah, on January 25, 2025. It started at around 11:30 in the morning, and ran for about twenty-five minutes. Nawaf bin Ayyaf probed the winning team to reveal the conversations that took place throughout the design and construction process, the role of collaborative practices in today's landscape, and the active blurring of disciplines in the pursuit of contemporary and culturally resonant work.

NBA: I want to start light heartedly here.

I know that you were friends even before *AlMusalla Prize* and that you always tried to find a way to work together. Why did you feel like the time was ripe for collaboration? What was it about this project that brought you together?

NF: It essentially mirrors something that Rayyane said recently, which was about the understanding that this project is not architecture, it's not art, and it's not engineering. It's all those fields coming together where we've worn each other's hats. Personally, I was constantly thinking about structural performance, but also ornament and function, and how these elements can come together. Really, our very initial sketches and thoughts prevailed throughout and it was extremely… almost didactic,

Makes a quick chopping motion to indicate successive steps

and very much consistent throughout the process.

Makes a sweeping motion

Where the conversations that we had as a team were only adding to the richness of the process and also the final product.

Makes a motion like the accretion of layers

NBA: Can you guys take us through some of those earlier conversations and brainstorming sessions about how the ideas for the project came to be?

RT: If we trace it back to its genesis, I remember when Nicolas reached out early last year after receiving an invitation that was really about proposing a thought piece. We always wanted to collaborate, but we were waiting for the right opportunity that brings art and architecture together. I know that Nicolas also wanted to work with Hanif Kara of AKT II, so we were keeping those energies or strategies in mind.

I think the invitation to respond to this thought piece was open enough and allowed for those three fields to come together. I remember personally that it was February 2024 and I was in Beirut when Nicolas reached out, so I told him: "just come over and let's talk about it." Very quickly, we started pulling books out of my library, like Annie Albers' *On Weaving*, a book of poetry by Etel Adnan, and some architecture books. All of a sudden, I felt that, without prescribing it too much, there was an ease in thinking both holistically, but also more generally, about the ideas that were of interest to us.

NBA: To build on the point Nicolas had raised,

Addressing RT to his left

I know that you personally like to stress on this project as being a sort of merging of the roles of architect, engineer, and artist where you have worn each other's hats at some point during the project.
I'm kind of curious about some of lessons that can be extracted on some of the ways in which this dynamic relationship, between the different collaborators, can be emphasized to present a holistic approach to an architectural proposal.

RT: I would say that I personally owe a lot to the classes on the history of art and architecture that I took at the American University of Beirut, they really introduced this idea of these fields as being unified

Crossing his fingers together

This came through when we studied Sinan, or polymaths like Da Vinci who wore different hats. I was always very moved and attached to that idea, or kind of practice, and I didn't see these fields as separate from each other. Personally, I felt that this project was almost an excuse to stress on that kind of unified practice

Brings his right index and thumb together and thrusts them forward

and I feel one can see it in the result, right? But this was not evident only in the result, but also in our process, as we were kind of weaving it together. It is very important, I think, for all of us to be reminded that these fields are actually one in the same, right? That when you're talking about structure,

Stressing on "Strucure"

you are talking about ornament or when you're talking about architectural principles of spatial organization, you are also talking about structure and aesthetics.

Stressing on "Aesthetics"

It was not that the architect would propose the building, the engineer would make it stand, and then the artist would decorate it. You can see this in the project at every level, from the smallest detail to the overall structure; it operated seamlessly at these different scales.

CB Nods in agreement

CB: And I would also like to add, that we looked at all the technical aspects holistically, not just the technical aspects of the structure, but even those pertaining to human comfort. So, one of our main objectives was to ensure that people were comfortable in the space. Jeddah can get hot, so we looked at the relationship of our *musalla* to the canopy above its position under it,

Motions his right hand toward the Hajj Terminal canopy

and where the sunlight comes through the oculus. So, we positioned things in a precise way to ensure that we had more sunlight come through in the earlier cooler months, as opposed to the later months, when the sun is higher in the sky and it's hotter, so that there's more shade coverage.

NBA: Thinking about the position in relationship to the sun also acknowledges ideas around time and transience that are embedded in the making of the *AlMusalla Prize*, and the *Rooted Transience* project by extension. Your On Weaving proposal was really reflective of that, as it really highlighted the *musalla* as a transient and adaptable space, and put so much emphasis on its afterlife and legacy. You thought of its time in the biennale as just one of the life's transient moments. By this process of yours, can you describe how this structure actually becomes a journey, and how can it be seen as resonating with your existing work that tends to challenge well-established narratives about our collective built environments?

NF: It is a challenge to conceive of a structure that is in perpetual movement,

Making a rotating movement with his hand

and that will be in different contexts every step of the way. So, how do you conceive of a *musalla* that is built here in this iconic space for four months, but also one with an unknown afterlife somewhere else?

Shapes his right hand into a bowl and moves it slightly up and down, emphasizing rootedness

NBA: This builds on the historical continuum of *musalla* spaces being conjoined with ideas of ephemerality and temporality serving their purpose for a limited time when needed.

NF: Absolutely, and it really comes down to the idea of the threshold. How do you create and then immerse yourself in a space that has a specific environment where you would convey this idea of communal gathering and spirituality through transience? This is very much reflected in the way we thought about the structure as being assembled and disassembled over time, along with materiality. There was a lot of research that went into questions of modularity, of what kind of materials we would want to work with, and how it would come together. But most importantly, what is the experience that we want to convey?

Points to his partner, CK, on his right

As a practice, we are very much driven by context. Usually, it's the context that informs our structures but, in this case, it was a kind of a reversal of thinking, because we had to think of it as an internal, almost inverted, design process that could respond to multiple contexts and conditions. As a result, it does, to a certain extent, act as an addition to the Hajj Terminal, in a way, it is in conversation with it, but the modularity of it can also allow for multiplicity, adaptability, and many other imagined conditions.

NBA: What do you think, Rayyane, would be the potential in tapping into this expansive view of the *musalla*? How might it affect how we perceive other transient typologies, especially those that are native to our region? By that, I mean transient typologies that transcend fixed architectures. How do you think this exercise with the *musalla* actually can further the understanding of the transient elements in the architecture discipline and its discourse?

RT: I've been thinking a lot about this idea of time, and how the brief we received, if one looks at it closely, is almost inviting you to think of a contradiction. It's an invitation to think of a structure that will be used during the run of the Islamic Arts Biennale, which is four months, but because of the brief, we also had to think of a ten to fifteen-year life cycle of the *musalla*, in its structure and materials. So, throughout the process, it was very important and interesting for us to hold and examine both timelines at once, a short exhibition timeline and a building timeline. This is also another way in which you can think of art, architecture, and engineering together because when you engineer something like a temporary structure, you activate one part of the brain, and when you engineer a building with a specific life cycle, it's different not only because of its materials, but also because of its thought processes and logics. To hold both truths at once has been for us, as a group, very important and interesting. And, I think some of the solutions that might not be visible right now, might become more apparent when the structure actually moves to another location where it has to spend a bit more time.

Personally, I think that the element in our project that maybe shifts some of the perspectives you mention around fixed architecture is actually found in the weave.

Weaves his fingers together

As a material, the weave has a very different time scale than the glue-laminated palm wood. So, for me, when you look at the structure itself, it is the past, present, and future all at once, not only in the techniques that are used to make it but it is somehow hard to date and place in time. So, the ethos of transience is somehow able to generate a structure that is contextual and contemporary, that sits in its time. But, philosophically, the act of transience is almost an eternal act, somehow the structure has to exist eternally. This in-betweenness, that the structure finds itself in, was very important for our thinking and communicates how we see it constructed and finished.

NBA: Along those lines, Nicholas, what would you imagine are some of the architectural possibilities that can emerge when we reorient ourselves toward spatial practices that are deeply rooted in transience, in adaptability, and in this sort of dynamicism of what architecture can convey?

NF: I think transience works very well with the concept of reclamation. When you think of modularity, adaptability, or even adaptive reuse, you as an architect and a designer, or almost anyone who's experiencing the space, reclaims it somehow. In this project, we had to imagine that the skeleton that we are proposing can be inhabited, reclaimed, and used in multiple ways. At the end of the day, what we are offering for the public is a series of frames or invitations for them to reimagine the *musalla*, by offering multiple possibilities, in its function, effect, or how it performs.

NBA: What you all managed to conceive is a revolutionary prototype that advances the discourse, not just on the typology, but also in the realm of pavilion competitions in general. You have exhibited great sensitivity in the approach and a wonderful understanding of the local context. Your design has the potential to provide a remarkable blueprint for a more sustainable future of regional architecture; it also a really fitting first take on our grand pursuit to attempt to define the elusive typology of a *musalla*. If there was one key takeaway from all the many lessons learned during the process, what would each of you like that to be?

CB: We had a concept about the foundations, which I would have loved to implement, but what we did on the ground was also ingenious, because it will provide the foundations for future *musalla* projects.

NBA: In a poetic way, you helped lay the ground for future iterations of the *AlMusalla Prize*, both symbolically and in terms of actual structural foundations.

CB agrees

You also posed a question, throughout the project about waste materials, or perceived waste materials, and how might we put those to use.

CB: Absolutely. It's a wider question for the world to ponder. How can you change waste into a beautiful product? Another waste material that we would have loved to incorporate would have been core drills from coral stone.

Mimics a cylindrical shape with his hands

We would have loved to use the coral stone to tension the fabric. So, there are these things that we had to give up along the way that might be used as launchpads for future projects.

RT: For me, the key takeaway is this is a project that makes you rethink the concept of tradition, which is always romanticized or kind of approached in a nostalgic way, that things are further from us in time.

NBA: Even commercialized.

RT: Absolutely, overly so, and frozen in time, as if tradition exists only in the past. The proposal managed to simultaneously blend the presence of craft and the presence of the overly engineered and machine element, simultaneously, while still being true and paying tribute to practices that are specific to the region. The project was bold and daring enough to push those practices toward a future common imaginary. This is a radical take, not only on the concept of tradition, but also on the idea of preservation.

NF: To follow up on what Rayyane was saying, the project successfully conveys the preservation of meaning and what it means for us as designers, engineers, and artists, to imagine a set of very honest practices that look back at the past, to really think through a continued legacy. The project is essentially a response to a very specific practice that embraces technology and artistry, pushing boundaries for these simultaneous skills and attitudes to coexist. It really is about the preservation of meaning toward the future.

CK: The design brief itself was extremely challenging and radical; to invite people to reimagine a very important kind of space. Our response to this serious challenge was also rooted in seriousness. We took on a few simple ideas and allowed them to both expand and also conceptually weave. For example, we took one material, the glue-laminated palm wood, and made the most out of it. Even the structure, it’s a strong architectural gesture based on a very simple idea of revealing the frame. As architects, it’s the most humbling thing to do, to be honest about what we're doing and reveal it.

The project would not have been what it is without the process. The sheer fact that this was a competition enabled us to act quickly and to impose on ourselves a seriousness at every level. Once we arrived at our initial idea, we kept testing ourselves: Are we true to that initial idea or not? The collaborative aspect of this competition really reinforced this feedback loop. Throughout, there was always someone who would come and say: Are we being true to the initial idea, the initial concept?

Noura Al Sayeh-Holtrop

Beyond the Religious Soundscape

On a recent plane ride, in a very dimmed cabin, I turned around and noticed one of the neighboring passengers praying in her seat. She was slightly tilted as if facing Makkah while kneeling in *sujood;* it felt as if the whole cabin had become a space for prayer. Enveloped in her devotion, the sterile buzzing space of the airplane was transformed into a spiritual chamber.

The overlapping of the spiritual and the urban has always been synonymous with the Islamic world, where the calls to prayer, Friday sermons, and the late-night prayers of the Taraweeh during Ramadan have permeated cities with their spiritual sound waves for centuries. Through sound, Islam spreads beyond the confines of a designated physical space. In essence, the whole world is considered a mosque and any space can be transformed through prayer into a mosque

The musalla, a space of prayer and introspection, presents a spatial archetype that has the potential to reintroduce the spiritual within the increasing commercialization of contemporary cities. While the mosque acts as a representation and collective expression of the Muslim community, the musalla responds to the individual prayer needs of Muslims, as a space of introspection and silence, a refuge from the profane.

Yet nowadays, the sounds of the *adhan*, the call to prayer, also resonate in the non-places of hypermodernity: airports, malls, supermarkets, banks, and more. Against these generic spaces, the superposition of the religious on the secular is sometimes uneasy. The sound of the adhan in the midst of a crowded mall suddenly jolts the spiritual against mass consumerism. Most shoppers continue unfazed – two different realities collide in a sealed space and the spheres of the personal and public intertwine with sound: the reading of the Holy Qur'an in the specific tone of voice on the loudspeaker of someone's phone clashes with the noise of another person's TikTok feed nearby.

In the same way that a sterile airplane cabin can transform through prayer and silence, any place can become a musalla. In our interconnected and digital world, its contemporary form is more than a question of physical space and architecture, it is a question of the synchronicity of spaces, societal behaviors, and the resonance of sound.

When one considers that there are as many Muslims in some neighborhoods of European cities as there are in some neighborhoods in the Arab world, it is necessary to rethink ideas of the place and shape of spiritualism in Islam. In the liminal space of sound, akin to the liminal space of the musalla, how can we reimagine the role and place of the religious and spiritual within the contemporary world? How does this affect the relationship between religion and the public realm beyond the traditional soundscapes of Islam?

Written on February 9, 2025

←*Image:* Moath Alofi, *The Last Tashahud*, 2017→

Epilogue
Juxtapositions, Paradoxes, Dichotomies, and Reclamations

Nawaf bin Ayyaf

with poetry by Jood AlThukair

What power can a word with an endless range of possibilities and interpretations hold? The word *musalla* was mentioned in the Holy Qur'an in just one single verse. In contrast, it was used in this publication 176 times; from the holistic wide-lens of historical investigation and a detailed dissection of its etymological roots, all the way up to the specificities of how its fleeting historical connotations can be contemporarily inferred. In the folds of this book, we have seen the word stretched and strained, sometimes bearing beyond what it can fathom and possibly should sustain. Yet, soon after embarking on this research journey, we swiftly realized that we are faced with a true enigmatic space that holds within it countless multiplicities at its core – which, in turn, opens the door for it to be conceived ever so elastically and loosely.

This, in itself, underscores the profound necessity and urgency of this project on *Rooted Transience,* which captures the essence of the *musalla* – embodying both stasis and change. In our collective hands lies the hefty responsibility and duty of attempting to unlock this elusive architectural typology, even if that means succumbing ourselves while probing to multiple juxtapositions and seemingly-unnecessary paradoxes. Instead of taking the possibly wiser route of trying to tame it, we are consciously choosing – perhaps rather impetuously – to further inflate an already-dilated typology with our approach to highlight the contrasting dichotomy between a *musalla's* ephemerality and the enduring omnipresence inherent in it.

Despite being interchangeably used on occasions, a *musalla* is not to be confused with a mosque; emphasizing this distinction was a starting point that drove this project. As we have seen throughout this book, in contrast to its much more analyzed and dissected counterpart, a *musalla* is a transient and fleeting sanctuary for prayer that is closely conjoined with the conceptual ideas of temporality and ephemerality, as well as the physical ideas of adaptability and flexibility. Whereas, in complete opposition, it does not get any more permanent and everlasting than the mosque; as it is naturally considered as a form of *waqf* (endowment) – meaning it is a building that cannot be sold, abandoned, or demolished except in rare cases.

Part of the arduous allure of defining the *musalla* typology lies in just how much it does not seek to assert nor over-impose; how it does not wish to be perpetual nor everlasting, but rather how it seeks to exist when a prayer need arises, then ceases to exist when that need becomes obsolete. Not only is the typology a disappearing one, but at times it is also re-emergent. Whether its cycle of re-emergence is of daily or seasonal recurrence, once a *musalla* leaves it does not necessarily vanish for good. This candid ability to naturally reappear once needed is a true testament to the typology's overpowering dynamism, as much as its profound complexity. It is precisely here, then, that the *AlMusalla Prize*[1] boldly intervenes, to address the illusory vagueness of its seeming demise, with an overemphasis on the *musalla's* afterlife and legacy.

[1] Shortlisted architects for the inaugural *AlMusalla Prize 2025*: AAU Anastas, Asif Khan, Dabbagh Architects, EAST Architecture Studio (winners in collaboration with Rayyane Tabet and AKTII), and the Office of Sahel AlHiyari

With an awareness of the temporary nature of present-day biennials, combined with the ephemeral nature of the typology itself, the *Al Musalla Prize* was adamant from the very start about its pursuit to create a disruptive competition for a *musalla* that would have a second life beyond the span of the Islamic Arts Biennale. By doing so, it doubled down on both the transitory, yet perpetual, potential of the typology itself, as well as the continual potential for biennials beyond their closing day. By giving the participating architects, whose voices permeate throughout the book, a clean slate to envision how and where their proposed *musalla* might materialize for its afterlife beyond the biennial, the *Al Musalla Prize* is also consciously disrupting a paradigm that usually confines architects to work within a specific time and place. Instead, the prize, in its inaugural edition, was structured around morphing the designers into actual partners in the long-term programming of their projects.

By seeking to define the undefinable and to bring the intangible into form, the *Al Musalla Prize* was clear in seeking not a hollow monument devoid of meaning and stripped of purpose, but a sacred space to cradle the most profound of all human acts: worship.

every phantom seed
begins with the
heart just as

the old peach wish
in earth's
bruised core fracture

more ويحمل القلب
البذرة
الأولى

does prayer
make sound?
or does whisper

in vernacular
heart? mud-filled
& upright

stuck between the ribs

at the masjid a woman folds in secret crouch rough salt throat

& tells me she was once a mountain

فأين يذهب الدعاء إن ابتلعته الأرض؟

↑ Jood AlThukair, *Ablution: First Heart*, 2025
Structured in the same numerical order of *wudhu'*, this poem explores the weaving of fragments and origins into threads of possibility. It examines language, body, and the sacred in a quiet inquiry of how prayer moves between realms.

Aligned with the overarching theme of yet another biennial; the *mother* of them all, the AlMusalla Prize was invited to showcase *Rooted Transience* at the 19th Venice Architecture Biennale 2025, titled: *Intelligens. Natural. Artificial. Collective.* curated by Carlo Ratti. This opportunity to test our hypothesis and present it to a broader architecture-minded audience holds a certain poetry of its own: on the face of it, the invitation is steeped in a long-standing tradition and historical continuum of cross-cultural exchange between Venice and the East.

As a city, Venice, was always considered a gateway toward the East. It was closely conjoined and linked with the Islamic world until the fall of Constantinople in 1453, which severely hampered their ability for trade and interaction with it. From an architectural perspective, the intertwining of Venice and the East has manifested in myriad ways. From the graceful sweep of pointed arches to the intricate mosaics and ornate carvings that echo Byzantine and Islamic artistic traditions, it is evident to the discerning eye just how deeply Venice has drawn from the architectural repertoire of the East, incorporating some of their design principles into its own architecture and urban fabric, and at times, even claiming them. While using it as the paragon of pre-Renaissance humanism, for ideological reasons in his *The stones of Venice,* John Ruskin spoke of the *corruption* of the West and *authenticity* of the East, positioning Venice as a vibrant melting pot where Eastern influences are believed to have been absorbed and transformed, turning the city into a symbol of how contradictory traditions could converge in creative and meaningful ways for artistic development.[2] Before carrying on any further, it is important to note that my referencing of Ruskin's deployment of the term authenticity is not intended as an endorsement. On the contrary, I would argue that we need to acknowledge that authenticity is itself a reified term and an unattainable goal which, though seemingly promulgated as an objective standard of reality, is subject to constant misapprehension. The late architect and historian Stanford Anderson once referred to authenticity as the third rail of architectural debate: a place to venture at one's peril.[3]

[2] Ruskin, John. *The stones of Venice* v. J. Wiley, 1851.

[3] Fixler, David N. "Kahn's Modernism and its Renewal." docomomo journal 58 (2018): 4-5

This intricate narrative of interdependence between Venice and the East, woven through the fabric of the built environment, runs deep within the very history of the Venice Architecture Biennale itself. In its second iteration in 1982/83, the theme *Architecture in Islamic Countries* was chosen by curator Paolo Portoghesi, who himself was in the midst of a personal journey of discovering Islamic architecture. At around the time, Portoghesi was commissioned to design the Grand Mosque of Rome that took more than twenty years to build, making it the largest mosque outside of the Islamic world, Russia, or India when it was finally completed in 1995. Portoghesi seemed to develop this into a habit, as was also responsible for France's biggest mosque, the Grand Mosque in Strasbourg, albeit a few decades later in 2012.

← Section featuring the works of Iraqi Architect Mohamed Makiya at the Second Venice Architecture Biennale (1982). His featured works include the Kuwait State Mosque (1977) and the Rafidain Bank, Kufa (1968). Photo: Giorgio Zucchiatti. Courtesy Archivio Storico della Biennale di Venezia, ASAC.

← Section on the works of Egyptian Architect Abdel-Wahed El-Wakil at the Second Venice Architecture Biennale (1982). His featured works include Sulaiman Palace (1979) and Island Mosque (1980) both in Jeddah, and the Khashoggi Residence (1973) in Taif. Photo: Giorgio Zucchiatti. Courtesy Archivio Storico della Biennale di Venezia, ASAC.

← The 1982 Venice Architecture Biennale mainly paid homage to four prominent architects and their contribution to Islamic Architecture (Fernand Pouillon, Louis Kahn, Le Corbusier, and Hassan Fathy) via dedicated sections at the catalogue and exhibition, this image is of the Hassan Fathy homage section. Photo: Giorgio Zucchiatti. Courtesy Archivio Storico della Biennale di Venezia, ASAC.

Portoghesi saw the 1982 biennial as a chance to engage in dialogue. He envisioned it as an opportunity to issue a collective call that urged the cultural world to dismantle barriers and bridge over divisions, working together to resolve conflicts of juxtapositions and false perceptions that have long kept the two-worlds apart. He details the grand ambition of leveling the field as follows:

"The biennale exhibition does not set out to make a fashionable choice, privileging only one aspect of the complex and multifaceted reality that characterizes the built works of Islamic countries. Rather, it prioritizes quality, whether the design is the work of Western experts or those who are increasingly expressing their own indigenous culture. The point of view is Western - it could hardly be otherwise - but it stems from a participatory approach rather than an illusionary assertion of superiority." [4]

For the *AlMusalla Prize* to be showcased at the 19th edition of the Venice Architecture Biennale is, in essence, a reclamation of a long-lost and misconceived narrative; a chance to shift a perspective no longer dominated by the Western gaze, but one that could just as easily come from within. For *Rooted Transience,* we are carrying with us fragments from a prize that seeks to enrich the architecture discipline at large, ironically won by a practice called EAST. In an attempt of intellectual reclamation, we find ourselves stepping into and taking-over the Abbazia di San Gregorio on the Venice Grand Canal; a waterway that gently curves eastward, reaching out toward the Mediterranean, via the Adriatic Sea, and then the world. Armed with a deep and locally-rooted knowledge of a subject often overlooked by the perceived West; we are also not making a fashionable choice, as Portoghesi put it, but are issuing a call to provoke a type of dialogue similar to the one he envisioned but has since disappeared: a form of dialogue that surpasses linguistic differences, even going as far as questioning our mere comprehension even of language itself.

[4] Thomas, Helen, ed. *Architecture in Islamic Countries - Second International Exhibition of Architecture Venice 1982/83: Selections from the Catalogue for the Second International Exhibition of Architecture Venice 1982/83.* 2023. Gta Verlag.

↗ Jood AlThukair, *Earth Autopsy,* 2025
This poem stretches our understanding of language, revealing its elasticity as an infinite container of prayer. It invites us to a speculative reading – how would the birds or trees pray? Here, this poem collapses the foundations of language, pushing us to listen beyond imaginations and allowing ecosystems to speak for themselves.

the first earth spoke in Arabic
kneeled & prayed for rain in Arabic
cracked its wrinkled skin in Arabic
did it splinter   Arabic?

نطقت الأرض الأولى بالعربية
ركعت وسجدت وهمست وتجعّدت
ثم تشققت وتفتحت: مطر غيم سيل
شتات ثم ثبات   نحو السماء نحو الفضاء

how did earth syntax after the Great Flood?

whatislightwhatisspacewhatiscompass   whatistimewhatisfirewhatisboat

if it sent prayer into the sky
which bird grammared it?
broken clay wing
supplicating

لحظة،

the earth will language itself:

أرض   مطر

جناح

طين

قوس/قوسين

شجر

أرض أرض أرض

سفر أو ماء: سماء

في بحر الرياح

في في في في في في

آمين

At its core, *Rooted Transience,* and the *Al Musalla Prize* by extension, poses the profound question of what possibilities can unfold when architecture turns toward spatial practices that are grounded in adaptability. And what better venue to accommodate and host an intellectual interrogation, which taps into the dichotomy between temporality and rootedness, than the paradoxical masterpiece of the Western Hajj Terminal? Designed by Fazlur Rahman Khan of Skidmore, Owings & Merrill (SOM) in 1982, the terminal stands as one of his most celebrated architectural and engineering feats; and he has had plenty of them. Though an engineer, Khan somehow mastered the art of weaving his structures into a historical and architectural narrative; whether it was the Sears (now Willis) Tower which echoed Chicago's rich skyscraper legacy, or the Hajj Terminal which drew inspiration from the local nomadic tent tradition.

↙Fazlur Rahman Khan, Partner at SOM, seen here inspecting the Teflon-coated fiberglass roof units used in the Hajj Terminal. © SOM

Perhaps more so functionally than spatially, the *AlMusalla Prize* was extremely self-conscious of the fact that it would be hosted within the vast embrace of the Hajj Terminal and beneath its soaring canopies: how does one decontextualize a design intervention in one of the twentieth century's most iconic feats of engineering? And, more provocatively, why even propose the creation of a dedicated space for prayer within a project that, from its inception, had intentionally resisted the very notion of such a designation?

It is precisely here that one might trace the common thread that links the competition's vision to the very space that housed and gave birth to it. Though they differ in scale and scope, both the Hajj Terminal and the *AlMusalla Prize* share a deeper kinship: they are spaces of temporary gathering and assembly whenever a need arises; and they are spaces of flow; whether it is the flow of people pouring into the terminal from all over the world, enroute to Makkah to perform Hajj, or the flow of people to a *musalla* anxious to receive the spiritual cleansing that a prayer promises.[5] Each respectfully challenges the rigid paradigms of established typologies and disciplines. The Hajj Terminal defied the conventional airport paradigm by pioneering a tectonic gathering place that intentionally functions more like a village than a terminal. Similarly, as explored plentifully throughout this publication, the *AlMusalla Prize* also finds itself entrenched in a parallel struggle of its own; advocating for a reimagining and a redefining of a new typology for prayer... that is not a mosque.

[5] Manuel Castells, *The Space of Flows*, Wiley, 2009.

[6] Cantacuzino, Sherban, ed. *Architecture in Continuity: Building in the Islamic World Today.* Aperture, 1985.

"This tent," once said Khan about the Hajj Terminal, *"does not copy tents of the past–it is a form for the future, and here it caters for today's needs–air travel."* [6]

Just as the rise of modern modes of transportation had driven the ever-growing influx of pilgrims to Jeddah, prompting Fazlur Rahman Khan to pragmatically harness new technologies to challenge conventional paradigms and existing disciplines, we argue that the development of modern modes of urbanization have similarly disrupted the way the spatiality of a *musalla* is conceived and represented. Hence, from one notion of temporary to another, *Rooted Transience* suggests that the concept of temporary in one historical context cannot be equated with that of another.

In this light, the *musalla* becomes not just a space, but a reflection on the nature of temporality itself; how it is shaped by the unique historical and geographical conditions which propelled it and in which it exists. When asked if he ever considered temporary structures for the Hajj Terminal – such as tents, for example, that could be dismantled after the Hajj – Khan admitted he did, but only briefly:

"We considered a convertible structure, one that would dismantle, but it would need repair as wear and tear on it was inevitable. And just think of the size of it: 450,000 square meters of covered space! What an operation that would be. So, we decided on a permanent structure that you do not have to worry about for fifty years." [7]

[7] Khan, Hasan-Uddin, ed. *Hajj Terminal. In Mimar 4: Architecture in Development.* Singapore: Concept Media Ltd., 1982

↑ Fazlur Rahman Khan, middle, seen here wearing a ghutra and igal - local Saudi head scarf used by men - on top of his western attire, in what looks like a photo taken in Saudi Arabia. © SOM

By paradoxically creating a permanent structure from the most temporary typology in existence, Fazlur Rahman Khan was admittedly having fun playing with architectural juxtapositions and contradictions back in 1982; and with *Rooted Transience,* we are perhaps forty-three years late to the party. In this essay alone, the word *musalla* was used twenty-seven times. By attempting to uncover its multiplicities and seeking to prove its elasticity, we found ourselves engaging with a fleeting and ghostly typology with a mind of its own. Exploring it has allowed us to raise questions that reach far beyond its inflated confines and into the heart of the architecture discipline itself; questioning some of the discipline's core foundations, probing its merits, and countering some of its prevailing narratives. The potential here is vast, and the challenge immense, yet this endeavor is but a seed; a humble beginning to lay the first stones on a long path ahead; one that seeks to root a space that is, by nature, transient.

Snapshots of Al Musalla Prize

March 2024

Shortlisted architects site visit to the AlMusalla site, the Western Hajj Terminal.

Asif Khan and Zaure Aitayeva getting lost under the canopies of the Western Hajj Terminal during AlMusalla shortlisted architects site visit.

Jury chair and shortlisted architects on site visit

June 2024

Final jury deliberation session.

Final jury deliberation session.

October 2024

AlMusalla presentation in Art Basel Paris

November 2024

The testing of natural colors on ropes to find the right pigmentation at production factory.

January 2025

First individual prayer in the *musalla*, by a worker tasked with ramming the ground around the *musalla* site.

Al Musalla Prize 2025 jury members and shortlisted architects, at the *Al Musalla Prize* dinner celebration at Jeddah Albalad during opening week of the Islamic Arts Biennale 2025.

Nawaf bin Ayyaf and Nicolas Fayyad during the final days of construction leading up to the opening.

April 2024

Snapshot from a mid-stage jury review.

May 2024

AlMusalla Prize chair and jury members, and Francis Kere, at the Pritzker Architecture Prize

July 2024

Conceptual model of the winning *musalla*, at OMA Rotterdam Offices, while workshopping the Islamic Arts Biennale scenography and *Musalla* placement.

September 2024

First prototype for the weave, set to determine density and opacity.

First prototype for the developed building material on site.

Silhouette of Nicolas Fayyad, of EAST Architecture Studio, against the ropes which makes the weave.

Weaving prototype to determine scale, color pigmentation, and a weave joinery system.

Jury members and winning team of the inaugural *AlMusalla Prize 2025* in the courtyard of the *musalla*

First communal prayer in the designated prayer space of the *musalla*, a day prior to opening.

A solitary man praying during the Islamic Arts Biennale. Photo by Marco Cappelletti 2025

Biographies
Jury

Nawaf bin Ayyaf
Chair

Chair of the AlMusalla Prize and a Senior Advisor for the Saudi Ministry of Culture, Prince Nawaf combines a firm academic background with a richly diverse professional experience. He holds a Master's of Architecture Studies degree (SMArchS) from MIT at the Aga Khan Program for Islamic Architecture, and a Master's of Design Studies degree (MDes) from Harvard GSD in Critical Conservation.

He is a published researcher with works featured in numerous architectural publications, journals, and conferences, and he has lectured at renowned institutions such as UNESCO, Harvard Graduate School of Design, Harvard Center for Middle Eastern Studies and the Royal College of Art in London. He has also practiced multi-scaled urban development in setting as wide-ranging as in NGOs like the World Bank, consulting firms such as Accenture, international design practices like Moriyama & Teshima, and in local institutions such as RCRC and MOC.

Farrokh Derakhshani

Director of the Aga Khan Award for Architecture, Farrokh Derakhshani specializes in the contemporary architecture of Muslim societies. He lectures widely and serves on boards and committees of several cultural institutions. In 2018, he was named an International Fellow of RIBA.

Derakhshani trained as an architect and planner at the National University of Iran and later continued his studies at the School of Architecture in Paris. Since 1982, his association with the Aga Khan Award has brought him into contact with architects, builders, and planners throughout the world.

His professional work has included the design and construction management of large-scale public works and infrastructure projects in Iran, as well as architectural design in Paris and Geneva.

Azra Akšamija

Artist, architectural historian and author, Azra Akšamija's multi-disciplinary practice investigates the potency of art and architecture to facilitate the process of transformative mediation in cultural or political conflicts.

Akšamija holds two Master of Architecture degrees from Graz Institute of Technology (2001) and Princeton University (2004), and a Ph.D. in History, Theory, and Criticism in Architecture from MIT (2011).

She received the Aga Khan Award for Architecture in 2013 for her design of the prayer space in the Islamic Cemetery Altach, Austria, the Art Award of the City of Graz in 2018, and an honorary doctorate from the Montserrat College of Art in 2020.

Lina Ghotmeh

Reflecting her lived experience in Beirut, Lina Ghotmeh's architecture practice, Lina Ghotmeh – Architecture, is driven by an "Archaeology of the Future." Her projects are materially sensitive and in symbiosis with nature.

Ghotmeh studied architecture at the American University of Beirut and the École Spéciale d'Architecture in Paris, and she currently holds the Kenzo Tange Professor Design Critic at the Harvard University's Graduate School of Design.

Notable projects include *Stone Garden* tower in Beirut, which was exhibited at the 17th Venice Biennale, and the Estonian National Museum, a Mies Van der Rohe Award nominee. Her awards include the Schelling Architecture Prize (2021) and the Tamayouz "Woman of Outstanding Achievement" Award (2020).

Ali Malkawi

Professor of Architectural Technology at Harvard University, Ali Malkawi advocates for energy-efficient strategies while educating the next generation of Graduate School of Design students in building simulation, energy conservation and sustainability.

An international scholar, Malkawi has a Bachelor of Science in architectural engineering and environmental design from Jordan University of Science and Technology, a Master of Architecture from the University of Colorado, and a PhD from Georgia Institute of Technology in architectural technology/ artificial intelligence.

Previously a professor at the University of Pennsylvania, Malkawi founded and directed the TC Chan Center for Building Simulation and Energy Studies. At Harvard, he was elemental in establishing the Harvard Center for Green Buildings and Cities (CGBC).

Biographies
Shortlisted Architects

AAU Anastas

AAU ANASTAS is an international architectural practice based in Bethlehem & Paris.The studio includes architects, interior designers, civil, electrical and mechanical engineers.

The practice's work is defined by punctilious attention to the site insertion and details of every project, with the aim at generating an architecture that is socially, culturally and intellectually coherent.

Asif Khan Studio

Asif Khan Studio is an architecture and exhibition design specialist with fourteen years experience delivering cultural projects and immersive experiences for museums, galleries, Olympic Games and World Expos. The studio is an SME, currently employing thirty members of staff.

The Studio is currently working on the National Liverpool Museums Waterside Transformation, new Museum of London at West Smithfield, the Barbican Centre regeneration, Tselinny Centre of Contemporary Culture in Almaty and the recently opened Dubai Expo 2020 public realm and entrance portals.

Notable previous projects include the "MegaFaces" pavilion at the Sochi 2014 Winter Olympics which won the Cannes Lion Grand Prix for Innovation, the Coca-Cola Beatbox at London 2012 Olympics, a finalist entry in the international competition for the new Guggenheim Museum Helsinki from 1700 anonymous designs.

Dabbagh Architects

Dabbagh Architects is an award-winning Architectural design practice with office in Dubai and Abu Dhabi in the UAE. It is recognized regionally for its contemporary design and quality-driven service.

The practice was established in 2008 in Dubai, becoming one of the first in the Gulf to become an RIBA Chartered Practice in 2015. It set out to create a timeless Architecture that enhances people's lives. It addresses themes of identity, place and context through its contemporary and innovative approach to architecture.

Dabbagh Architects are renowned for their culturally sensitive, contextual designs. In addition to cultural projects, Dabbagh's portfolio covers diverse sectors including commercial, residential as well as educational. The practice is also known for its quality-driven design.

Office of Sahel AlHiyari for Architecture

Office of Sahel Alhyari for Architecture (OSAA) is an award-winning architectural practice based in Amman, Jordan. The practice is led by principal architect Sahel AlHiyari. The firm's work covers a wide spectrum of design related disciplines ranging from urban design, interior and furniture design, to architectural installations and exhibition design. OSAA's diverse portfolio has been published and exhibited internationally. OSAA addresses the particularities, challenges and limitations of each project as instrumental aspects that are internalized within the design discourse and approach. The synergies between design, materiality, and technique with the cultural context create an architecture that proposes diversity, change, and place-related transformation. The research driven practice focuses on works that evolve from the cultural and morphological landscapes of each specific context. OSAA's work therefore regards context, with its traditions and conventions, as aspects subject to redefinition and reinvention.

Biographies
Winning Collaborators

EAST Architecture Studio

EAST Architecture Studio is an award-winning collective practice committed to architectural design and experimental research. Under the banner of preservation as practice, the studio yields innovative built environments of various scales ranging from master planning to interior design and adaptive reuse, engaging contemporary society with traditional culture. EAST Architecture Studio is a recipient of the Aga Khan Award for Architecture, and winner of the first edition of the *AlMusalla Prize 2025.*

The studio's work is a testament to a visionary approach and sensitive interpretation of history and culture, notably in projects like the highly praised Niemeyer Guest House Renovation in Tripoli, Lebanon. EAST Architecture Studio's work was showcased internationally, namely at the 17th Architecture Biennale in Venice, the Royal Institute of British Architects (RIBA), and the Chicago History Museum, and widely published in the likes of *Wallpaper Magazine, The Architectural Review,* and *Architectural Record.*

Rayyane Tabet

Drawing from experience and self-directed research, Rayyane Tabet explores stories that offer an alternative understanding of major socio-political events through individual narratives. Informed by his training in architecture and sculpture, his work investigates paradoxes in the built environment and its history by way of installations, interventions, and performances that reconstitute the perception of physical and temporal distance.

In recent years, Tabet has had solo exhibitions at the MUDAM Museum (2023), Walker Art Center (2021), Sharjah Art Foundation (2021), Storefront for Art and Architecture (2020), Parasol Unit Foundation of Contemporary Art (2019), The Metropolitan Museum of Art (2019), The Louvre Museum (2019), Carée d'Art Musée d'Art Contemporain (2018) and at the Kunstverein Hamburg (2017). His work was featured in numerous international group shows, among which the 80th Whitney Biennial (2022), the 7th Yokohama Triennial (2020), the 2nd Lahore Biennial (2020), the 21st Sydney Biennial (2018), Manifesta 12 (2018), the 15th Istanbul Biennial (2017), the 32nd Sao Paolo Biennial (2016), the 10th and 12th Sharjah Biennial (2011, 2015) and the 2nd New Museum Triennial (2012).

AKT II

AKT II is a progressive, design-led structural and civil engineering firm with current and complete projects in forty-four countries worldwide. The practice operates from its central London headquarters of over three hundred people, with regional offices in Manchester and Cambridge.

Christopher Blust

Christopher Blust is a design director with over fifteen years of experience. He contributes a broad strategic vision across AKT II's global portfolio: from the unprecedented restoration at Shrewsbury Flaxmill Maltings, and the forthcoming retrofit of London's New Zealand House, to the iconic new Zayed National Museum in Abu Dhabi.

Biographies
Contributors

Hanif Kara

Professor Hanif Kara OBE is a practicing Structural Engineer and Professor in Practice of Architectural Technology at the Graduate School of Design, Harvard. He is recognized for linking design, research, education, and practice. He co-tutored a Diploma Unit at the Architecture Association, London from 2000 to 2004 and was a Visiting Professor of Architectural Technology at KTH Stockholm from 2007 to 2012.

As Design Director and co-founder of AKT II (est. 1996), his particular design-led approach and interest in innovative form, pushing material uses, sustainable construction and complex analysis methods have allowed him to work on numerous pioneering projects at the forefront of many challenges facing the built environment.

Khaled Azzam

Khaled Azzam is the Director of The Prince's School of Traditional Arts in London. He is an architect by training and maintains his practice through offices in Cairo and Jeddah. He has built houses, schools, mosques, offices, commercial buildings and royal residences. These projects apply the principles of traditional Islamic design and construction techniques, acquired from academic research and practice, with the aim of establishing a contemporary expression for the architecture of the Arab/ Islamic world. The integration of architecture, the arts and education is not only seen in his architectural profession but also in his academic career through the development of education projects, programs, and institutions.

Nasser Rabbat

Nasser Rabbat is the Aga Khan Professor and Director of the Aga Khan Program for Islamic Architecture at MIT. His interests include Islamic art and architecture, urban history, heritage studies, Arab history, contemporary Islamic art, and post-colonial criticism. He teaches lecture courses on various aspects of Islamic architecture and seminars on Orientalism and colonialism; Issues in Islamic Urbanism; Historiography of Islamic Architecture; Late Antiquity and the foundation of Islamic architecture; Reading Ibn Khaldun; (Re)constructing Memory; Urbicide; and Balancing Globalism and Regionalism in the Arabian Gulf.

Rabbat has published more than a hundred scholarly articles and several books on topics ranging from Mamluk architecture to Antique Syria, 19th century Cairo, Orientalism, and urbicide. His most recent books are *Taqiy al-Din al-Maqrizi: Wijdan al-Tarikh al-Masri* (2024); *Nasser Rabbat: Critical Encounters* (2023); *Writing Egypt: Al-Maqrizi and His Historical Project* (2023); *'Imarat al-Mudun al-Mayyita* (The Architecture of the Dead Cities) (2018), and an online book, *The Destruction of Cultural Heritage: From Napoléon to ISIS*, co-edited with Pamela Karimi (2016). His co-edited book, *Construction as Destruction: The Case of Syria* will be published in 2025 by AUC Press. He is currently editing a book on the cultural history of Syria to be published by Edinburgh University Press. His next book project is a history of Mamluk Cairo, which is under contract with AUC Press.

Noura Al Sayeh-Holtrop

Noura Al Sayeh-Holtrop is an architect and curator based in Bahrain. She was the co-curator of Reclaim, Bahrain's first participation at the 12th Venice Architecture Biennale in 2010 that was awarded a Golden Lion, and the Deputy Commissioner General for Bahrain's National Pavilion since the Expo Milan in 2015. Since 2015, she has been heading the *Pearling, Testimony of an Island Economy* UNESCO World Heritage project, which was awarded the Aga Khan Award for Architecture for the 2019 cycle. She has built a number of temporary and permanent installations, and worked as an architect in Jerusalem, Amsterdam, and New York. Her work has been exhibited internationally at several biennals and exhibitions of which the Lisbon Triennale, the Venice Architecture Biennale, the London Design Festival, the Seoul Biennale for Architecture and Urbanism and the Jeddah Islamic Art Biennale.

She is currently at the Bahrain Authority for Culture and Antiquities (BACA) as Advisor for Heritage Projects, where she is responsible for overseeing the planning and implementation of cultural institutions and museums, as well as advising on urban rehabilitation strategies. She holds a Master's Degree in Architecture from the École Polytechnique Fédérale de Lausanne and is a board member of the Palestinian Museum in Birzeit, Palestine.

Wesam Al Asali

Wesam Al Asali is an architect and researcher specializing in building crafts and construction technology. He is an Assistant Professor and Director of Materials and Methods at IE School of Architecture and Design. He earned his Ph.D. from the University of Cambridge in 2021 and was a Global Fung Fellow at Princeton University (2021–2022) before joining IE University.

Wesam's work explores the histories and applications of scarcity-driven experimentation in vernacular, indigenous, and local construction methods. In practice, he engages with heritage knowledge to develop environmentally sensitive designs. In 2010, he co-founded IWlab, a research hub investigating Syrian ecologies of making and dwelling. In 2020, he co-founded CERCAA, a social enterprise based in Valencia, Spain, dedicated to training architects in local building crafts across Spain and the Middle East.

His research and practice have earned multiple awards, including the Royal Institute of British Architects (RIBA) President's Medal for Research (2021), Clare Hall's Salje Award for best PhD thesis (2022), and the Journal of the Society of Architectural Historians' Founders' Award (2022). In 2024, he was named a DigitalFutures awardee for the Middle East, and IWlab received the Global Award for Sustainable Architecture.

Ziad Jamaleddine

Ziad Jamaleddine is a co-founder of L.E.FT Architects (New York/Beirut) and an assistant professor at Columbia University, GSAPP. He is the recipient of the Emerging Voices Award from the Architectural League of New York (2010), and was selected as one of the Nine Arab American Architects You Should Know by the AIA (2024). Jamaleddine is a practitioner and scholar with a research focus on mosque architecture. His writings have been published in *Places Journal* (2020), *Journal of Material Cultures in the Muslim World* (Brill, 2024), and *International Journal of Islamic Architecture* (Intellect, 2025). His research and design work has been exhibited at Oslo Architecture Triennale (2016), Milan Architecture Triennale (2018), Sharjah Architecture Triennale (2019), and most recently Jeddah Islamic Art Biennale (2023). L.E.FT was selected in 2025 to the AD100, The Best Designers in the Middle East and North Africa. L.E.FT's work includes Shakib Arslan Mosque, Lebanon (2017), winner of the Interfaith Design (AIA) & Partners of Sacred Places Award (2018), and the Al Fozan Award for Mosque Architecture (2020), and the Office of Religious and Spiritual Life and Contemplative Practices, Vassar College (2023), winner of the Interfaith Design (AIA) & Partners of Sacred Places Award: Adaptive Re-Use (2024)

Editors' Acknowledgments

Rooted Transience could not have materialized without the contributions from a myriad of individuals and institutions.

Our gratitude goes to the HH Prince Badr bin Farhan AlSaud, Saudi Minister of Culture, HE Rakan Altouq, Assistant Minister and Vice Chairman of the Diriyah Biennale Foundation, and Aya Al-Bakree, CEO of Diriyah Biennale Foundation for their trust in our collective efforts in planting the seeds for the story of *musalla* spaces.

We would like to acknowledge the work of friends, colleagues, and scholars who have actively shaped this publication, and challenged us to think about our work in inspiring new ways: Hanif Kara, Khaled Azzam, Nasser Rabbat, Noura AlSayeh-Holtrop, Wesam Al Asali, and Ziad Jameleddine and for providing their insightful reflections on *musalla* spaces.

For those whose conversations we were fortunate enough to record and transmit: Ali Malkawi, Asif Khan, Azra Akšamija, Charles Kettaneh, Christopher Blust, Elias and Yousef Anastas, Farrokh Derakhshani, Lina Ghotmeh, Nicolas Fayad, Rayyane Tabet, Sahel AlHiyari, and Sumaya Dabbagh.

Jood AlThukair for filling our book with her poetry and Moath Alofi for allowing us to borrow from his lens.

Dina Hirzallah and Nada Barqawi for their talents and assisting us in bringing *Rooted Transience* to the Abbazia di San Gregorio. Omar Darwish for assisting us with the research, hinting towards new lines of inquiry on a daily basis.

Farida Alhusseini, Niyanar Ajram, Sara Al-Tunisi, Talal Al-Obaid, and Omar Diab at the Diriyah Biennale Foundation for their patience, encouragement, and unyielding support.

Nour Salamé at Kaph Books, for her guidance. Zeina Assaf, for her careful and collaborative reading. Dr Mohamed Ait Mihoub for translating the book into our beautiful Arabic language,
Mohammad Hamdan for Arabic copyediting, and Nadim Zablit for ensuring the images communicate flawlessly.

The designers behind bytwo: Abdullah Kenani and Mohammed Alruways for their experimental design spirit, along with type designer Wael Morcos for his spontaneous generosity.

الشكر والتقدير

لم يكن لكتاب "*عابرٌ متجذّر*" أن يكتب له النجاح لولا مساهمات عدد لا يُحصى من الأفراد والمؤسسات.

نتقدم بجزيل الشكر والامتنان لسمو الأمير بدر بن فرحان آل سعود، وزير الثقافة السعودي، ومعالي الأستاذ راكان الطوق، مساعد وزير الثقافة ونائب رئيس مجلس أمناء مؤسسة بينالي الدرعية، والسيدة آية البكري، الرئيس التنفيذي لمؤسسة بينالي الدرعية، على ثقتهم بجهودنا الجماعية في غرس بذور قصة فضاءات المصلى.

نود أن نتقدم بالشكر الجزيل لأصدقائنا وزملائنا والباحثين الذين أسهموا بفاعلية في صياغة هذا الكتاب، وشجعونا على التفكير في عملنا بطرق جديدة ومُلهمة: حنيف كارا، وخالد عزام، وناصر رباط، ونورة السايح-هولتروب، ووسام العسلي، وزياد جمال الدين على إسهاماتهم الثاقبة في فضاءات المصلى.

شكر خاص لمن حالفنا الحظ بتسجيل ونقل حواراتهم: علي ملكاوي، آصف خان، أزرا أكشاميا، شارل كتانة، كريستوفر بلست، إلياس ويوسف أنسطاس، فاروخ درخشاني، لينا غطمة، نقولا فياض، ريان تابت، سهل الحياري، وسمية الدباغ.

لا بد من شكر جود الذكير لإثراء كتابنا بشعرها، ومعاذ العوفي لسماحه لنا بالاقتباس من عدسته.

نود أيضا أن نشكر دينا حرزالله وندى برقاوي لموهبتهما ومساعدتهما لنا في إثراء معرض "*عابرٌ متجذّر*" في أبازيا سان غريغوريو و عمر درويش لمساعدتنا في البحث، ملمحًا إلى آفاق جديدة من البحث.

لا يسعنا نسيان فريدة الحسيني، نيانار عجرم، سارة التونسي، طلال العبيد، وعمر دياب من مؤسسة بينالي الدرعية على صبرهم وتشجيعهم ودعمهم المتواصل.

نور سلامة من دار كاف للنشر على توجيهاتها. زينة عساف على قراءتها المتأنية والمتعاونة. الدكتور محمد آيت ميهوب على ترجمة الكتاب إلى لغتنا العربية الجميلة، ومحمد حمدان على التدقيق اللغوي، ونديم زبليط على ضمان طباعة الصور بدقة عالية.

و في الختام، شكر خاص لعبدالله الكناني محمد الرويس من "*باي تو*" على روحهما التصميمية التجريبية، بالإضافة إلى مصمم الخطوط وائل مرقص على كرمه العفوي.

نورة السايح-هولتروب

نورة السايح-هولتروب هي مهندسة معماريّة وقيّمة فنيّة مقيمة في البحرين. وقد اضطلعت بخطّة أمينة مشاركة لمعرض "استعادة"، وهو أوّل مشاركة للبحرين في بينالي البندقيّة للعمارة الثاني عشر في سنة 2010، وقد توّج بجائزة الأسد الذهبي؛ وهي نائبة المفوّض العام لجناح البحرين الوطني، منذ معرض إكسبو ميلانو في عام 2015. ومنذ عام 2015، ترأست مشروع "اللؤلؤ، شهادة على اقتصاد الجزيرة" المدرج في مواقع التراث العالمي لليونسكو، وقد حصل على جائزة الآغا خان لدورة 2019. وقامت نورة السايح-هولتروب ببناء عدد من المنشآت المؤقّتة والدائمة، وعملت مهندسة معماريّة في القدس، وأمستردام، ونيويورك. وقد عُرضت أعمالها على النطاق الدوليّ في العديد من البيناليّات والمعارض الدوليّة، من بينها ترينالي لشبونة، وبينالي البندقيّة للهندسة المعماريّة، ومهرجان لندن للتصميم، وبينالي سيول للهندسة المعماريّة والعمران، وبينالي جدّة للفنّ الإسلامي. تعمل نورة السايح-هولتروب حالياً في هيئة البحرين للثقافة والآثار في منصب مستشارة المشاريع التراثيّة، حيث تتولّى مسؤوليّة الإشراف على تخطيط وتنفيذ المؤسّسات الثقافيّة والمتاحف، علاوة على تقديم المشورة بشأن استراتيجيات إعادة التأهيل الحضري. وهي حاصلة على درجة الماجستير في الهندسة المعماريّة من المدرسة الفيدراليّة للفنون التطبيقيّة في لوزان، وهي عضو في مجلس إدارة المتحف الفلسطيني في بير زيت، فلسطين.

وسام العسلي

وسام العسلي (سوريا، إسبانيا) هو مهندس معماريّ وباحث متخصّص في الحرف اليدويّة وتكنولوجيا البناء. وهو أستاذ مساعد ومدير الموادّ والأساليب في كليّة لهندسة المعمارية والتصميم بجامعة معهد إدارة الأعمال، في إسبانيا (IE). حصل على درجة الدكتوراه من جامعة كامبريدج في عام 2021، وكان زميلًا في برنامج زمالة فونغ العالميّة المقدَّم من جامعة برينستون (2021-2022) قبل أن ينضمّ إلى جامعة معهد إدارة الأعمال، في إسبانيا (IE).

تستكشف أعمال وسام العسلي تاريخَ وتطبيقات التجريب القائم على الندرة في أساليب البناء التقليديّة والأصليّة والمحليّة. أما من الناحية العمليّة، فيعتمد في أعماله على المعرفة التراثيّة لتطوير تصاميم صديقة للبيئة. وفي عام 2010، شارك في تأسيس مختبر IWlab، وهو مركز أبحاث متخصّص في دراسة بيئة التصنيع والإسكان السوريّة. وفي عام 2020، شارك في تأسيس مركز CERCAA، وهو مؤسّسة اجتماعيّة مقرّها في مدينة فالنسيا بإسبانيا، وقد أُنشئت لتدريب المهندسين المعماريّين على حِرف البناء المحليّة، في إسبانيا والشرق الأوسط.

فازت بحوثه وأنشطته بجوائز عديدة، نذكر منها وسام رئيس المعهد الملكي للمهندسين المعماريّين البريطانيّين (RIBA) للبحث (2021)، وجائزة كلير هول سالجي لأفضل أطروحة دكتوراه (2022)، وجائزة مؤسّسي مجلّة جمعيّة المؤرّخين المعماريّين (2022). وفي عام 2024، حصل على جائزة المستقبل الرقمي (Digital Futures) للشرق الأوسط، وحصل مختبر IWlab على الجائزة العالميّة للهندسة المعماريّة المستدامة.

زياد جمال الدين

زياد جمال الدين هو مؤسّس مشارك لشركة "ليفت أركيتيكس" (L.E.FT Architects) (نيويورك/بيروت)، وأستاذ مساعد في جامعة كولومبيا (GSAPP). حصل على جائزة الأصوات الناشئة من رابطة الهندسة المعماريّة في نيويورك (2010)، وتم اختياره من المعهد الأمريكي للمهندسين المعماريّين (AIA) كواحد من "تسعة مهندسين معماريّين عرب أمريكيّين يجب أن تعرفهم" (2024). يجمع جمال الدين بين ممارسة الهندسة المعماريّة والبحث والتدريس الأكاديميّ، وتركز بحوثه على عمارة المساجد. وقد نُشرت كتاباته في مجلّة الأماكن (2020) (Places Journal)، ومجلّة الثقافات الماديّة في العالم الإسلامي (Material Cultures in the Muslim World) (بريل، 2024)، والمجلّة الدوليّة للعمارة الإسلاميّة (International Journal of Islamic Architecture) (إنتلكت، 2025). وتم عرض أعماله البحثيّة والتصميميّة في ترينالي أوسلو للعمارة (2016)، وترينالي ميلانو للعمارة (2018)، وترينالي الشارقة للعمارة (2019)، ومؤخّراً في بينالي جدّة للفنّ الإسلامي (2023). وتم اختيار شركة "ليفت أركيتيكس" L.E.FT في عام 2025 لجائزة AD100 لأفضل المصمّمين في الشرق الأوسط وشمال إفريقيا. ومن المشاريع التي أنجزتها شركة "ليفت أركيتيكس" L.E.FT، نذكر مسجد شكيب أرسلان في لبنان (2017)، الحائز على جائزة التصميم المشترَك بين الأديان (AIA) وشركاء الأماكن المقدّسة (2018)، وجائزة الفوزان لعمارة المساجد (2020)، بالإضافة إلى جائزة مكتب الحياة الدينيّة والروحيّة والممارسات التأمّليّة بكليّة فاسار (2023)، وفاز كذلك بجائزة التصميم المشترَك بين الأديان (AIA) وجائزة شركاء الأماكن المقدّسة: في مجال إعادة الاستخدام التكيّفي (2024).

المساهمون

حنيف كارا

البروفيسور حنيف كارا هو مهندس إنشائيّ ممارِس لهذه المهنة، وهو كذلك أستاذ يدرّس في كليّة الدراسات العليا للتصميم بجامعة هارفارد، مختصّ في مجال ممارسة التكنولوجيا المعماريّة. وقد عُرف بربطه بين التصميم والبحث والتعليم والممارسة. شارك في الفترة الممتدّة بين عاميْ 2000 و2004 في إدارة وحدة الدبلوم في جمعية الهندسة المعماريّة في لندن، وكان أستاذًا زائرًا في المعهد الملكي بستوكهولم حيث قدّم دروساً في التكنولوجيا المعماريّة، من سنة 2007 إلى سنة 2012.

وبصفته مدير التصميم والمؤسّس المشارك لشركة أكت II (AKT II) (تأسّست عام 1996)، فإنّ منهجه المميّز الذي يقوم على التصميم والاهتمام بالأشكال المبتكرة واستخدام الموادّ والبناء المستدام وطرق التحليل المعقّدة، قد مكّنه من العمل في العديد من المشاريع الرائدة التي تصدّرت طليعة المشاريع التي عالجت التحدّيات العديدة التي تواجه البيئة المبنيّة.

خالد عزام

خالد عزام هو مدير "مدرسة الأمير للفنون التقليدية في لندن. وهو مهندس معماري بالتدريب، ويدير مكتبه في القاهرة وجدة. بنى منازل ومدارس ومساجد ومكاتب ومبانٍ تجارية ومساكن ملكية. وتطبق هذه المشاريع مبادئ التصميم والبناء الإسلامي التقليدي، المستمدة من البحث والممارسة الأكاديمية، بهدف إرساء مفهوم معاصر للعمارة في العالم العربي/الإسلامي. ولا يقتصر تكامل العمارة والفنون والتعليم على مهنته المعمارية فحسب، بل يمتد إلى مسيرته الأكاديمية أيضًا من خلال تطوير مشاريع وبرامج ومؤسسات تعليمية.

جود الذكير

جود الذكير باحثة وشاعرة حاصلة على منحة رودس (2022) و على درجة الماجستير في الأدب المقارن والترجمة النقدية من جامعة أكسفورد.

معاذ العوفي

تولد معاذ العوفي في المدينة المنورة بالمملكة العربية السعودية عام 1984 ، وهو فنان وباحث ومستكشف. يشغل حاليًا منصب رئيس البرامج الثقافية في هيئة تطوير المدينة المنورة. بالإضافة إلى إدارة مركز المدينة للفنون ، فإن معاذ هو أيضًا مؤسس الاستوديو الفني المثباء ، والشريك المؤسس لفريق Erth Team ، وهي مجموعة إنتاج مدربة ومتخصصة في رحلات السفاري والتصوير الجوي ووثائق السفر.

طوال حياته المهنية ، عرض معاذ أعماله في جدة والرياض والدمام والبحرين وعمان ولندن وباريس وبروكسل وموسكو ونيو مكسيكو ويوتا وسيول.

ناصر رباط

ناصر رباط هو أستاذ ومدير برنامج الآغا خان للعمارة الإسلاميّة في معهد ماساتشوستس للتكنولوجيا. تشمل اهتماماته الفنّ، والعمارة الإسلاميّة، والتاريخ الحضريّ، ودراسات التراث، والتاريخ العربي، والفنّ الإسلاميّ المعاصر، والنقد الما بعد الكولونيالي. ويقوم ناصر رباط بإلقاء محاضرات في جوانب مختلفة من العمارة الإسلاميّة، ويشرف على عدّة ندوات حول الاستشراق والاستعمار؛ وقضايا التخطيط العمرانيّ الإسلاميّ؛ وتاريخ العمارة الإسلاميّة؛ والعصور القديمة المتأخّرة وأساس العمارة الإسلاميّة؛ وقراءة ابن خلدون؛ و (إعادة) بناء الذاكرة؛ وإبادة المدن؛ والتوازن بين العولمة والإقليميّة في الخليج العربي.

وقد نشر البروفيسور رباط ما يزيد على مائة مقال علمي، والكثير من الكتب التي تتّصل بموضوعات تنطلق من العمارة المملوكة، وصولاً إلى سوريا القديمة، ومروراً بالقاهرة في القرن التاسع عشر، والاستشراق وإبادة المدن. ونذكر من أحدث مؤلّفاته كتابه "تقيّ الدين المقريزي: وجدان التاريخ المصري" (2024)؛ ومؤلَّف "ناصر رباط: لقاءات حرجة" (2023)؛ ودراسته "كتابة مصر: المقريزي ومشروعه التاريخي" (2023)؛ وبحثه "عمارة المدن الميّتة" (2018)، والكتاب الذي قام بتحريره بالاشتراك مع باميلا كريمي، ونشر على الشبكة العنكبوتيّة "تدمير التراث الثقافي: من نابليون إلى داعش" (2016). وستنشر مطبعة الجامعة الأمريكية بالقاهرة خلال سنة 2025، كتاباً شارك في تحريره بعنوان "البناء بوصفه تدميراً: حالة سوريا". ويقوم ناصر رباط حالياً بتحرير كتاب عن التاريخ الثقافي لسوريا، ستقوم مطبعة جامعة إدنبرة بنشره. وله مشروع كتاب قادم يتناول بالدرس تاريخ القاهرة المملوكيّة، وقد تعاقد بشأنه مع مطبعة الجامعة الأمريكيّة بالقاهرة.

الفريق الفائز

إستوديو إيست للهندسة المعماريّة

إستوديو إيست للهندسة المعماريّة (EAST Architecture Studio) هو شركة معماريّة جماعيّة حائزة على جوائز عديدة، تعمل في مجال التصميم المعماريّ والبحث التجريبيّ. يتّخذ هذا الإستوديو من ممارسة الحفاظ شعاراً له، وانطلاقاً من هذا الشعار أنتجت الشركة بيئات مبنيّة مبتكَرة على مستويات مختلفة، تتراوح من التخطيط الرئيسي إلى التصميم الداخلي وإعادة الاستخدام التكيّفي، دافعةً بذلك المجتمع المعاصر إلى الانخراط في استعادة العلاقة مع الثقافة التقليديّة. وقد فاز إستوديو إيست للهندسة المعماريّة بجائزة الآغا خان للعمارة، وبالنسخة الأولى من جائزة المصلّى 2025.
وتكشف الأعمال التي أنجزها الإستوديو عن مقاربة ثاقبة البصيرة، وتفسير حسّاس للتاريخ والثقافة، لاسيما في عدد من المشاريع ،مثل مشروع تجديد بيت ضيافة نيماير في مدينة طرابلس بلبنان، الذي حاز تقديراً كبيراً.

تم عرض أعمال إستوديو إيست للهندسة المعماريّة على النطاق الدوليّ، لاسيما في بينالي البندقيّة للهندسة المعماريّة السابع عشر، والمعهد الملكيّ للمهندسين المعماريّين البريطانيّين (RIBA)، ومتحف شيكاغو للتاريخ، وقد نُشرت الدراسات المتعلّقة بهذه الأعمال على نطاق واسع أيضاً، في مجلة "ورق الجدران" (Wallpaper Magazine) ومجلة "المراجعة المعماريّة" (Architectural Review)، ومجلّة "السجلّ المعماري" (Architectural Record).

ريان تابت

يعتمد ريان تابت (من مواليد 1983 في قرية عشقوت بلبنان) على خبرته الذاتيّة وبحوثه الشخصيّة، ليستكشف القصص التي تقدّم من خلال الروايات الفرديّة، فهماً بديلاً للأحداث الاجتماعيّة والسياسيّة الكبرى. وتستلهم أعماله التدريب الذي تلقّاه في الهندسة المعماريّة والنحت، وظهر ذلك في تركيز مشاريعه على استكشاف مفارقات البيئة المبنيّة وتاريخها من خلال ما أنجزه من تركيبات، وتدخّلات وعروض، تلتقي جميعاً في إعادة بناء تصوّر المسافة الماديّة والزمانيّة.
وقد أقام تابت في السنوات الأخيرة، مجموعة من المعارض الفرديّة نذكر منها معارضه في متحف مودام (2023)، ومركز ووكر للفنون (2021)، ومؤسّسة الشارقة للفنون (2021)، وواجهة متجر للفنّ والعمارة (Storefront for Art and Architecture 2020)، ومؤسّسة براسول يونيت للفنّ المعاصر (Parasol Unit Foundation of Contemporary Art) (2019)، ومتحف المتروبوليتان للفنون (2019)، ومتحف اللّوفر (2019)، ومتحف كاري دار للفنّ المعاصر (Carée d'Art Musée d'Art Contemporain) في مدينة نيم بفرنسا (2018) وجمعيّة الفنون (Kunstverein) بهامبورغ. (2017). كما ظهرت أعماله في العديد من المعارض الجماعيّة الدوليّة، نذكر منها بينالي ويتني 80 (2022)، وترينالي يوكوهاما 7 (2020)، وبينالي لاهور 2 (2020)، وبينالي سيدني 21 (2018)، وبينالي مانيفستا 12 (2018)، وبينالي إسطنبول 15 (2017)، وبينالي ساو باولو 32 (2017)، وبينالي الشارقة 10 و12 (2011، 2015)، وترينالي المتحف الجديد 2(2012).

أكت II (AKT II)

هي شركة هندسة مدنيّة وإنشائيّة تقدميّة تعمل أساساً في التصميم، ولديها مشاريع منجزة وأخرى قيد التنفيذ في 44 دولة حول العالم. تدير الشركة أعمالها انطلاقاً من مقرّها الاجتماعي في مكتبها الرئيسي بلندن، ويضمّ أكثر من 300 شخص، وله مكاتب إقليميّة في مانشستر وكامبريدج.

كريستوفر بلست

يملك كريستوفر بلست ما يزيد على 15 عاماً من الخبرة. وبوصفه مدير تصميم، فهو يساهم بخبرة استراتيجيّة واسعة النطاق عبر محفظة "أكت II " العالميّة: بدءًا من إنجاز مشروع الترميم غير المسبوق لمصنع شروزبري فلاكسميل للشعير، وصولاً إلى التجديد الذي ينتظر الفراغ منه قريباً للبيت النيوزيلندي في لندن، وإنجاز متحف زايد الوطني الجديد في أبوظبي.

المعماريون المتأهلون للجائزة

أنسطاس AAU

هو مكتب هندسة معماريّة دوليّة مقرّه في بيت لحم بفلسطين، وباريس. ويضمّ إستوديو هذا المكتب مهندسين معماريّين، ومصمّمي ديكور داخليّ، ومهندسين مدنيّين، وكهربائيّين، وميكانيكيّين. ترتكز طبيعة الممارسة التي يختصّ بها هذا المكتب، على الاهتمام الدقيق بالتكامل بين المبنى والموقع، والاعتناء بأدقّ تفاصيل كلّ مشروع، سعياً إلى توليد بنية متماسكة اجتماعيّاً وثقافيّاً وفكريّاً.

إستوديو آصف خان

يختصّ إستوديو آصف خان في الهندسة المعماريّة، وتصميم المعارض، وهو يتمتّع بخبرة 14 عاماً في مجال تقديم المشاريع الثقافيّة والتجارب الغامرة لفائدة المتاحف، والمعارض، والألعاب الأولمبيّة، والمعارض العالميّة. هذا الإستوديو هو عبارة عن شركة صغيرة ومتوسّطة الحجم، توظّف حاليّاً 30 موظّفاً. وينكبّ الاستوديو في الوقت الحالي على مشاريع عديدة منها تحويل الواجهة البحريّة لمتاحف ليفربول الوطنيّة، وإنجاز متحف لندن الجديد في ويست سميثفيلد، وتجديد مركز باربيكان، وإنجاز مركز تسيليني للثقافة المعاصرة في ألماتي، والمنطقة العامّة وبوّابات الدخول لمعرض إكسبو دبي 2020.

ومن أبرز المشاريع التي سبق للإستوديو إنجازها، نذكر جناح "ميغافيس" (Mega Faces) (وجوه ضخمة) في دورة الألعاب الأولمبيّة الشتويّة التي دارت في سوتشي 2014، وقد فاز هذا الجناح بجائزة كان ليون الكبرى للابتكار، وجائزة كوكاكولا بيتبوكس في أولمبياد لندن 2012، وبلغ هذا الجناح مرحلة الدور النهائي في المنافسة الدوليّة لمتحف جوجنهايم الجديد في هلسنكي، وقد تقدّم إليها بين 1700 تصميم لا تحمل أسماء أصحابها.

الدبّاغ للهندسة المعمارية

الدبّاغ للهندسة المعمارية هي شركة تصميم معماري حائزة على جوائز عدة ولها مكاتب في دبي وأبو ظبي بالإمارات العربية المتحدة. وتشتهر الشركة إقليميًا بتصميماتها المعاصرة وخدماتها المتميزة.

تأسست الشركة عام 2008 في دبي، لتصبح من أوائل الشركات في منطقة الخليج التي تحصل على شهادة المعهد الملكي للمهندسين المعماريين البريطانيين (RIBA) عام 2015. سعى المكتب إلى ابتكار هندسة معمارية تُحسّن حياة الناس ومُعالجة مواضيع الهوية والمكان والسياق. تشتهر الدبّاغ للهندسة المعمارية بتصميماتها التي تُراعي السياق الثقافي وبالإضافة إلى المشاريع الثقافية، تُغطي محفظة الأعمال قطاعات متنوعة، بما في ذلك المشاريع التجارية والسكنية والتعليمية.

مكتب سهل الحياري للهندسة المعماريّة

مكتب سهل الحياري للهندسة المعماريّة (OSAA) هو شركة معماريّة حائزة على جوائز عديدة، ومقرّها العاصمة الأردنيّة، عَمّان. يدير هذه الشركة المهندس المعماري الرئيسي سهل الحياري. وتشمل الأعمال التي تنجزها الشركة مجموعة واسعة من التخصّصات ذات الصلة بالتصميم، بدءًا من التصميم الحضريّ إلى التصميم الداخليّ وتصميم الأثاث، مروراً بالمنشآت المعماريّة وتصميم المعارض. وقد تمّ نشر وعرض المحفظة المتنوّعة لمكتب سهل الحياري للهندسة المعماريّة (OSAA) على النطاق الدولي. فهذا المكتب يتناول ما يتّصل بكل مشروع ينجزه من خصوصيّات وتحدّيات وقيود، باعتبارها جوانب مفيدة تُستوعب داخل خطاب التصميم ونوعيّة المقاربة المحدّدة لتنفيذه. إنّ أوجه التآزر بين التصميم والموادّ المستعملة في البناء والتقنية من جهة، والسياق الثقافي من جهة أخرى، من شأنها أن تنشئ بنية توفّر التنوّع والتغيير والتحول المرتبط بالمكان. وتركّز الممارسة المتمحورة حول البحث، على إنجاز أعمال يقع تطويرها انطلاقاً من المناظر الطبيعيّة الثقافيّة والمورفولوجيّة الخاصّة بكل سياق محدد. وعلى هذا النحو، فإن الأعمال التي ينجزها مكتب سهل الحياري للهندسة المعماريّة تأخذ بعين الاعتبار السياق الذي يتنزّل فيه المشروع، بتقاليده ومواضعاته، بوصفها جوانب قابلة لإعادة التعريف وإعادة الابتكار.

علي ملكاوي

علي ملكاوي هو أستاذ تقنية العمارة بجامعة هارفارد، يدعو إلى تبني إستراتيجيات كفاءة الطاقة مع تثقيف الجيل القادم من طلاب كلية الدراسات العليا للتصميم في مجال محاكاة البناء والحفاظ على الطاقة والاستدامة. بصفته باحثاً دولياً، حصل على درجة البكالوريوس في العلوم في الهندسة المعمارية والتصميم البيئي من جامعة العلوم والتكنولوجيا الأردنية، ودرجة الماجستير في الهندسة المعمارية من جامعة كولورادو، ودرجة الدكتوراه من معهد جورجيا للتقنية في تقنيات العمارة/ الذكاء الاصطناعي. عمل سابقاً كأستاذ في جامعة بنسلفانيا، وأسس وأدار مركز «تي سي تشان» لمحاكاة البناء ودراسات الطاقة. وكان من الأعمدة الأساسية التي أسهمت في إنشاء مركز هارفارد للمباني والمدن الخضراء في جامعة هارفارد

لجنة التحكيم

نوّاف بن عيّاف

رئيس اللجنة

رئيس لجنة التحكيم في جائزة المصلى ومستشار أول في وزارة الثقافة السعودية. هو خبير باحث في التنمية الحضرية والدراسات المعمارية وممارسات التراث الثقافي. حاصل على درجتي ماجستير من معهد ماساتشوستس للتقنية ومن كلية التصميم في جامعة هارفارد. تم نشر أبحاثه وأعماله في العديد من مجلات وكتب الهندسة المعمارية، كما ظهرت في عدد من المؤتمرات المتخصصة. كما قد درّس وألقى محاضرات في مؤسسات مرموقة مثل اليونسكو، وكلية التصميم ومركز الدراسات الشرق أوسطية في جامعة هارفارد، والكلية الملكية للفنون في لندن. كما مارس الأمير نواف التنمية الحضرية على نطاقات متعددة، في منظمات غير حكومية مثل البنك الدولي، وشركات استشارية عالمية، ومكاتب تصميم رائدة عالمياً ومحلياً.

فاروخ درخشاني

فاروخ درخشاني هو مدير جائزة الآغا خان للعمارة، ومتخصص في العمارة المعاصرة للمجتمعات الإسلامية. يلقي محاضرات في عدة أماكن ويشارك في مجالس ولجان العديد من المؤسسات الثقافية. في عام 2018، تم تعيينه زميلاً دولياً في المعهد الملكي للمعماريين البريطانيين. تدرب درخشاني كمهندس معماري ومخطط في جامعة شهيد بهشتي الإيرانية ثم واصل دراسته في كلية العمارة في باريس. منذ عام 1982، جعله ارتباطه بجائزة الآغا خان على اتصال بالمهندسين المعماريين والبناة والمخططين في جميع أنحاء العالم. شمل عمله المهني تصميم وإدارة بناء مشاريع الأشغال العامة والبنية التحتية واسعة النطاق في إيران، فضلاً عن التصميم المعماري في باريس وجنيف.

أزرا أكشاميا

أزرا أكشاميا هي فنانة ومؤرخة معمارية ومؤلفة، تستكشف أعمالها متعددة التخصصات قوة الفن والعمارة في تسهيل عملية الوساطة التحويلية في الصراعات الثقافية أو السياسية. حصلت على درجتي ماجستير في الهندسة المعمارية من معهد غراتس للتكنولوجيا (2001) وجامعة برينستون (2004)، ودكتوراه في التاريخ والنظرية والنقد في الهندسة المعمارية من معهد ماساتشوستس للتقنية (2011). نالت جائزة الآغا خان للتصاميم المعمارية عام 2013 عن تصميمها لمساحة الصلاة في المقبرة الإسلامية في ألتاش، النمسا، وجائزة الفن لمدينة غراتس عام 2018، ودكتوراه فخرية من كلية مونتسيرات للفنون في 2020.

لينا غطمة

تعكس أعمال لينا غطمة للهندسة المعمارية وجودها الانتمائي وتجربة عيشها في بيروت، وهي مؤسِّسة شركة «لينا غطمة للعمارة» التي يدفعها مفهوم «علم الآثار من أجل المستقبل»، تهتم مشاريعها بمواد الطبيعة وتتناغم معها. درست الهندسة المعمارية في الجامعة الأمريكية في بيروت والمدرسة الخاصة للهندسة المعمارية في باريس، وهي تشغل حالياً منصب أستاذة نقد التصميم (كرسي كنزو تانغ) في كلية الدراسات العليا للتصميم بجامعة هارفارد. ومن بين مشاريعها البارزة: برج «ستون جاردن» في بيروت، والذي عُرض في بينالي البندقية السابع عشر، والمتحف الوطني الإستوني، المرشح لجائزة «ميس فان دير روه». حصدت جوائز عدة، من بينها: جائزة شيلينغ للهندسة المعمارية (2021) وجائزة فئة «نساء الإنجاز المتميز» من مؤسسة تميُّز (2020).

في هذه الصورة التي يبدو أنّها التُقطت في المملكة العربيّة السعوديّة، يظهر فضل الرحمن خان في الوسط، وهو يرتدي الغترة والعقال - غطاء الرأس السعودي المحلّي الذي يستخدمه الرجال - فوق ملابسه الغربيّة. SOM ©

لقد عمل فضل الرحمن خان على مفارقة كبيرة، إذ أنشأ هيكلاً دائماً انطلاقاً من نمط يُعدّ أكثر الأنماط المؤقتة الموجودة. وهو بهذا العمل، قد استمتع بلا شكّ باللّعب على التجاورات والتناقضات المعماريّة منذ سنة 1982؛ ولعلّنا بإنجازنا مشروع «عابر متجذّر» في هذه السنة، نكون قد استمرينا على نمط اللعب ذاته، ولو كنّا متأخرين ثلاثة وأربعين عاماً عن فضل الرحمن خان.

كلمة مصلّى قد وردت في هذا المقال وحده، سبعاً وعشرين مرّة. أثناء محاولتنا الكشف عن تعدديّة المصلّى وإثبات مرونته، وجدنا أنفسنا أمام نمط شبحيّ وعابر، ذي طبيعة خاصّة به. فلقد سمح لنا استكشافها بإثارة أسئلة تتجاوز حدودها المضخّمة، وتتغلغل في صلب تخصّص العمارة ذاته؛ من خلال التشكيك في بعض أسسه الرئيسيّة، والوقوف على مزايا معارضة بعض خطاباته السائدة. إنّ الإمكانات المتاحة هنا هائلة، والتحدّي جسيم، بيد أنّ هذا المشروع ليس في الحقيقة سوى بذرة؛ إنّه بداية متواضعة لوضع اللّبنة الأولى في طريق طويل ممتدّ أمامنا؛ وهو مسار يهدف إلى تجذير دعائم فضاء جُبِل على أن يكون سريع الزوال بطبعه.

الموضة، مفضّلاً جانباً واحداً من الواقع المعقّد والمتعدّد الأوجه الذي يميّز الأعمال التي تم إنشاؤها في البلدان الإسلاميّة. بدلاً من ذلك، يؤكّد المعرض على إعطاء الأولويّة للجودة، سواء أكان التصميم من عمل خبراء غربيّين، أم من إنجاز أولئك الذين يعبّرون بشكل متزايد عن ثقافتهم الأصليّة. إنّ وجهة النظر التي قام عليها المعرض غربيّة - ولا يمكن أن تكون غير ذلك - لكنّها تنبع في الآن ذاته من نهج تشاركيّ، لا من التأكيد الوهميّ على التفوّق»[4].

إنّ جائزة المصلّى التي تمّ تقديمها خلال الدورة التاسعة عشرة لبينالي البندقيّة للعمارة، هي في جوهرها استعادة لسرديّة مفقودة فُهمت فهماً سيئاً لمدّة طويلة من الزمن؛ إنّها فرصة سانحة لتغيير المنظور، ولا نعني به المنظور الذي تهيمن عليه النظرة الغربيّة فحسب، بل المنظور الذي قد ينبع من الداخل أيضاً. أمّا في ما يتعلّق بمشروع «عابر متجذّر»، فقد جلبنا معنا أجزاء من جائزة تهدف إلى إثراء التخصّص المعماريّ العالمي والدخول في صلبه، ومن المفارقات أنّ شركة تدعى EAST (الشرق) هي التي فازت بهذه الجائزة. وفي سياق المسعى إلى القيام باستعادة فكريّة بواسطة هذه الجائزة وهذا المشروع البحثي، وجدنا منصة تحاور في دير سان غريغوريو على القناة الكبرى في البندقيّة؛ وهي ممرّ مائيّ يتعرّج بلطف نحو الشرق، ويمتدّ إلى البحر الأبيض المتوسط، عبر البحر الأدرياتيكيّ، ومن ثمّ ينفتح على العالم بأسره بكل شاعرية. إنّنا متسلّحون بمعرفة محلّية متعمّقة في موضوع غالباً ما أهمله الغرب المتصوّر؛ فلا نختار نحن أيضاً الموضة، كما قال بورتوغيسي، ولكنّنا نوجه دعوة لإعادة إطلاق نوع من الحوار المماثل لذلك الذي تطلّع إليه، والذي اختفى منذ ذلك الحين.

إنّ مشروعي جائزة المصلى و «عابر متجذّر»، يطرح في الأساس سؤالاً عميقاً يتعلّق بما يمكن أن يظهر من إمكانات عندما يتجه التفكير المعماري نحو الممارسات المكانيّة القائمة على القدرة على التكيّف. فهل ثمّة من مكان يحتفي بسؤال فكريّ يستثمر ثنائيّة الزمانيّة والتجذّر، أفضل من التحفة الفنيّة التي تحمل اسم صالة الحجّاج؟ قد عمل على تصميمها فضل الرحمن خان من شركة سكيدمور، أوينغز آند ميريل المعماريّة (SOM) واكتمل بناءها في عام 1981، ويُعدّ هذا المبنى أحد أشهر أعماله المعماريّة والهندسيّة العديدة. على الرغم من كون فضل الرحمن خان مهندساً في المقام الأوّل، وليس معمارياً، فقد أتقن فنّ دمج هياكله داخل سرديات تاريخيّة ومعماريّة؛ سواء كان ذلك في برج سيرز (ويليس الآن)، الذي ردّد تصميمُه أصداء من التراث الغنيّ لناطحات السحاب في شيكاغو، أو في صالة الحجاج التي استوحاها من التقاليد المحلّية للخيام البدويّة.

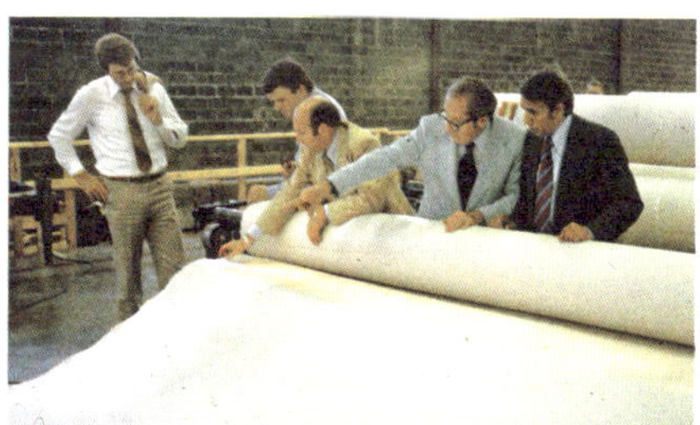

يظهر في هذه الصورة فضل الرحمن خان، الشريك في SOM، وهو يتفقّد وحدات السقف المصنوعة من الألياف الزجاجيّة المطليّة بالتيفلون، والمستخدمة هنا، في محطّة الحجّ. SOM ©

لقد توجّست جائزة المصلّى من حقيقة أنّها ستتمّ استضافتها في محطّة الحجّ الضخمة وتحت مظلاّتها الشامخة: فكيف يمكن إخراج التدخّل التصميمي المعماريّ المطلوب من الجائزة من سياق أحد أكثر الأعمال الهندسيّة شهرةً في القرن العشرين؟ بل إنّ السؤال الأكثر إلحاحاً من سابقه، هو لماذا يُقترح، من الأساس، إنشاء مكان مخصّص للصلاة داخل مشروع قاوم عمداً منذ بدايته تلك الفكرة؟

هنا بالتحديد يمكن للمرء أن يتتبّع الخيط المشترَك الذي يربط الرؤية التي انبنت عليها المسابقة، بالفضاء ذاته الذي استضافتها ومنحها الحياة. فعلى الرغم ممّا بينهما من اختلاف في الحجم والنطاق، فإنّ صالة الحجّاج وجائزة المصلّى تجمع بينهما قرابة أعمق: فهما فضاءان للتجمّع والاجتماع المؤقّتين، كلّما دعت الحاجة إلى ذلك؛ وهما فضاءان خاصّان بالتدفّق، سواء أتعلّق الأمر بتدفّق جموع الناس الذين يأتون من جميع أنحاء العالم إلى المحطّة، وهم في طريقهم إلى مكّة لأداء فريضة الحجّ، أو بتدفّق الأفراد المتّجهين إلى المصلّى، حريصين على تلقّي التطهير الروحي الذي تعد به الصلاة . فكلاهما (صالة الحجاج والمصلّى) يتحدّى بكل احترام النماذج الأصليّة الجامدة والراسخة للأنماط المعماريّة. فقد تحدّى مبنى صالة الحجّاج نموذج المطار التقليديّ، من خلال اختراع مكان للتجمّع التكتوني الذي يعمل عمداً بوصفه قريةً أكثر من كونه محطّةً. وبالمثل، كما تمّ استكشافه بإسهاب في هذا الكتاب، فإنّ جائزة المصلّى تجد نفسها غارقة هي أيضاً في صراع موازٍ خاصّ بها؛ فهي تدعو إلى إعادة اختراع وإعادة تعريف نمط جديد لمكان الصلاة[5]... وهو ليس مسجداً.

لقد قال فضل خان ذات مرّة عن محطّة الحجّ: «هذه الخيمة لا تحاكي خيام الماضي؛ إنّها شكل من أشكال المستقبل يلبّي احتياجات اليوم، ألا وهي: النقل الجويّ»[6].

ومثلما أدّى ظهور وسائل النقل الحديثة إلى تزايد تدفّق الحجّاج إلى جدّة، ممّا دفع فضل الرحمن خان إلى استغلال التقنيات الجديدة بشكل عمليّ لكسر رتابة النماذج التقليديّة والقائمة، فكذلك نؤكّد نحن الآن أيضاً أنّ تطوّر أنماط التحضّر الحديثة قد أدخل تغييراً جذرياً على الطريقة التي يتمّ بها تصوّر مكانيّة المصلّى وتمثيلها. وعلى هذا النحو، فإنّ مشروع «عابر متجذّر» يبيّن من خلال التباين بين فكرة مؤقّتة إلى أخرى، أنّ مفهوم المؤقّت في أحد السياقات التاريخيّة لا يمكن مضاهاته بمفهوم آخر للمؤقّت مندرج في سياق تاريخيّ مختلف. في ضوء ذلك، يكفّ المصلى عن أن يكون مجرّد فضاء فحسب، بل يصبح انعكاساً لطبيعته الزمانيّة ذاتها؛ والكيفيّة التي تشكّلت وفقها من خلال الظروف التاريخيّة والجغرافيّة الفريدة التي دفعتها والتي وجدت فيها. عندما سُئل فضل خان عمّا إذا كان قد فكّر في السابق، في إنشاء هياكل مؤقّتة لصالة الحجّاج - مثل الخيام، على سبيل المثال، التي يمكن إزالتها بعد الحجّ - أقرّ بأنّه قد فكّر في ذلك فعلاً، ولكن لفترة وجيزة فقط:

«لقد تصوّرنا هيكلاً قابلاً للتحويل يمكن تفكيكه، لكنه سيتطلّب إصلاحات، إذ كان التآكل والتلف أمراً لا مفرّ منه. فلكُم أن تتخيّلوا حجمها: 450 ألف متر مربع من المساحة المغطّاة! يا لها من عمليّة ضخمة! ولذلك اخترنا الهيكل الدائم، فلن يكون علينا أن نقلق بشأنه لمدّة خمسين عاماً»[7].

4 Thomas, Helen, ed. Architecture in Islamic Countries - Second International Exhibition of Architecture Venice 1982/83: Selections from the Catalogue for the Second International Exhibition of Architecture Venice 1982/83. 2023. Gta Verlag.

5 Manuel Castells, *The Space of Flows*, Wiley, 2009.

6 Cantacuzino, Sherban, ed. *Architecture in Continuity: Building in the Islamic World Today*. Aperture, 1985.

7 Khan, Hasan-Uddin, ed. *Hajj* Terminal. In *Mimar 4: Architecture in Development*. Singapore: Concept Media Ltd., 1982

من وجهة نظر معماريّة، فإنّ التشابك بين البندقيّة والشرق قد تجلّى بطرق لا تحصى ولا تعدّ. فمن رشاقة انحناءة الأقواس المدبّبة، إلى الفسيفساء المركّبة والمنحوتات الزخرفيّة التي تجسّم التقاليد الفنيّة البيزنطيّة والإسلاميّة، يتّضح للعين الثاقبة مدى اعتماد البندقيّة على الذخيرة المعماريّة الشرقيّة، مدمجةً بعض مبادئ التصميم الشرقيّة في هندستها المعماريّة ونسيجها الحضريّ، بل لقد عمدت في بعض الأحيان إلى ادّعاء ملكيّتها لها. ففي الوقت الذي قام فيه جون روسكين في مؤلَّفه «أحجار البندقيّة» ولأسباب أيديولوجيّة معيّنة، باعتماد البندقيّة نموذجاً للإنسانيّة قبل عصر النهضة، نراه يتحدّث في الآن ذاته عن فساد الغرب وأصالة الشرق، منزِّلاً البندقيّة في منزلة بوتقة انصهار نابضة بالحياة، حيث يُعتقد أنّ التأثيرات الشرقيّة قد تمّ استيعابها وتحويلها، فتحوّلت المدينة بذلك إلى رمز يؤكّد إمكانيّة تقارب التقاليد المتناقضة بعضها من بعض، بواسطة طرق إبداعيّة وذات معنى، من أجل تحقيق التطوّر الفنيّ [2]. ومن المهمّ قبل أن نتابع في هذا السياق، أن أوضّح أنّ إشارتي إلى استخدام روسكين لعبارة «الأصالة» لا تحمل تأييداً لرأيه. بل على العكس من ذلك، إنّني أزعم أنّه من الضروريّ الاعتراف بأنّ الأصالة في حدّ ذاتها هي مصطلح معقد وهدف بعيد المنال، وعلى الرغم من الترويج لهذا المفهوم كمعيار موضوعيّ للواقع، فإنّه غالباً ما يثير سوء الفهم على الدوام. لقد سبق للمهندس المعماريّ والمؤرّخ الراحل ستانفورد أندرسون أن عرّف ذات مرّة الأصالة بأنّها الطريق الثالثة للنقاش المعماريّ: فهي مكان للمغامرة يقتحمه كلّ فرد على مسؤوليّته الخاصّة[3].

إنّ هذا السرد المركّب للترابط بين البندقيّة والشرق، الذي حبك خيوطه نسيجُ البيئة المبنيّة، متجذّر بعمق في تاريخ بينالي البندقيّة للهندسة المعماريّة نفسه. فخلال نسخته التاريخية الثانية في عام 1982-1983، تم اختيار موضوع «الهندسة المعماريّة في البلدان الإسلاميّة» كعنوان رئيسي للنسخة من قبل القيم الفني باولو بورتوغيسي - الذي كان قد انخرط هو نفسه في رحلة شخصيّة لاكتشاف العمارة الإسلاميّة. حيث في هذا الوقت نفسه تقريباً، كان قد كُلّف بورتوغيسي بتصميم مسجد روما الكبير، الذي استغرق بناؤه أكثر من عشرين عاماً، ممّا أهّله ليكون أكبر مسجد خارج العالم الإسلامي وروسيا والهند، عندما فرغ منه أخيراً سنة 1995. كما أنّ بورتوغيسي كان قد اضطلع كذلك بالإشراف على بناء أكبر مسجد في فرنسا، المسجد الكبير في ستراسبورغ، وإن تمّ ذلك بعد بضعة عقود، في عام 2012.

قسم من معرض يضمّ أعمال المهندس المعماريّ العراقيّ محمد مكية، وقد وقع عرضها في بينالي البندقيّة للعمارة الثاني (1982)، حول موضوع «الهندسة المعماريّة في البلدان الإسلاميّة»، بإشراف باولو بورتوغيسي. ومن بين أعمال مكية المعروضة تصاميمه لمسجد دولة الكويت (1977) ومصرف الرافدين في الكوفة (1968). صورة: جورجيو زوكياتي. بإذن من أرشيف بينالي البندقية التاريخي، ASAC.

قسم من المعرض خُصّص لأعمال المهندس المعماري المصري عبد الواحد الوكيل، في بينالي البندقيّة للعمارة الثاني (1982)، حول موضوع «الهندسة المعماريّة في البلدان الإسلاميّة» ، بإشراف باولو بورتوغيسي. ومن أعمال الوكيل المعروضة، تصاميمه لقصر سليمان بجدّة (1979) ومسجد الجزيرة (1980)، وكذلك مسكن خاشقجي بالطائف (1973). صورة: جورجيو زوكياتي. بإذن من أرشيف بينالي البندقية التاريخي، ASAC.

من بين القائمة الطويلة للمهندسين المعماريّين المميَّزين، أشاد بينالي البندقيّة عام 1982 بشكل أساسيّ بأربعة مهندسين معماريّين بارزين - ثلاثة منهم غربيّون - وبمساهمتهم في العمارة الإسلاميّة وهم (فرنان بويّون، ولويس كان، ولو كوربوزييه، وحسن فتحي)، وذلك من خلال تخصيص أقسام لهم في الكتالوج والمعرض. وتوضّح هذه الصورة القسم الذي خُصّص تكريماً لحسن فتحي في بينالي البندقيّة للعمارة في دورته الثانية (1982)، وحمل عنوان «الهندسة المعماريّة في الدول الإسلاميّة» ، برعاية باولو بورتوغيسي. صورة: جورجيو زوكياتي. بإذن من أرشيف بينالي البندقية التاريخي، ASAC.

لقد رأى بورتوغيسي في بينالي 1982 فرصةً للانخراط في الحوار. فقد ارتأى أنّ هذا البينالي فرصة لإصدار نداء جماعيّ يحثّ العالَم الثقافيّ على كسر الحواجز والتغلّب على الانقسامات، عن طريق العمل معاً لحلّ النزاعات الناجمة عن التجاور، والتصوّرات الخاطئة التي فصلت بين العالَمين لفترة طويلة. وقد شرح بورتوغيسي على نحو مفصّل، طموحه الكبير لتحقيق تكافؤ الفرص بين كل المشاركين، فقال:

«لا يسعى المعرض الذي يقام كل سنتين إلى الخروج باختيار يماشي

[2] Ruskin, John. *The stones of Venice* v. J. Wiley, 1851
[3] Fixler, David N. "Kahn's Modernism and its Renewal." *docomomo journal* 58 (2018): 4–5

مميَّزة تتردّد على مكبّر صوت هاتف شخص مّا، مع ضجيج مقطع تيك توك يجلجل في هاتف شخص آخر يوجد على مقربة من المكان.

على هذا النحو، فكما يمكن تحويل مقصورة الطائرة المعقّمة من خلال الصلاة والصمت إلى غرفة للصلاة، فكذلك يمكن لأيّ مكان أن يصبح مصلّى. ففي عالَمنا الرقميّ المترابط بعضه مع بعض، لا يستمدّ شكله المعاصر وخصائصه المميَّزة من مجرّد كونه فضاءً مادياً ملموساً وهندسة معماريّة، بل هو أكثر من ذلك إذ يتعلّق بمسائل عديدة من بينها تزامن الفضاءات، والسلوكات المجتمعيّة، وصدى الصوت.

عندما نأخذ في الاعتبار أنّ عدد المسلمين في بعض الأحياء داخل المدن الأوروبية يماثل عددهم في بعض أحياء العالم العربي، يتبيّن لنا أنّه من الضروريّ إعادة النظر في الأفكار السائدة حول مكانة الروحانيّة وشكلها في الإسلام. فكيف يمكننا في الفضاء الحَدّي للصوت، الشبيه بالفضاء الحَدّي للمصلّى، أن نعيد صياغة التصوّر الخاصّ بمكانة الديني والروحاني ودورهما في العالم المعاصر؟ وكيف يؤثّر ذلك في العلاقة القائمة بين الدين والمجال العامّ، بعيداً عن دائرة المشاهد الصوتيّة التقليديّة في الإسلام؟

خاتمة: نوّاف بن عيّاف
حول التجاورات، والمفارقات، والثنائيات، والمطالبات

أيّ قوة يمكن أن تمتلكها كلمة ذات إمكانات وتأويلات لا حصر لها؟ فكلمة «مُصلّى» لم يرد ذكرها في القرآن الكريم إلاّ في آية واحدة. وفي المقابل، جرى استخدامها 176 مرّةً في هذا الكتاب؛ بدءاً من المنظور الشامل والواسع المتّصل بالتحقيق التاريخيّ والتحليل التفصيليّ لجذورها اللغويّة الاشتقاقيّة، وصولاً إلى خصوصيّات الكيفيّة التي تُستخلص وِفقها الدلالات التاريخيّة العابرة التي يمكن أن توحي بها هذا الكلمة اليومَ. وقد رأينا هذا المصطلح يتمدّد في صفحات هذا الكتاب ويتمطّط، متجاوزاً أحياناً ما لا يحتمله وما قد لا يحسن به تحمّله من معانٍ. ومع ذلك، وبعد وقت قصير من الشروع في هذه الرحلة البحثيّة، أدركنا بسرعة أنّنا نقف أمام فضاء يكتنفه الغموض حقّاً وحقيقةً، وتكمن في جوهره وجوه وضروب لا حصر لها من التعدّديّة، وهي بدورها تمهّد السبيل ليكون تصميم المصلّى على هذا القدر الكبير من المرونة والفضفضة.

وهذا في حدّ ذاته يؤكّد على الضرورة الشديدة والحاجة الملحّة إلى إنجاز هذا المشروع الموسوم بعنوان «عابر متجذّر»، الذي أحاط بجوهر المصلّى نفسه - مجسّداً دلالتيْ الجمود والتحوّل في الآن ذاته. فقد وقعت على عاتقنا جميعاً مسؤوليّة جسيمة فرضت علينا واجب السعي إلى الكشف عن هذا النمط المعماريّ الذي يمتنع عن التحديد، وإن اقتضى ذلك الاستسلام لتجاورات كثيرة، ومفارقات تبدو في ظاهرها غير ضروريّة. فبدلاً من اتّباع مسار محاولة ترويض هذا النمط والتي قد تكون أكثر حكمةً، اخترنا بوعي - وربما في شيء من التهوّر - المضي في زيادة تضخيم نمط هو في أصله شديد الاتّساع، من خلال مقاربتنا التي تهدف إلى تسليط الضوء على الثنائيّة القائمة على المفارقة بين زوال المصلّى من جهة، وحضوره الكليّ المستديم الكامن فيه في جوهره من جهة أخرى.

وعلى الرغم من جريان الحديث عن المسجد والمصلّى في بعض الأحيان وكأنّهما أمر واحد، فإنّه لا ينبغي أبداً الخلط بينهما؛ وكان الإلحاح على ضرورة هذا التمييز بين المصلّى والمسجد هو نقطة الانطلاق لهذا المشروع. فمثلما رأينا بين طيّات هذا الكتاب، وعلى نقيض المسجد الذي حظي بتحليل وشرح أوسع نطاقاً، فإنّ المصلّى هو ملاذ عابر وسريع الزوال يؤدّي فيه الناس الصلاة، ويرتبط ارتباطاً وثيقاً بالتصوّرات المفاهيميّة المتعلّقة بالزمنيّة والزوال، علاوةً على المفاهيم الحسيّة المتّصلة بالقدرة على التكيّف والمرونة. بينما، وفي تعارض تامّ مع المسجد، فإنّ المصلّى لا يضاهي المسجد في ديمومته وخلوده؛ ذلك أنّ المسجد يُعتبر في أصل طبعه وقفاً، أي بناء لا يجوز بيعه أو تركه أو هدمه إلاّ في حالات نادرة جداً.

إنّ جزءاً من الجاذبيّة المركّبة الجوانب لتعريف نمط المصلّى، يكمن في غياب أيّ رغبة لديه في إثبات أو فرض نفسه؛ وفي رغبته ألاّ يكون دائماً أو أبديّاً، مؤثراً على ذلك قدرته على أن يوجد كلّما نشأت الحاجة إلى إقامة الصلاة، ومن ثَم يسعه الإختفاء من الوجود ما إن تنته تلك الحاجة ويمرّ عليها الزمن. وسواء أكانت دورة ظهور المصلّى يوميّة أم موسميّة، فإنّ اختفاءه لا يعني بالضرورة زواله إلى الأبد. إن هذه القدرة الصريحة على الظهور مرّة أخرى بشكل سلس بمجرّد قيام الحاجة إلى ذلك، هي بمثابة شهادة تثبت حيويّة هذا النمط الجارفة، وهي في الوقت نفسه دليل على ما يتّسم به من تعقّد عميق. وهنا بالتحديد تدخّلت جائزة المصلّى[1] بجرأة، لتعالج الغموض المخادع المتمثّل في اختفائه الظاهري، من خلال التأكيد على حياة المصلّى الآخرة وإرثه.

وإدراكاً من جائزة المصلّى للطبيعة المؤقّتة للبيناليات المعاصرة، جنباً إلى جنب مع الطبيعة المؤقتة لنمط المصلّى نفسه، فقد أصرّت الجائزة منذ البداية على تشكيل مسابقة ثوريّة موضوعها تصميم مصلّى قادر على عيش حياة ثانية بعد انتهاء بينالي الفنون الإسلاميّة. بذلك، عزّزت الجائزة الاستفادة من الإمكانات المؤقّتة، ولكن الدائمة، الكامنة في النمط نفسه، ومن احتمالات الاستفادة من إمكانات البينالي حتى بعد اختتامه. ومن خلال تزويد المهندسين المعماريّين المشاركين في المسابقة، والذين تتجلّى أصواتهم طيلة هذا الكتاب، بمساحة فارغة مفتوحة لوضع تصوّراتهم عن كيفيّة ومكان تجسيد مصلّياتهم المقترحة في حياتها الآخرة بعد اختتام البينالي، فإنّ جائزة المصلّى تُدخل كذلك بعداً إضافياً، واعياً ومتعمَّداً، على النموذج الأصليّ الذي يحصر عمل المعماريّين بصفة عامّة في إطار زماني ومكاني محدّد. فعلى نقيض هذا النموذج السائد، تمحورت الجائزة خلال نسختها الأولى حول تحويل المصمّمين إلى شركاء حقيقيّين في وضع البرمجة الطويلة المدى لمشاريعهم.

إنّ سعي هذه الجائزة إلى تعريف ما لا يمكن تعريفه وإضفاء شكل على ما هو غير ملموس، يبيّن بوضوح أنّ هدفها الأساسيّ لم يكن إنشاء نصب تذكاريّ مجوّف خالٍ من المعنى والغرض، بل لقد سعت في المقام الأوّل إلى إنشاء فضاء مقدّس يضمّ بين جوانبه أعمق الأعمال البشريّة: العبادة. وبما أنّ مشروع «عابر متجذّر» يندرج في سياق عنوان بينالي آخر، فقد دعيت جائزة المصلّى لعرض هذا العمل وإطلاق هذا الكتاب في بينالي البندقيّة للعمارة التاسع عشر 2025، الموسوم بعنوان: «ذكاء. طبيعي. صناعي. جماعي»، الذي ينظّم من القيم الفني كارلو راتي. إنّ هذه الفرصة لاختبار فرضيّتنا وتقديمها إلى جمهور أوسع من المعماريّين المختصين والمهتمين، تحمل في طيّاتها شاعريّة مخصوصة: فمنذ الوهلة الأولى، تبدو هذه الدعوة مندجة في تقليد عريق ومسار تاريخيّ متواصل من التبادل الثقافيّ بين مدينة البندقيّة والشرق.

لطالما اعتُبرت البندقيّة بوّابةً منفتحة إلى الشرق. وكانت مرتبطة ارتباطاً وثيقاً بالعالَم الإسلامي، إلى حدود سقوط القسطنطينيّة عام 1453، ممّا أعاق التجارة والتفاعل مع هذه المدينة إعاقة كبيرة. وإذا تناولنا الأمر

[1] المعماريّون الذين وصلوا إلى القائمة لجائزة المصلّى في دورتها الأولى 2025 هم: AAU أنسطاس، وآصف خان، ودبّاغ للهندسة المعماريّة، واستوديو EAST للهندسة المعمارية (الفائزون بالتعاون مع ريان ثابت وAKTII)، ومكتب سهل الحياري؛ أما أعضاء لجنة تحكيم جائزة المصلى في هذه الدورة الافتتاحيّة 2025 فهم: أزرا أكشاميا، وفاروخ درخشاني، ولينا غطمة، وعلي ملكاوي، ونواف بن عياف (رئيساً).

للمصلّى، هذا الفضاء المراوغ لعمليّة التصنيف. فإذا كان ثمّة استنتاج رئيسيّ يمكن استخلاصه من جميع الدروس العديدة المستفادة خلال مجمل المراحل التي قطعها المشروع، فما الذي يودّ كلّ واحد منكم أن يكون ذلك الاستنتاج؟

ك ب: كان لدينا تصوّر عن أسس الهيكل وددت كثيراً لو نفّذناه، ولكن ما قمنا به على أرض الواقع كان في منتهى البراعة أيضاً، لأنّه سيشكّل أسساً تسير عليها مشاريع المصلّى المستقبليّة.

ن ب ع: لقد ساهمتم بطريقة شاعريّة في وضع الدعائم التي ستقوم عليها النسخ القادمة من جائزة المصلّى، سواء أكان ذلك من الناحية الرمزيّة أم من حيث الأسس الهيكليّة الفعليّة. (يومئ ك ب موافقاً). ولقد طرحتم كذلك سؤالاً تردّد طيلة مراحل إنجاز المشروع وانصبّ على مسألة موادّ النفايات، أو موادّ النفايات المتوقّعة، والطريقة التي ينبغي أن نسلكها حتى يتسنّى لنا استخدامها.

ك ب: قطعاً. هذا سؤال أوسع مدًى يجب على العالَم بأجمعه أن يفكّر فيه. فكيف لك أن تحوّل النفايات إلى منتَج جميل؟ وأذكر من موادّ النفايات الأخرى التي وددنا دمجها، النفايات التي تخلّفها المثاقب الأساسيّة عند حفر الحجر المرجانيّ (يرسم بيديه حركة تحاكي الشكل الإسطواني). فقد كنّا نرغب لو أتيح لنا أن نستخدم الحجر المرجانيّ لشدّ القماش. فكما تلاحظ، هناك عدّة أفكار توجّب علينا أن نتخلّى عنها طيلة المسار الذي قطعه المشروع، لكنّها يمكن أن تشكّل في المستقبل نقطة انطلاق للمشاريع القادمة.

ر ت: بالنسبة إليّ، ما أستخلصه هو أنّ هذا المشروع يجعلك تعيد التفكير في مفهوم التقاليد التي دائماً ما يقع إضفاء طابع رومانسيّ عليها، أو يُتعامل معها بطريقة نوستالجيّة يغلب عليها الحنين إلى الماضي، فتظهر الأشياء وقد نأت عنّا كثيراً في الزمن.

ن ب ع: حتى وإن تمّ تسويقها.

ر ت: بالتأكيد، هناك إفراط في ربط مفهوم التقاليد بالماضي، فهو متجمّد في الزمن، كما لو أنّ التقاليد لا توجد إلاّ في الماضي. وقد نجح مقترحنا في المزج بشكل متزامن وفي وقت واحد بين حضور الصناعة اليدويّة، ووجود العنصر المفرط في طابعه التقنيّ والميكانيكي، مع المحافظة في الوقت نفسه على الحقيقة والحرص على مطابقة الواقع، وتكريم الممارسات المعماريّة التي تختصّ بها المنطقة. بيد أنّ المشروع كان جريئاً وشجاعاً بما فيه الكفاية، لدفع هذه الممارسات نحو مستقبل متخيَّل مشترَك. وهذه مقاربة جذريّة، لا في ما يتعلّق بمفهوم التقاليد فقط، ولكن في ما يخصّ فكرة المحافظة أيضاً.

ن ف: متابعةً لما كان يقوله ريان، أذكر أنّ المشروع قد نجح في نقل المحافظة على المعنى، وما يعنيه ذلك بالنسبة إلينا بوصفنا مصمّمين ومهندسين وفنّانين، هو أن نبتكر مجموعة صادقة جدّاً من الممارسات التي تعود إلى الماضي، للتفكير تفكيراً حقيقيّاً في تراث ما زال مستمراً في الحاضر. فهذا المشروع يُعدّ في الأساس استجابةً لممارسة مخصوصة للغاية، تحتضن التكنولوجيا والفنّ، وتعزّز التعايش بين هذه المهارات والمواقف المتزامنة وتدفعه إلى أقصى حدّ ممكن. فمناط الأمر يتعلّق في حقيقة الأمر بالحفاظ على المعنى وادّخاره لمواجهة المستقبل.

ت ك: إنّ كراسة الشروط نفسها كانت طموحة وجذريّة إلى حدّ بعيد؛ فقد قامت على دعوة الناس إلى إعادة ابتكار تصوّر جديد لصنف مهمّ جدّاً من الفضاءات. وبالمثل فإنّ استجابتنا لهذا التحدّي الجسيم اتّسمت بأقصى درجات الجدّية هي أيضاً. فقد استعدنا بعض الأفكار البسيطة، وعملنا على تحقيق أمرين في الوقت نفسه: تمكين تلك الأفكار من التوسع من جهة، وجعلها تتآلف معاً مكوّنةً نسيجاً مفاهيمياً من جهة أخرى. فعلى سبيل المثال، أخذنا مادّة بناء، وهي خشب النخيل الرقائقيّ، فاستفدنا من ميزاتها إلى أقصى حدّ. وهكذا فإنّ الهيكل نفسه كان عبارة عن لفتة معماريّة قويّة قائمة على فكرة بسيطة للغاية تتمثّل في الكشف عن الإطار الخشبيّ. وبوصفنا مهندسين معماريّين، فإنّ أبرز مظاهر التواضع أن نكون صادقين في ما يتعلّق بما نقوم به، فلا نتردّد في الكشف عنه.

والحقّ، أنّه ما كان لهذا المشروع أن يكون على ما هو عليه لولا هذا المسار الذي اتّبعناه. فمجرّد العلم بأمر المسابقة، استحثّنا على التصرّفِ بسرعة، والتزامِ الجديّة في جميع مستويات المشروع. وما إن توصّلنا إلى تحديد الفكرة الأوّليّة التي انطلقنا منها، حتى واظبنا على محاسبة أنفسنا، فكنّا لا ننفكّ عن التساؤل في ما بيننا: هل نحن صادقون مع هذه الفكرة الأوّليّة أم لا؟ وقد ساهم الجانب التعاونيّ المميَّز لهذه المسابقة، في توسيع دائرة هذه التعليقات فعلاً. فطيلة المدّة التي قضّيناها في إنجاز المشروع، تعوّدنا على أن يظهر على الدوام شخصٌ مّا يأتي ويقول متسائلاً: هل نحن صادقون مع الفكرة الأوّليّة، مع المفهوم الأوّليّ؟

خاطرة: نوار السابح-هولتروب

المُصلّى: ما وراء المشهد الصوتيّ الدينيّ

قمت مؤخّراً برحلة على متن الطائرة، وكان مقعدي في مقصورة شديدة العتمة، وحانت منّي التفاتة إلى الخلف، فلمحت راكبة مجاورة لي، وهي تصلّي في مقعدها. كانت مائلة قليلاً، كما لو أنّها تولّي وجهها ناحيةَ مكّة المكرّمة وهي في حالة سجود؛ فشعرتُ فجأة كأنّ المقصورة بأكملها أصبحت مكاناً للصلاة. وإذا بفضاء الطائرة المعقّم الذي يدوّي فيه الطنينُ، قد تحوّل إلى حجرة روحيّة، بعد أن غمره خشوعُها.

لقد كان التداخل بين الروحانيّ والحضريّ خاصيّة ملازمة دوماً للعالَم الإسلامي، فطيلة قرون طويلة، ظلّ الأذان وخطب الجمعة وصلاة التراويح الليليّة خلال شهر رمضان، تتغلغل في أعماق المدن غامرةً إياها بموجاتها الصوتيّة الروحيّة. فمن خلال الصوت، انتشر الإسلام بعيداً عن حدود الفضاء الملموس المحدّد، المخصّص للصلاة. ذلك أنّ الإسلام في جوهره، يعتبر العالَم كلّه مسجداً ويمكن تحويل أيّ فضاء إلى مسجد بمجرّد أن تُقام فيه الصلاة.

يجسّم المُصلّى، وهو فضاء مخصّص للصلاة والتأمّل الذاتي، نموذجاً مكانيّاً أوّليّاً، يمتلك قدرة كبيرة على إعادة إدماج الجانب الروحانيّ في صلب دائرة التسويق التجاريّ المتزايد للمدن المعاصرة. وفي حين يؤدّي المسجد دوره بوصفه تمثيلاً وتعبيراً جماعيّين عن المجتمع المسلم، فإنّ المصلّى ينهض أساساً بوظيفة تلبية حاجات المسلمين الفرديّة إلى مكان يؤدّون فيه صلواتهم: فهو فضاء للتأمّل والصمت، وملجأ يلوذ إليه الفرد بعيداً عن الدنيويّ الزائل.

ومع ذلك، فإنّ أصوات الأذان، وإقامة الصلاة، يتردّد صداها اليومَ أيضاً في ما يسمّى باللاّأماكن التي أوجدتها الحداثة المفرطة، ونعني بها: المطارات، ومراكز التسوّق الكبرى، ومحلاّت السوبر ماركت، والبنوك، وما إلى ذلك. ولكن في مقابل نجاح هذه المساحات العامّة في تحقيق التناضد بين الدينيّ والعلمانيّ، فإنّ هذا التناضد بين البعدين يكون أمراً محرجاً في بعض الأحيان. فارتفاع صوت الأذان وسط مركز تجاريّ مزدحم، يخضّ فجأة الجانب الروحانيّ في الفرد، ضدّ النزعة الاستهلاكيّة الجماعيّة. بيد أنّ معظم المتسوّقين يظلّون منكبّين على ما هم فيه من بيع وشراء ولا يبدون أيّ انزعاج - وبذلك يتصادم واقعان مختلفان في فضاء واحد مغلق، وتتشابك المجالات الشخصيّة والعامّة مع الصوت المرتفع: فيتداخل صوت قراءة القرآن الكريم مع نبرة صوت

ن ب ع: إنّ التفكير في تحديد موقع المصلّى انطلاقاً من علاقته بالشمس، ينطوي على الإقرار أيضاً بالأفكار المتعلّقة بالزمن وسرعة الزوال، التي تمّ تضمينها في إنشاء جائزة المصلّى ومشروع "عابرٌ متجذّر" على سبيل التوسّع. لقد جسّم مقترحكم الحامل عنوان "عن النسيج" هذا الأمر حقّاً، إذ سلّط الضوء فعلاً على المصلّى باعتباره فضاءً سريع الزوال وقابلاً للتكيّف مع أيّ مكان، وركّز كثيراً على حياته الآخرة وتراثه. لقد اعتبرتم هذه الفترة الزمنيّة التي قضّاها المصلّى في البينالي بمثابة إحدى لحظات الحياة الزائلة. فهل يمكنكم من خلال المراحل العمليّة التي قطعها مشروعكم، وصفَ كيف يصبح هذا الهيكل في الواقع رحلة، وكيف يمكن أن يُنظر إليه بوصفه متوافقاً مع عملكم الحاليّ الذي يميل إلى تحدّي الروايات الراسخة حول بيئاتنا المبنيّة الجماعيّة؟

ن ف: إنّه لمن باب التحدّي أن تضع تصميماً لهيكل يتّصف بأنّه في حركة دائمة (يقوم بحركة دوّارة بيده)، وقد يُقحم في سياقات مختلفة، خلال كل مرحلة من مراحل عمليّة إنجازه واستخدامه. فكيف يتسنّى إذن تصميم مصلّى يتمّ بناؤه هنا (يشكّل يده اليمنى في هيئة وعاء ويحرّكها قليلاً نحو الأعلى والأسفل، مع التركيز على الإيحاء بمعنى التجذّر)، في هذا الفضاء الرمزيّ لمدّة أربعة أشهر، إضافة إلى حياة أخرى مجهولة تنتظره بعد تفكيكه، وسيُنقل خلالها إلى مكان آخر لا نعرف عنه شيئاً؟

ن ب ع: إنّ ما ذكرتَه الآن يستند إلى خاصيّة الاستمراريّة التاريخيّة لفضاءات المصلّى المرتبطة بفكرتيْ سرعة الزوال والزمنيّة، اللّتين تخدمان الغرض من إقامة هذه الفضاءات لفترة محدودة، متى دعت الحاجة إلى ذلك.

ن ف: بالضبط تماماً، والأمر يتعلّق حقّاً بفكرة العتبة. فكيف يمكنك أن تنشئ ثم تنغمس في فضاء ذي بيئة مخصوصة، تنقل من خلالها هذه الفكرة المتعلّقة بتجمّع مجموعات مجتمعيّة معيّنة وبالروحانيّة، عن طريق ما هو سريع الزوال؟ وقد تجلّى هذا بوضوح إلى حدّ كبير في الطريقة التي فكّرنا بها في الهيكل، باعتبار أنّه سيجمّع ثم يفكّك بمرور الوقت، فضلاً عن أهميّته من زاوية الموادّ التي سيصنع منها. فتمّ في هذا السياق إجراءُ الكثير من البحوث التي انصبّت على مسائل تتعلّق بقابليّةِ التقسيم، ونوعِ الموادّ التي نرغب في العمل بها، وكيف يمكن دمجُها معاً. ولكن الأهمّ من كل ذلك هو أنّنا تساءلنا قبل كل شيء، عن ماهيّة التجربة التي نريد أن ننقلها؟ أمّا من حيث الممارسة (يشير إلى شريكه، تشارلز كناله ، على يمينه)، فقد كنّا مدفوعين إلى حدّ كبير بالسياق. وفي الحقيقة، إنّ السياق هو الذي يوجّه عادةً الهياكل التي ننشئها، ولكن في تجربتنا هذه كان الأمر ضرباً من انقلاب في مسار التفكير، لأنّه كان علينا أن نفكّر فيه باعتباره عمليّة تصميم داخليّة معكوسة تقريبًا، من الداخل إلى الخارج، ويمكنها الاستجابة لسياقات وظروف متعدّدة. ونتيجة لذلك، فقد بني المشروع، إلى حدّ مّا، وكأنّه إضافة إلى محطّة الحجّ، إنّه في حوار معها بشكل من الأشكال، ولكنّ خاصيّة قابليّة التقسيم التي يتّسم بها تسمح أيضًا بالتعدّد والقدرة على التكيّف، والتفاعل مع ظروف أخرى عديدة يمكن تصوّرها مسبقاً.

ن ب ع: حسب رأيك يا ريان، ما هي إمكانيّة استغلال هذه الرؤية الأوسع للمصلّى؟ كيف يمكن أن يؤثّر ذلك في كيفيّة تصوّرنا للأنماط العابرة الأخرى، لاسيما تلك الموجودة في منطقتنا؟ وأعني بذلك الأنماطَ الوقتيّة التي تتجاوز البنى المعماريّة الثابتة. فكيف تتصوّر أن يتاح لهذه الممارسة الخاصّة بالمصلّى أن تعزّز فهم العناصر العابرة في مجالِ الهندسةِ المعماريّة وخطابِها؟

ر ت: لقد أمعنت التفكير طويلاً في مسألة الزمن هذه، وكيف أنّ الملخّص الذي تلقّيناه، إذا نظرنا إليه عن كثب، فهو يكاد يدعوك إلى مواجهة تناقض. فلقد تضمّن هذا الملخّص دعوة للتفكير في الهيكل الذي سيتمّ استخدامه خلال فترة بينالي الفنون الإسلاميّة الذي يستمرّ أربعة أشهر، ولكن التزاماً بكراسة الشروط، توجّب علينا أيضاً أن نفكّر في دورة حياة المصلّى التي تمتدّ من عشرة أعوام إلى خمسة عشر عاماً، سواء في هيكله أم موادّه. لذلك، كان من المهمّ جداً والمثير للاهتمام بالنسبة إلينا طوال مرحلة الإنجاز، أن نحتفظ ونفحص كلا الجدولين الزمنيّين معاً في وقت واحد، وأقصد بالجدولين: الجدول الزمنيّ القصير الخاصّ بالمعرض، والجدول الزمني الخاصّ بالبناء. وكانت هذه التجربة طريقة أخرى للتفكير هي أيضاً، في التقاء الفنّ والهندسة المعماريّة والهندسة معاً، فعندما تصمّم مشروعاً مثل هيكل مؤقّت، فإنك تفعّل جزءاً واحداً من الدماغ، أما عندما تصمّم مبنى ذا دورةِ حياةٍ محدَّدة، فإنّك تجد نفسك أمام هيكل مختلف، لا بسبب موادّه فحسب، ولكن بسبب اختلاف مسارات التفكير والمنطق الخاصّة به أيضًا. لقد كان التمسّك بالحقيقتين في وقت واحد أمرًا مهمّاً ومفيداً جدّا بالنسبة إلينا كمجموعة. وأعتقد أنّ بعض الحلول التي قد لا تكون مرئيّة في الوقت الحاليّ، قد تصبح أكثر وضوحاً عندما ينتقل الهيكل إلى موقع آخر حيث يتوجّب عليه قضاء المزيد من الوقت هناك.

وأعتقد شخصيّاً أن المقوّم الأساسيّ في مشروعنا الذي قد يغيّر بعض وجهات النظر التي ذكرتَها حول الهندسة المعماريّة الثابتة، يكمن في النسيج فعلاً (يشبك أصابعه بعضها في بعض). فإذا تناولنا النسيج من حيث هو مادّة إنشاء، بان لنا أنّ له نطاقاً زمنيّاً مختلفاً تمامًا عن خشب النخيل الرقائقي الملصَق. لذلك فعندما تنظر إلى الهيكل نفسه، يبدو لي أنّه يمثّل الماضي والحاضر والمستقبل في آن واحد، ولا يتجلّى ذلك في التقنيات المستخدَمة في صنعه فحسب، بل في صعوبة تأريخه وتحديد موقعه في سلّم الزمن كذلك. وعلى هذا النحو، فإنّ إيتوس (السجايا) سرعة الزوال قادرة بطريقة مّا على توليد بنية سياقيّة ومعاصرة، متجذّرة في زمنها. أما من الناحية الفلسفيّة، فإنّ فعل التلاشي يكاد يكون فعلاً أبديّاً، فيجب بطريقة أو بأخرى، أن يبقى الهيكل إلى الأبد. لقد حاز هذا الفاصل البين-بين، الذي يقع فيه الهيكل، أهميّة كبيرة في تفكيرنا ونحن نخطّط للمشروع، وهو يوضّح الطريقة التي تخيّلناه عليها عندما يتمّ تشييده ونفرغ منه.

ن ب ع: في هذا السياق أسألك نقولا، ما هي في رأيك بعض الإمكانات المعماريّة التي يمكن أن تظهر عندما نعيد توجيه أنفسنا نحو الممارسات المكانيّة المتجذّرة بعمق في مفهوم الزوال، والقدرةِ على التكيّف، وهذا النوع من الحيويّة التي يمكن أن تنقلها الهندسة المعماريّة؟

ن ف: أعتقد أنّ خاصيّة الزوال تعمل بشكل جيد مع مفهوم الاستعادة. فعندما تفكّر في قابليّة التقسيم، أو القدرة على التكيّف، أو حتى في إعادة الاستخدام التكيّفي، فأنت، بوصفك مهندساً معماريّاً ومصمّماً، أو لنقلْ كلّ من يختبر الفضاء على وجه التقريب، ستستفيد من خاصيّة الاستعادة بطريقة مّا. فقد توجّب علينا في هذا المشروع، أن نستحضر في أذهاننا أنّ الهيكل العظميّ الذي اقترحناه يمكن أن يُسكن، ويستعاد بعد تفكيكه، ويستخدم مجدَّداً بطرق متعدّدة. إنّ ما نقدّمه للجمهور في نهاية المطاف، هو سلسلة من الأطر أو الدعوات التي تستحثّهم على إعادة ابتكار المصلّى، من خلال تقديم إمكانات متعدّدة، وظيفةً، وتأثيراً وأداءً.

ن ب ع: إنّ ما تمكّنتم جميعاً من تصميمه هو نموذج أوّليّ ثوريّ يعزّز عمليّة تطوير الخطاب، لا في مستوى التصنيف فحسب، ولكن أيضًا في مجال مسابقات الأجنحة بصفة أعمّ. لقد أظهرتم حساسيّةً كبيرة في مقاربة موضوع المسابقة، وفهماً رائعاً للسياق المحلّي. إنّ تصميمكم يتميّز بقدرته الكبيرة على تقديم نموذج باهر لبناء مستقبل أكثر استدامةً للهندسة المعماريّة الإقليميّة؛ وهو يُعتبر كذلك خطوة أولى ملائمة جدّاً في سعينا الحثيث نحو محاولة ضبط تصنيف محدّد

164: استُنبط نظام التجميع وأُخذت الموادّ المستخدمة فيه من المصدر الطبيعيّ ذاته، وهو مخلّفات سعف نخيل التمر التي كان ستنتهي إلى الإتلاف والحرق لولا استغلالنا لها. فقد تمّ دمجها بالكامل ضمن مجموعة من العناصر البنائيّة، ووضعت بطريقة متناضدة ومتشابكة، واضطلعت بدور تأطير المناطق وتشكيل الفضاء. وإنّ ما يُعتبر نفايات هو في الحقيقة انعكاس للقيود التي نفرضها على رؤيتنا. وفي ذلك رسالة إلى العالم: فلا شيء في الوجود يمكن اعتباره نفاية- وإنما كلّ ما في الأمر أنّه مادّة بناء تنتظر أن تولد من جديد.

172: نتصوّر أنّ مشروع "عن النسيج" سيمثّل في المستقبل سقالةً ثقافيّةً، مائلة وعابرة في الوقت نفسه، تتجذّر في الزمان والمكان من أجل أن تضع على منصّة واحدة برامج تتعلّق بمجالات مختلفة، فتصبح بذلك قناة تنقل أجزاء من الماضي، مع العمل في الآن ذاته على زرع بذور ستثمر مزيداً من البحث والتعاون في المستقبل.

حوار: نوّاف بن عيّاف مع إيست وريّان تابت وكريستوفر بلست

عن التفكير المتشابك

نوّاف بن عياف: أريد أن أبدأ هذا الحوار دون تحفّظ. أعرف أنّكم كنتم أصدقاء حتى قبل جائزة المُصلّى، وأنّكم حاولتم دائماً إيجاد وسيلة مَا لإنجاز عمل تشتركون فيه معاً. فلماذا اعتبرتم أنّه قد حان الوقت المناسب للتعاون بينكم؟ ما الذي جمعكم في هذا المشروع؟

نقولا فيّاض: إنّ هذا التعاون يجسّد بشكل أساسيّ ما قاله ريان مؤخّراً، ومفادُه أنّ هذا المشروع ليس عمارة هندسيّة ولا فنّاً ولا هندسة. بل إنّ هذه المجالات كلّها تجتمع معاً في هذا العمل، إذ ارتدى كلٌّ منّا قبّعة الآخر. شخصيّاً، كنت دائماً أُولي اهتماماً بالأداء الهيكليّ، ولكن بالزخرفة والناحية الوظيفيّة أيضاً، وبالطريقة التي تتيح لهذه العناصر أن تجتمع معاً كذلك. بالفعل، لقد رجحت كفّة رسوماتنا وأفكارنا الأولى طوال الوقت وكانت شديدةً... شبهَ تعليميّة (يقوم بحركة سريعة ترسم عمليّة القطع، للإشارة إلى الخطوات المتعاقبة) ومتّسقةً جدّاً طوال المراحل التي استغرقها المشروع (يقوم بحركة بيده توحي باتّساع المدى والتعميم)، إذ مثّلت المحادثات التي أجريناها في إطار الفريق مصدر إثراءٍ للمسارِ الذي سلكه المشروع (يقوم بحركة توحي بمعنى تراكم الطبقات) و للمنتَجِ النهائيّ أيضًا.

ن ب ع: هل بوسعك أن تخبرنا عن بعض تلك المحادثات وجلسات العصف الذهني السابقة، وكيف أدّت إلى ظهور الأفكار التي انبنى عليها المشروع؟

ريان تابت: إذا عدنا إلى المرحلة الجنينيّة من هذا العمل، فإنّي أتذكّر عندما اتّصل بنا نقولا في بداية العام الماضي إثر تلقّيه دعوة كانت في الواقع عبارةً عن طلب تقديم مقال فكريّ. وفي الحقيقة لقد كانت تحدونا دائماً الرغبةُ في التعاون مع بعض، لكنّنا ظللنا ننتظر الفرصة المناسبة للجمع بين الفنّ والهندسة المعماريّة. وكنت على علم بأنّ نقولا يريد العمل أيضاً مع حنيف كارا من مكتب "أدامس كارا تايلور " (AKT) ، لذلك كنّا نحتفظ بتلك الطاقات أو الإستراتيجيّات في أذهاننا، منتظرين الوقت المناسب لتنفيذها. وأتصوّر أنّ الدعوة لكتابة هذا المقال الفكريّ كانت مفتوحة بما فيه الكفاية، فسمحت لهذه المجالات الثلاثة بأن تلتقي معاً في عمل واحد. أذكر شخصيّاً أنّ ذلك قد حدث في فبراير 2024، وكنت آنذاك في بيروت عندما اتّصل بي نقولا فقلت له: "تعال ولْنتحدّث في الأمر". وبسرعة فائقة، شرعنا في العمل وبدأنا بجذب بعض الكتب من مكتبتي، مثل كتاب "عن النسيج" لآني ألبرز، وديوان شعر لإيتيل عدنان، وكتب أخرى في مجال الهندسة المعماريّة. وفجأة، شعرت، ودون الإسهاب في وصف ذلك، أنّ ثمّة سهولة كبيرة بيننا في التفكير معاً بشكل تكامليّ، وبصفة عامّة لقد شملت هذه السهولة كلّ المسائل التي تمثّل نقطة اهتمام مشتركة بيننا.

ن ب ع: مواصلةً للنقطة التي أثارها نقولا (يتوجّه بالحديث إلى ر ت على يساره) أشير إلى أنني أعلم أنّك ترغب شخصيّاً في التأكيد على هذا المشروع باعتباره نوعاً من الاندماج بين أدوار: المهندس المعماريّ، والمهندس، والفنّان، إذ تبادلتم قبّعات بعضكم بعضاً في مرحلة مّا من مراحل المشروع. يستولي عليّ الآن شعور حبّ الاطّلاع لمعرفة بعض الدروس التي يمكن استخلاصها، في ما يتعلّق ببعض الطرق التي يمكن من خلالها تأكيد هذه العلاقة الحيويّة، بين مختلف المتعاونين، لتقديم مقاربة تكامليّة لمقترح معماريّ واحد.

ر ت: أودّ أن أقول إنّني مَدين شخصيّاً بالكثير من الاعتراف بالجميل لدروس تاريخ الفنّ والهندسة المعماريّة التي تلقّيتُها في الجامعة الأمريكيّة ببيروت، فقد أدخلوا بالفعل هذه الفكرة القائلة بأنّ هذه المجالات موحَّدة في ما بينها (قال ذلك وهو يضع أصابعه متشابكةً بعضها في بعض). وقد تجلّى هذا عندما درسنا آثار المعماريّ العثماني سنان، أو بعض الموسوعيّين مثل دافنشي، الذين كانوا يضعون قبّعات مختلفة في الوقت نفسه. لقد أثّرت فيّ هذه الفكرةُ دائماً وطالما تعلّقتُ بها، وبهذا النوع من الممارسة، فلم أعتبر هذه المجالات منفصلة بعضها عن بعض. وقد شعرت شخصيّاً أن هذا المشروع يكاد يكون مجرّد مبرّر للتأكيد على هذا النوع من الممارسة الموحَّدة (يجمع سبّابة وإبهام يده اليمنى معاً ويدفعهما إلى الأمام)، ولديّ انطباع بأنّه يمكن معاينة ذلك في النتيجة التي توصّلنا إليها، أليس كذلك؟ لكنّ ذلك لم يكن جليّاً في مستوى النتيجة النهائيّة فحسب، بل في صلب المسار الذي سلكه عملُنا أيضاً، لأنّنا كنّا ننسجه معاً بشكل من الأشكال. أتصوّر أنه من الأهميّة بمكان أن نتذكّر جميعاً بأنّ هذه المجالات ليست في الحقيقة إلاّ مجالاً واحداً في الآن ذاته، أليس كذلك؟ فأنت عندما تتحدّث عن الهيكل، تجد نفسك تتحدّث (يشدّد في نطق هذه الكلمة) في الوقت نفسه عن الزخرفة، أو عندما تتحدّث عن المبادئ المعماريّة للتنظيم المكاني، فهذا يدفعك إلى أن تتحدّث (يشدّد في نطق هذه الكلمة) أيضاً عن الهيكل والجماليّات. فلم يقم عملُنا على الصيغة المعتادة التي تقتضي أنّ المهندس المعماريّ هو الذي يقترح البناء، والمهندس هو الذي يجعله قائم الذات، ثم يأتي الفنّان ويزخرفه. وما أقوله الآن يظهر في المشروع على جميع المستويات، من أصغر التفاصيل إلى الهيكل العام؛ لقد أُنجز بسلاسة في هذه المستويات المختلفة.

كريستوف بلست: (يومئ برأسه موافقاً)
أودّ من ناحيتي أيضاً أن أضيف أنّنا نظرنا إلى جميع الجوانب الفنيّة بشكل كليّ، ولا أقصد بذلك الجوانب الفنيّة في هيكل المشروع فقط، ولكن تلك الجوانب المتعلّقة براحة الإنسان كذلك. بناءً عليه، ارتكز أحد أهدافنا الرئيسيّة على أخذ كل التدابير التي تضمن شعور الناس بالراحة في المكان. فبما أنّ مدينة جدّة قد تسجّل درجات حرارة عالية، فقد درسنا علاقة المصلّى الذي صمّمناه بالمظلّة أعلاه (يشير بيده اليمنى نحو مظلّة محطّة الحج)، وأخذنا بعين الاعتبار موقعه في الأسفل، ومكان مرور ضوء الشمس عبر الكوّة. على هذا النحو، قمنا بتحديد موقع المصلّى بدقّة لضمان وصول المزيد من ضوء الشمس في الأشهر الأولى الباردة، وذلك على عكس الأشهر اللاّحقة عندما تكون الشمس أعلى في السماء ويكون الجوّ أشدّ حرارةً، فنكون في حاجة إلى مزيد من الظلّ.

الدائريّ حول الكعبة المشرّفة، وهي أقدس الأماكن المرجعيّة. وعلى سبيل الاستلهام من النسيج أيضاً، انبنى هذا التصميم على الشبكات في مستويات متعدّدة. فعلى مستوى الحجم الأكبر المستوحى من مزارع النخيل، اتّبع المبدأ التوجيهي للمجال شبكةَ مقاس تمتدّ على 6 × 6 م.

ويتكوّن التصميم النهائي من قاعدة ذات جانبين، ترتفع بشكل تدريجيّ من الأرض نحو السماء، وتصبح أقلّ سمكًا كلّما اقتربت من مظلّة صالة استقبال الحجاج.

ويشبه مظهر المصلّى شكل النَّوْل، وفي ذلك حرص على إحياء تقاليد النسيج، والإشادة بتجسيمه خصائص الصناعة اليدويّة. إنّ المصلّى كيان قائم الذات مستقلاً بنفسه، ولكنّه في الوقت نفسه قابل للتقسيم ويمكن إعادة استخدامه مرات متعدّدة، فهو يجمع بين أدوار مختلفة في وقت واحد، ذلك أنّه هيكل ووظيفة وزخرفة معاً. ويدعو فناء المصلّى المفتوح الزائرين إلى الجلوس، والتجمّع، والصلاة جماعيّاً أو فرديّاً. وتمّ إضفاء طابع من الحيويّة على الألوان الترابيّة التي تشكّل الجزء الخارجيّ من المصلّى من خلال توظيف اللّون الداخلي للمبنى، حيث استُخدمت أصباغ طبيعيّة وقع استخراجها من النباتات المحليّة والإقليميّة، لإضاءة الفضاء بالألوان الأحمر والأزرق والأخضر والأصفر الفاقع.

إن طبيعة المصلّى القائمة على خاصيّة التجزئة تجعله مفتوحاً على التأويل وإعادة التفسير، وعلى الخيال وإعادة التصوّر. فكلّ جزء منه هو بمثابة دعوة عامّة مفتوحة للزوّار: فهذا مكان للصلاة، وهذه منصّة للفنون والحرف اليدويّة، وذلك فضاء مخصّص للعرض، وتلك حديقة عامّة. وجميع هذه الأجزاء تتضافر بعضها مع بعض لتنشئ بذور تعاون يمتدّ في الزمن إلى ما بعد العمر القصير الذي سيقضيه هذا الهيكل في صالة استقبال الحجاج.

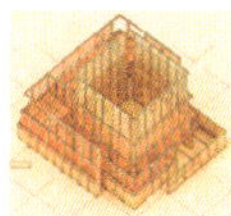

139: يضطلع هيكل المصلّى بدور توفير غطاء وقائيّ يحيط بالمساحات المشترَكة، وهو يتوسّط في الوقت نفسه مناطق التداخل مع بيئة محطّة الحج، وبذلك يقوم الهيكل بالربط بين المجالين الخارجيّ والداخليّ. وإنّ الإطار المعدني الذي يحتضن بيئته المحيطة ويبتعد عنها في الآن ذاته ليبثّ الشعور بالصفاء، يتيح أمام المرء فرصاً جديدة للانغماس في التأمّل.

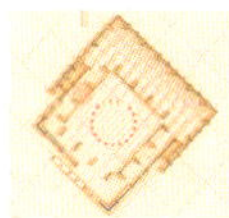

141: أصبح النسيج نموذجاً إبداعيّاً. ففي المخطّط، تتداخل وتتشابك فضاءات مختلفة الأحجام. وقد تضافرت معاً لتوفّر لنا جودة تجريبيّة تتطلّب الاستمراريّة، والتكرار، والنظام.

142: التزمت المقاربة المعتمَدة في تصميم موادّ البناء، بمبدأ الاستدامة، ونعني بذلك: التزوّد بالمنتجات الطبيعيّة والمحليّة. وقد تعزّز ذلك من خلال اعتماد مبادئ الخفّة، وقابليّة التوسّع، والبساطة. وقد اعتبرنا أشجار النخيل المحلّية، مادّة بناء منخفضة الكربون، غير مستغلّة على النحو الأمثل.

144: يحيل كتاب "عن النسيج" على التجريد في الهندسة المعماريّة، الذي يُعرَف من خلال مسار عمليّة النسج، لا الأسلوب. فالجانب التأثيريّ والزخرفة هما منتجان ثانويّان لعمليّات التصنيع. وتتضافر الطبقات والرقائق المعدنيّة وأعمال التركيب/التفكيك لتشكّل معاً مجموعاً معمارياً يتحدّث لغة النسيج.

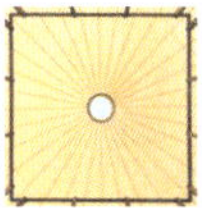

151: إنّ مشروع "عن النسيج" هو عمل ضخم وحميميّ في الآن ذاته، إذ يقدّم للزوّار تجربة تشاركيّة وشخصيّة إلى حدّ بعيد، مجسّماً بذلك صورة مصغّرة من فضاء محطّة الحجّ. وقد حُدّد موقع هيكل المبنى في الوسط تحت كوّة المظلّة، فأدّى هذا الاختيار إلى تمكين الهيكل من اختزال المسافة الفاصلة بين الأرض والسماء، مقدّماً رؤية مؤطّرة لما يوجد بينهما.

153: لقد صُمّمت الستائر المنسوجة من ألياف النخيل كما لو أنّها لوحة تجريديّة تبعث الحيويّة في الفناء الداخليّ، وقد صُبغت هذه الستائر جزئيّاً بمجموعة من الألوان ذات الأبعاد الزخرفيّة والسرديّة. وكانت النباتات الأصليّة المحليّة والإقليميّة مثل الحنّاء، والرمّان، والنيلة، والنبق، والمُخْمَليّة، المصادر الأساسيّة التي أُستُخرجت منها الألوان. إنّ هذه الأصباغ التي تُستخدم في ممارسات النسيج الإقليميّة، تجسّم العناصر الموجودة في الطبيعة مثل التربة، والمياه، والأشجار، وأشعّة الشمس. وعلى هذا النحو، فإنّ المشروع يُعدّ امتداداً للمهن التقليديّة التي ما تزال حيّة إلى يومنا هذا.

154: انبعث مشروع "عن النسيج" إلى الحياة كنظام قابل للتقسيم والتفكيك، قادر على أن تكون له حيوات عديدة فيما بعد "بينالي الفنون الإسلاميّة"، وهو بذلك يشكّك في الأفكار المتعلّقة بنفايات موادّ البناء - وقد كانت تلك الأفكار نفسها مصدراً إلهامياً أيضاً.

162: إنّ مساحة مشروع "عن النسيج" تقوم بإخفاء الفضاء والكشف عنه في الوقت نفسه، وهي تتكوّن من 200 كيلومتر من ألياف النخيل، المنسوجة والمجدولة يدويّاً. فطول الحبل يساوي المسافة الفاصلة بين جدّة ومكّة المكرّمة، وهكذا، فإنّ الغلالة التي تحيط بالهيكل هي صورة مصغّرة من طريق رحلة الحجّ.

فأدى ذلك إلى تقلص القصص التي ارتبطت بأعمال البناء الحيوية وتحولها إلى أشكال ثابتة.

فللرسم المساحي قدرة كبيرة على تمثيل المعرفةِ تمثيلاً سكونياً جامداً، من خلال تثبيت الأبعاد وفترات البناء وطرائق الاستخدام. على هذا النحو، قلب التصميم المفرط في تبسيط مبنى الجامع الأزهر، عصوره واتجاهاته ومخططاته المتعددة إلى مجرد مبنى من العصر الفاطمي موجه بشكل واضح، وأحادي الاستخدام. فإذا عدنا الآن إلى المُصلّى وقارنا بينه وبين ثبات الرسم المساحي الخاص بالمساجد، ألفينا المصلى على النقيض من ذلك، فهو فضاء ديني مرن - دائم الانفلات من مثل هذه المقاييس الصارمة - يوفر عدسة نقدية يمكننا اعتمادها لإعادة النظر في المساجد المعروضة رسومها في كتب المسح. ذلك أن المصلى لم يكن له تاريخياً أي حضور تصويري في دفاتر المسح، بسبب ما اختص به من ممارسات مكانية وزمانية. على هذا النحو، يتجلى لنا أن المصلّى ليس له تكوين هندسي محدد مسبقاً، ولا يقوم بين أقسامه اتساق صارم من شأنه أن ينشئ كلاً موحَّداً، ولا توجد فيه جدران مجوفة لتعيين حدود الفضاء أو الكشف عن أصول المكان. وعلى الرغم من أن المُصلّى موجه نحو مكة المكرمة، فإن اتجاهه العام المؤقت (الجهة) مرن وتقريبي. وعندما يشكل المصلّى فضاء ملموساً للتعبد، فإنه لا يترك أي أثر واضح المعالم يمكن وضع رسم خرائطي له أو دراسته أو تصنيفه بعد أن يختفي عن العيان. وهكذا يمكن القولُ إن المصلّى يوجد خارج علم التصنيف.

وإذا كان الرسم المساحي يزعم التقاط مختلف الفترات الزمانية المتعددة للبنى التاريخية لا لشيء إلا ليمحوها، فإن افتقار المصلّى إلى التمثيل المنهجي المتناسق لا يخلف لنا سوى فتراته الزمانية هو فحسب. إن مقاومة المصلى للمسح ورفضه الوقوع في قبضته، حفز على تطوير أشكال بديلة من المعرفة التاريخية الخاصة بأماكن العبادة الإسلامية - بما في ذلك المسجد الجامع الذي تقام فيه صلاة الجمعة - واستدعى استحداث أساليب جديدة لتمثيل تلك الفضاءات. فالممارسات الفراغية الموسومة بخاصية التراكم التي يجسدها المصلى - وهي ثابتة وتخضع لإعادة تصميم في الوقت نفسه- والمنافع المجتمعية التي تقدمها للمصلين، توفّر مصدراً غنياً لبناء هذه المعرفة الواسعة الأبعاد. ذلك أن تحرر أماكن العبادة الإسلامية من ثبات المسح والمخطط التصنيفي التركيبي، أتاح إمكان إعادة تشكيل صورتها في ضوء علاقتها بأوساطها الاجتماعية وسياقاتها الحضرية والبيئية. ومن شأن فهم هذه الروابطِ مجدَّداً، أن يثمر فصل المسجد عن التقليد التصنيفي الوظائفي الذي نشره الرسم التخطيطي على نطاق واسع. ذلك أن المرونة المتجددة التي تميز مخططات البناء وترتيب الفضاءات متناضدة بعضها إلى بعض، سيجعلان هذه المباني مفتوحة أمام طيف واسع من المستخدمين، قادرة على أن تلبي لهم حاجات كثيرة متنوعة. وبفعل تخلينا عن التركيز على طلب نقاء التصميم، سنتوقف في آخر المطاف عن البحث عن "الأصل" التصنيفي للمسجدِ. فبدلاً من ذلك، يمكننا أن نبدأ باستكشاف حلقات تاريخه المعماري المتشابكة والمدمجة بعضها في بعض، مستخلصين الدروس من ماضيه الأكثر تسامحاً وإن كان مجزأً، فاتحين أبواب المستقبل بعد أن ظلت مغلقة فيما مضى من الأزمنة.

أن يكون مسجد ما بلا مخطط مساحي فهذا لا يعني البتة أنه مسجد بلا تاريخ. بل إن الأمر على النقيض من ذلك، فمسجد من هذا القبيل هو في الحقيقة مسجد يسعى إلى كشف طبقات التاريخ التي حجبها الرسم المساحي. وهذا التاريخ ما زال ينتظر إعادة كتابته لا رسمه، ولتكن البداية من استكشافات تصميم المصلّى.

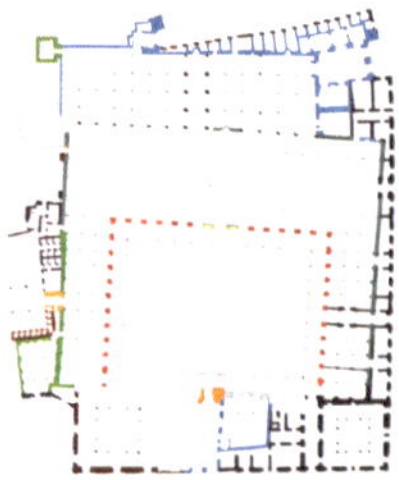

الصورة 1. كريزويل، الجامع الأزهر: عرض مختلف الفترات التي مرت بها العمارة الإسلامية في مصر، المصدر: كريزويل (1952). كلاسيكيات أفيري، مكتبة أفيري للهندسة المعمارية والفنون الجميلة، جامعة كولومبيا.

الصورة 2. كريزويل، الجامع الأزهر: مقترح لإعادة تصميم البناء الأصلي لجامع الأزهر، استناداً إلى كتاب "العمارة الإسلاميه في مصر"، المصدر: كريزويل (1952). كلاسيكيات أفيري، مكتبة أفيري للهندسة المعمارية والفنون الجميلة، جامعة كولومبيا.

الفائزون بجائزة المُصلّى 2025: عن النسيج

"عن النسيج" هو عنوان المقترح الفائز في مسابقة المصلّى، وقد أنجزه إستوديو إيست للهندسة المعماريّة بالتعاون مع ريان ثابت وشركة الهندسة الدوليّة AKT II، وقد استوحى أصحاب هذا المقترح عنوانه من كتاب يحمل الاسم نفسه لفنّانة النسيج المرموقة آني ألبرز. إنّ التصميم الذي أنجزه هذا الفريق هو امتداد للمقاربات النظريّة للحرف اليدويّة، وما يكمن فيها من قدرات على إنشاء مساحات للتعايش، حيث يصبح النسيج فعلاً صناعيّاً متعدّد المستويات. وقد تناول التصوّر الذي صيغ موضوعاً للنسخة الأولى من جائزة المصلّى، فكرة الصنع بوصفها عمليّة تجريد غامرة: فالشكل والفروق الدقيقة والظلال وبرنامج المؤلف ومقاصده، يتمّ التعبير عنها جميعاً باستخدام الأساليب نفسها المتّبعة في نسج الخطوط.

وفي سياق البحث الذي قام به أعضاء الفريق، استخلصوا أنّ المملكة العربيّة السعوديّة هي ثاني أكبر منتج لنخيل التمر في العالم. ومن ثمّ اكتشفوا أنه بمجرّد انتهاء عمر النبتة الإنتاجي، يعمد الناس عادة إلى قطع الأشجار أو حرقها أو رميها في مكبّ النفايات. وبذلك انتبه الفريق إلى أنّ السعف والألياف التي خلّفتها تلك الأشجار المحليّة وظلّت مهملة في النفايات، يمكن تحويلها إلى مادّة مستدامة صالحة لأن تُستعمل لصنع هيكل المصلّى والنسيج الذي يكسو جوانبه. وقد أعاد هذا القرار إحياء عادة استخدام أشجار النخيل في الحياة اليوميّة، وكان ذلك فيما مضى أمراً شائعاً على نطاق واسع في المملكة العربيّة السعوديّة، قبل أن يصير الوصول إلى الأخشاب الصلبة والموادّ البلاستيكيّة الوافدة من الخارج سهلاً في متناول جميع الناس.

إنّ المسار الذي اتّبعه تصميم مشروع "عن النسيج" أعاد توجيه سرد النسيج المحبوك باعتباره فنّاً ونظاماً وظيفيّاً، وسعى إلى التعريف بتراث النسيج الثقافي سواء المادي أو غير المادي - وهو أحد أعرق الحرف اليدويّة في المنطقة - بالتركيز خصوصاً على إبراز أدائه الهيكلي، وخصائصه الصناعيّه المتكرّرة والزائلة التي تقدّم بعداً لامحدوداً. فهذه الإحالة على اللّامحدود تردّد أصداء من طقوس "الطواف"

مرّة أخرى على إعادة بناء مطار مفتوح. إنّه أكثر الأعمال خرقاً للمعتاد، وقد جاء ثمرةَ الإيمان بشيء ما.

ل غ: هناك تجسيد لهذا الإيمان والفضاء الذي يخلقه ويجعله ذا قيمة رفيعة إلى أبعد حدّ.
لذلك، وعلى سبيل وضع خاتمة لحوارنا، أرى أنّ جائزة المُصلّى والمبادرات المماثلة لها، تعيد على نحو ما الإيمان (آ خ: بالضبط، بالضبط)، بأنّ دلالة الهندسة المعماريّة لا تقتصر على مجرّد كونها مظهراً وظيفيّاً واستهلاكيّاً فحسب، بل هي تتعلّق كذلك بتجربة الوجود بين الهنا والماوراء.

آ خ: إنّ الهدف الذي تسعى إليه جائزة المصلّى هو زرع بذرة من أجل الآخرين ومن أجل أنفسنا، وآمل أن تجد هذه البذرة أرضاً خصبةً تمكّنها من أن تغيّر قليلاً الاتّجاه الذي نسير فيه.

إستوديو آصف خان

لحصده المركز الثاني في المسابقة، حصل إستوديو آصف خان على تقدير لتصميمه المستوحى من فكرة «التوحيد»، وهو مفهوم يدعم جوانب الفن الإسلامي، والعمارة الإسلامية، ومساحة العبادة، والشعائر الدينية.

يتجسد هذا المفهوم بصورة أكبر في الكعبة، التي تعتبر مركز الأرض والتي تشير إليها كل قِبلة في كل من المساجد والمصليات البالغ عددها 3.6 مليون مسجد حول العالم. وأثناء صلاة المسلمين في مختلف بقاع العالم، يمكن رسم نحو 1.8 مليار خط في اتجاه واحد، مما يكشف عن ممارسة موحَّدة وطقس ثابت استمر لأكثر من 1400 عام.

إن مُصلّى إستوديو آصف خان عبارة عن هيكل مفتوح من أربعة جوانب مع سقف مدعوم في كل من زواياه الأربع. تشكل الجدران ثمانية أقسام دوارة يمكن فتحها في عدد من التكوينات المختلفة. اقترح فريقه استخدام تقنية الكربون أو الألياف الزجاجية كمادة أساسية لتحقيق شعور بانعدام الوزن. وفي وسط المساحة، داخل خزانة عرض، يبرز هيكل قرآن زجاجي. تم ترتيب الرمال المضغوطة المرصعة بالحجارة المحلية المصدرة خصيصاً لكل تركيب حول الهيكل.

إن مصدر الإلهام أدى إلى تقسيم شكل سداسي أُنشئ بواسطة 1.8 مليار خط موجهة إلى نقطة واحدة للنمط عبر جدران ألياف الكربون والستائر الفاصلة للمُصلّى. وكما هي الحال في الطبيعة بجميع مقاييسها، فإن الهندسة تحقق الهيكلية والتوافق بين العناصر المختلفة. يفترض مقترح التصميم الذي قدمه إستوديو آصف خان أنه إذا كان النظام البنيوي بجميع مقاييس الطبيعة هو انعكاساً للقدرة الإلهية، فإن الهياكل والفنون التي أنشأها الإنسان استجابةً لهذه الهندسة، تكاد تكون شكلاً من أشكال العبادة.

خاطرة: زياد جمال الدين

بدون رسم، ولكن ليس بدون تاريخ

كيف يتسنى لنا أن نستحضر إلى أذهاننا صورة المصلى والحال أن السجلات التاريخية الأرشيفية تفتقر إلى رسوم توثق الأشكال التي كان يظهر عليها في الماضي؟

قد يخطر ببالنا أن نسترشد بسجلات أرشيف الهياكل الدينية الأخرى، من قبيل المسح التصويري الذي أجراه كيبيل أرتشيبلد كاميرون كريزويل للجامع الأزهر الشريف، وقد اضطلع هذا العمل بدور أساسي في تحديد خصائص المعرفة التخصصية للعمارة الإسلامية. فإذا نظرنا إلى المسألة من زاوية تاريخية، تبين لنا أن الرسوم التخطيطية قد ساهمت في تشكيل نظام تصنيف ثابت لأماكن العبادة الإسلامية، بفضل إدراجها في الكتب المدرسية المعمارية. بيد أنّ المُصلّى، وهو فضاء مؤقت للعبادة، غائب عن هذا التاريخ البصري المكتوب بدقة سردية صارمة. في المقابل، يتجلى لنا أن هذه الثغرة التمثيلية الناتجة عن الافتقار إلى صور للمصلّى، تمنحنا رغم كل شيء القدرة على إمعان النظر في الإمكانات الفراغية والمادية والمخططاتية التي أتيحت أمامنا عندما تحرر هذا الفضاء التعبدي من الثقل التصويري المتصل بهيمنة المسجد بوصفه الفضاء التشريعي المرجعي، ومن ثم يمكن أن تنطلق عملية إعادة النظر في التاريخ التصنيفي الراسخ للمسجد.

فمنذ أواخر القرن التاسع عشر، اتبع إنشاء الرسوم التخطيطية في كتب المسح الخاصة بتاريخ العمارة الإسلامية أساليب علمية في مجال تمثيل المعالم، ولم تلبث تلك الأساليب أن عرفت تطوّراً كبيراً سهّل عملية التقاط رسوم مخططات المباني التاريخية المعقدةِ التقاطاً لم يفتأ يزداد دقة يوما بعد آخر. وبفضل استخدام هذه التقنيات، تم مع مرور الزمن وصف الطبقات المتعددة لما شهدته المباني من توسع ومراكمة وتجديد، وقد وظف هذا الوصف لغايات دراسية. ذلك أن الرسوم التخطيطية كانت أداة فعالة في ميدان التحليل المقارن لمختلف المباني، ومن ثم استخدمها التصنيف النموذجي للمساجد في مختلف أنحاء جغرافيا العالم الإسلامي ممتدة الأطراف.

إن الرسم الأصلي الذي أنجزه كريزويل للجامع الأزهر الشريف، وأعاد استنساخه في كتابه «العمارة الإسلامية في مصر» (1952-1959)، يجسد هذه الطريقة في التمثيل والمعرفة التخصصية التي جاءت ثمرة لها. فالرسم الورقي الكبير والمتقن ذو المقاس 70 × 85 سم أنجز وفق مقياس 1: 300، واستخدمت فيه تقنية الجيوب المطوية، واعتمد فيه نظام محدد لتوزيع الألوان يرمز فيه كل لون إلى فترة معينة من مختلف العهود التي مر بها تشييد المبنى، بدءاً من سنة 1130 إلى سنة 1894. وتمتد الخطوط المركزية على طول شكل مبنى الجامع، سعياً إلى تبيين التناظر الذي يقوم عليه هيكل المبنى والاتساق بين مداخله وسائر غرفه. وتعمل أبعاد الرسم التخطيطي التي قيست بدقة وقسطاس، على تعزيز الأدلة المؤيدة لفكرة قيام البناء على التركيبات الهندسية الأساسية وتناسب الأبعاد والإيقاعات. زد على ذلك، أن الرسم قد تضمن علامة أثبتت في شماله تشير إلى اتجاه القبلة نحو مكة المكرمة. وقد أدى تصوير كريزويل المبنى في دقة وعناية كبيرتين، إلى الإحاطة علماً بالحالة التي وجده عليها، وفتح في الوقت نفسه المجال أمام إجراء تحقيق يعيد تشكيل معالم ماضيه التاريخي. فبفضل ما توصل إليه كريزويل من تحديد جامع مانع شمل مختلف الفترات التي مر بها البناء، وما وضعه من أبعاد دقيقة، استطاع أن يقيم الحجة البينة على توفقه إلى اكتشاف آثار تعود إلى أصل المبنى وفق التصور الرائج، مفترِضاً أنه مستطيل الشكل دون ريب. فقد كان كريزويل يعتقد، شأنه في ذلك شأن معاصريه من العلماء، أن المساجد التي درسها لها أشكال أصلية "حقيقية" تجسم أنماطاً تصنيفية واضحة.

وقد أسقط كريزويل من رسمه كذلك السياق الحضري المحيط بالجامع الأزهر، فنصل المسجد عن أرضيته وخلفيته ليؤوله بوصفه كياناً مستقلاً. وقد أكد رسم مؤمثل لاحق موسوم بعنوان «مقترح لإعادة تصميم بناء الجامع الأصلي» هذا التفسير، وسمح بدراسة شكل المبنى انطلاقاً من مقارنته بمخططات المساجد الأخرى. والغريب في الأمر أن دقة رسم المسح الذي أنجزه كريزويل، قد سهلت في نهاية المطاف استخلاص رسوم تجريدية محتملة للجامع. وبفعل إعادة استنساخ هذه الرسوم ونشرها في كتب التاريخ خلال القرن العشرين، لم تلبث هذه الرسوم أن بسطت تدريجياً واختزلت في مجرد رسوم بيانية،

التفكيرُ في مشروع ما، بل إنّنا نستكشف ذلك في العمل الفنيّ الذي تعرضه؛ وبوسعنا الآن أن نشاهد هذا الأمر في الجناح الحالي أيضاً (تشير إلى المقترَح الفائز والمعروض بالقرب منهما).

وأتساءل: كيف يمكننا، بوصفنا مهندسين معماريّين، أن نقحم ذلك حقّاً خلال إنشاء فضائنا المبنيّ؟ كيف ستسير الأمور؟ اليوم، أعني أنّه يمكن العمل باستخدام الصناعة اليدويّة في صلب الطريقة التي نبني وفقها، سواء أكانت مصنوعة يدوياً أم باستخدام الآلة. على وجه التحديد، كيف ترى ذلك فعلياً في عملك؟ وهل ما زلت تعمل دائما باستعمال الصناعة اليدويّة في إطار ما تقوم به من هندسة معماريّة وما تنفّذه من مشاريع؟ وهل أنت قادر على الانتقال من القطع المصنوعة يدوياً إلى الهندسة المعماريّة؟

آ خ: أعتبر أنّ هذا السؤال هو سؤال العصر. وجهة نظري في هذا السياق هي أن أسعى في المقام الأوّل إلى أكون صادقاً مع نفسي. فبوصفي إنساناً أرى أنّكِ إذا تمكّنتِ من تحقيق نفسك واتّخذتها مركزاً لك، فسوف تكونين قادرةً على اكتشاف أسس عميقة، وهي في الأساس ما تركه لنا الأجداد من معارف.

إنّ البشر لم يتغيّروا منذ زمن طويل، أليس كذلك؟ لقد لبثنا على حالنا. فما زلنا نحبّ النسيج، وما زلنا نحبّ الخيوط، وما زلنا نحبّ العمل اليدويّ لأنّه بمثابة غذاء لنا. إنّنا نحبّ دائماً زراعة بعض الأشياء. ونحبّ الرقص، ونحبّ الموسيقى، ونحبّ نعومة الأشياء ورقّتها وخشونتها كذلك، ونحبّ تقطيعَ الأشياء وتشكيلَها من جديد. إنّ مرونة العالَم الذي يحيط بنا تغذّينا. وجميع ذلك هو، بشكل من الأشكال، ما تتوقّعه الإنسانيّة في العالَم، لأنّنا لم نغيّر حِمضنا النوويّ. إنّ في حوزتنا الآن في هذا العالَم أدوات كثيرة تبعدنا عن الأرض، وعن الطين، وعن الأنهار، وعن المذاقات التي تعوّدت عليها أفواهُنا، إنّها تبعدنا عن كلّ هذه الأمور. هذا صحيح، ولكن عندما تتناولين قهوة عربيّة أُعدّت يدوياً ويتاح لك أن تتذوّقي الهِيل، فستجدينها أفضل من القهوة العاديّة بطبيعة الحال. أعتقد أنّني أحاول دائمًا، أثناء ممارستي عملي، الاهتداءَ إلى طريقي نحو هذا... الذوق. إنّ الشوق يحدونا للعودة إلى الأشياء نفسها، مثل الخدوش الثابتة في الأرض، ومثل الملمس الذي يبعث فينا القشعريرة، والمتعة التي يشعر بها المرء وهو يمرر يده عبر الشعر، وهذا...

ل غ: والنور الذي يسطعه.

آ خ: النور الذي يسطعهم، وأشعّة الشمس وكلّ تلك العناصر الأساسيّة، إنّها ليست أموراً اصطناعيّة، بل هي جوهر ما يعنيه أن يكون المرء واعياً، وهذا هو ما يمنح البشر هويّتهم، ويجب علينا تعزيز ذلك اليومَ أكثرَ من أيّ وقت مضى، وسيكون الأمر أكثرَ صعوبة كلّما حقّقنا تقدّماً. لذلك، أحاول تحديد الأرضيّة المشترَكة بيننا.

ل غ: تحديد من نحن.

آ خ: تحديد من نحن، نعم بالضبط، ومن ثَمّ ستكون الهندسة المعماريّة بسيطة، يكفينا فقط أن نكون قناةً لما يحدّد من نكون.
ل غ: أتساءل كيف سيؤثّر الذكاء الاصطناعيّ في هذه الأمور.
آ خ: عندما رأيت صالة الحجّ لأوّل مرّة، عرفت أنّ هذا الهيكل قد رُسم باليد. فلا وجود لأيّ أثر لجهاز الكمبيوتر في تصميم هذا الهيكل. وإنّ في كلّ زاوية، وفي كلّ تفصيل، ضروباً من الاستنباط التي لا يمكن أن تحدث إلاّ عندما يقع تفاعلٌ بين العين واليد.

ل غ: ولكن في الوقت نفسه، سيسمح لك الذكاء الاصطناعي أن تنجز تصميماً يتضمّن قدراً كبيراً من التفاصيل لا تستطيع محاميلنا الحاليّة تحقيقه. نعم، على المرء أن يعود إلى يده، ولكن لو توفّرت نقطة التقاء بين الذكاء الاصطناعي واليد فسيكون أمراً ساحراً. وهذا يتطلّب تغييراً يشمل أنظمة القيم.

آ خ: أتصوّر أنّه... (متردّداً) مستقبل محتمل.
والسؤال الذي يطرح نفسه هو: ما هي قيمة الأشياء؟ وما هي الدلالة التي تكمن خلف شروعنا في تقييم عمل الكمبيوتر باعتباره مساوياً أو أفضل من عمل الإنسان؟ مع كلّ هذه الفوضى، ما معنى أن يكون المرء إنساناً، ونحن نعلم مدى صعوبة أن يكون المرء إنساناً، أيْ: أن نعيش ونحقّق بقاءنا بيولوجيّاً، ولكن هذا يعني كذلك أن يصبح المرء سيّداً على شيء ما. فنحن نناضل من أجل رفع هذه الراية والقول إنّنا نستطيع أن نفعل ما هو أفضل، وإنّنا قادرون بوصفنا فنّانين ومهندسين معماريّين، على أن ندفع إلى أقصى ما نستطيع حدودَ ما هو ممكن في عالَمنا. ولكن إذا بدأ أشخاص آخرون في تقدير عمل الكمبيوتر، دون الأخذ بالاعتبار أنّه لا يواجه أيّاً من صعوبات الحياة، فإنّنا نشرع حينها في التساؤل عن قيمة كلّ ما يفعله البشر. وأيّ نوع من المجتمع هذا الذي نعيش فيه؟

ل غ: هذا صحيح. وكما تعلم، فبوصفنا بشراً، فإنّنا نكافح أو نعمل دائماً على بناء إدراك للعالَم. إنّنا نعرّف الهندسة المعماريّة بأنّها وسيلة لبناء المعرفة باستمرار، ولكنّها وسيلة لفهم العالَم أيضاً. فإذا ألقينا نظرة على ما أنجزه بعض الفنّانين أو أشخاص مثل أينشتاين وإتقانهم للاكتشافات طوال حياتهم، فإنّه يتبيّن لنا أنّ ما قاموا به يتّصل في الحقيقة بفهم العالم أو استعادته من جديد.

آ خ : أتصوّر أنّ ماقام به هؤلاء الأفراد هو شكل من أشكال التضحية بالنفس من أجل الآخرين. فقد كرّسوا حياتهم يلاحقون تحقيق أمر يبعث السرور في الآخرين. إنّه شيء يشبه الإكراه تقريبًا، إذ يُفرض على كلّ فنّان عظيم... أن يندفع في هذه الرحلة. وبفضل عملهم، طوّروا إدراكنا لأصل الكون، وإدراكنا لطبيعة المادّة والجسم، وسائر الأمور الأخرى.
ل غ: نعم، إنّه على نحو مّا الإحساس بالتواضع، لوجود الإنسان على الأرض. إنّ الهندسة المعماريّة مهنة تسمح لنا أن نستمرّ دائماً في التساؤل وإعادة النظر في ما تحقّق، والبناء، وإعادة تشكيل البيئة بأسلوب جديد مختلف عمّا سبقه، وهي تتيح لهذا الحلم بأن يكون حاضراً في حياتنا على نحو ثابت.

آ خ: هذه هي اللّحظة الحقيقيّة فعلاً، إنّها الثورة الصناعيّة الجديدة، لكن أتصوّر أنّها أكثر هشاشةً ممّا نعتقد. لننظرْ إلى هذا المبنى الفريد من نوعه (ينظر إلى الوراء، وذراعاه مفتوحتان على آخرهما، للتأكيد على ضخامة محطّة الحجّ)، فمثل هذا الإنجاز لن يتحقّق مرّةً أخرى البتّة. ذلك أنّه لن يكون لدى أحدٍ القناعةُ أو الجرأةُ على المخاطرة بالإقدام

في "بينالي الفنون الإسلاميّة"، يخامرنا شعور بوجود حسّ حرفيّ يتجاوز الأصناف حقّاً، وكذلك الزمان والمكان. وقد استكشفتَ هذا على نحو جيّد في العمل الفنيّ الذي تعرضه الآن أيضًا، الكتاب الزجاجيّ، حيث كُتب النصُّ بخطّ اليد وأُلّف بأسلوب سرديّ. فأودّ أن أعرف المزيد عن كيفيّة إظهارك الفضاء داخل هذه القطعة اليدويّة نفسها. وماذا عن فكرة الصناعة اليدويّة هذه، وكيف تلعب دوراً في توليد عالَم جديد؟

آخ: هذا سؤال مذهل. إنّ الإسلام، في رأيي، هو بمثابة ولادة للفنّ المفاهيمي. فهو ينتقل من التجريد إلى المنطق والعلم والجماليّات والفنّ والطقوس. فجميع ذلك يمتزج بعضه ببعض ويندمج... إنّني أشعر أنّ الإسلام هو الفنّ الأسمى... والحقّ، أنّ هذا ما كان يمثّله الفنُّ في نهاية المطاف. لقد بدأ الأمر من الاعتقاد بوجود عالَم ماورائيّ؛ لقد كان ذلك طريقة لفهم شيء يتجاوز إدراكنا. كان ذلك بمثابة أداة، وسيلة للكشف والفهم.

↑ تصوير: ماركو كابيليتي، 2025

ل غ: نعم، ومن دون أن نفهم تمام الفهم، وهذا هو الجميل. إذن، أنت تعيش هذه الحالة، أليس كذلك؟ أنت تلازم دائمًا هذا النوع من الحالة التي تكون فيها تجريديًا، وهو بشكل ما أمر ساحر حقًا، أليس كذلك؟

آخ: هذا صحيح، وقد سبق لكِ أن قلتِ إنّه كان وسيطًا، وهذا صحيح تماما. لذلك فالقول إنّنا نوجد بين الاثنين، يعني أنّ البعض سوف يفهم أكثر، والبعض الآخر سوف يفهم أقلّ (تومئ ل غ برأسها موافقةً)، وسيجد أفراد المجتمع بأكمله أنفسهم في هذه الحالة الذهنيّة التي تشبه سحابة من المشاعر، إنّها ضرب من المشاركة...

ل غ: إنّه وجود ميتافيزيقيّ مشترَك، وربما أمكننا القول إنّ اللاّمرئيّ يجمع بيننا بطريقة ما، وإنّه قوّة لها حضور أوضح كثيراً من حضورنا نحن. وقد أحببت فعلاً الصورة التي تجسّد بها ذلك من خلال الأسلوب الذي قدّمت به مشروعك كنوع من السحابة التي يمكننا معاينتها، حتى وإن كانت تجربة افتراضيّة. أتصوّر أنّنا بوصفنا مهندسين معماريّين فإنّنا نخوض دائمًا المسابقات؛ فأحياناً نفوز وأحياناً لا، لكن أعتقد أنّ الأفكار والعمليّات الإبداعيّة لا تنقطع بانتهاء المسابقات بل تستمرّ معنا، من مشروع إلى آخر. وقد انتهى مشروعك بإنجاز هذا العمل الفنيّ الموجود هنا، ولكن لعلّه سيستمرّ في أشكال فنيّة مختلفة أيضًا.

آخ: لا أدري إن كنتِ قد مررت بهذه التجربة من قبلُ، ولكن يمكن لمشروع ما أن يمثّل بوّابةً نعبر منها إلى أمر آخر (تقاطعه ل غ: بالطبع، نعم). ومثلما تعلمين، ربما لم يكن الهدف الذي سعيت إليه منذ البداية هو النتيجة التي ذكرتها الآن، ولكنّ غرضي تعلّق ببساطة، بالسعي إلى مسايرة التيّار.

ل غ: إنّه جزء من الرحلة (آخ: هذا صحيح). في بعض الأحيان، لا يظهر الرابط على الفور، لكنّك سرعان ما تدركه في لحظة معيّنة. هذا جزء من هذا النوع من الرحلة المستمرّة التي نسعى إليها.

آخ: فلْنعد الآن إلى دراسة سورة النور. فأنا أحبّ كثيراً هذه السورة لأنّها الأكثر كونيّةً في رأيي. فبإمكان المسلم أو غير المسلم على حدّ سواء، أن يجد فيها معنًى لأنّها تنقل، من الناحية الإنسانيّة، شيئاً لا يمكن تمثّله ذهنياً، فهو، مثل الضوء نفسه، إنّه شبيه بـ... عظمة الله. وهكذا فإنّ فكرة جناح النور هي فكرة تعبّديّة؛ فإذا ما أمكننا الاهتداءُ إليه وتصوّره ذهنياً، فإنّ ذلك يُعدّ بمثابة عمل من أعمال التقوى. لقد كان هذا بالضبط الاستكشاف الذي قمتُ به، أما لماذا كان الزجاج هو الوسيلة المعتمدة، فذلك يعود إلى أنّ الزجاج مادّة قديمة. فهو تحت الأرض ولكنّه يتميّز بهذه الصفات الكونيّة؛ إذ إنّه مرسِل للضوء ومنبثق منه في الوقت نفسه؛ عليه ينعكس الضوء وعليه ينكسر أيضاً. وقد ورد ذكره عدّة مرّات في القرآن الكريم، صحبة المصباح والنور. هاتان الفكرتان، وقد ذكرتِ للتوّ الفكرة الثانية، وهي اليد، أصبحتا فكرتين في غاية الأهمّية. لقد أخذت اليد تختفي من عالَم الإنتاج، وصارت الصناعة اليدويّة معزولة عن المستخدِم. فنحن نشتري البضائع من المتاجر، دون أن يكون لدينا أيّ صلة بكيفيّة إنتاجها.

ل غ: وربما تظهر يدٌ أخرى لا نملك الآن القدرةَ على إدراكها. قد تكون أقلّ علاقة باللّمس.

آخ: نحن نشهد ظهور نوع من العالَم الرقميّ، ونذهب إلى المتاحف ونحضر التظاهرات الفريدة من نوعها مثل جائزة المصلّى لنذكّر أنفسنا بالعالَم الذي صنعه الإنسانُ ونجدّد علاقتنا به، ولكن في كثير من الأحيان تكون هندستنا المعماريّة بعيدة جداً عنه. أما في ما يتّصل بالمصلّى، فبإمكانك إعادة استعمال الصناعة اليدويّة. وهكذا فإنّ هذا الفعل اليدويّ القائم على صنع شيء باستعمال التكرار، وهو فعل تأمليّ، يشبه تكرار بعض الآيات في القرآن الكريم. ويبدو لي أنّه أمر مهمّ، ولهذا السبب فهو جناح من العمل الخطّي والتكرار. فكلّ نقطة ترتبط بنقاط أخرى، وهي جميعاً تتضافر بعضها مع بعض لتنقل المعنى من خلال علاقاتها الهندسيّة، ولكنّها كذلك ناقلات للضوء، تنبعث من حولنا وتخلق هذا الإحساس الشبيه بالسحابة. يمكنك أن تعتبري هذا العمل هندسةً معماريّةً مصغَّرةً، بوصفه مبنى، ثم انهار المبنى لأنّنا لم نفز في المنافسة ومن الآن فصاعداً، ستتضمّن الأعمال الفنيّة التي نعرضها جميع هذه الأفكار.

ل غ: عندما كنتَ بصدد وصف عمليّة ربط الخطوط، تذكّرت فعلَيْ الخياطة والنسج. أعتقد أنّ لحظة الخياطة، ونسج الأشياء بعضها مع بعض، والعمليّة التي تنجم عن ذلك، هي تجربة عميقة جداً. أحيانًا نستكشف ذلك في الهندسة المعماريّة، أو خلال المسار الذي يتّخذه

التخصّصاتِ لا تقيّده ضوابطُ المهنِ التقليديّةِ والتفكيرُ التخصّصيُّ المعزولُ.

أعتقد أنّ هذا هو المجالُ الذي تكمن فيه القوّةُ الحقيقيّةُ للتكنولوجيا، لا من زاويةِ ما تبنيه فحسْبُ، ولكن كذلك من زاويةِ طريقتِها في التأقلمِ والتفاعلِ، إلى أن تصبح في خاتمةِ المطافِ جزءاً أساسيّاً مندمجاً في إيقاعاتِ التجربةِ الإنسانيّةِ. فسواء أتعلّق الأمرُ بأماكنَ للصلاةِ، أم بمراكزِ نقلٍ، أم بهياكلَ مؤقّتةٍ، فإنّ التكنولوجيا التي تدوم على مرّ الزمن إنّما هي تلكَ التي تُصيخ السّمعَ في المقامِ الأوّلِ، ومن ثَمّ تشكّل نفسَها على النحو الذي يؤهّلها لتتأقلمَ في انسجامٍ مع العالَم الذي تعيش فيه.

حوار: لينا غطمة وآصف خان

عن النور والحرفة

لينا غطمة: كم هو أمر رائع أن ألتقيك يا آصف، فقد كان من دواعي سروري أن أكون بين أعضاء لجنة تحكيم جائزة المُصلّى، وقد انبهرت حقّاً بالمسار الذي اتّخذته بحوثُك، وبالطريقة التي توصّلت بها إلى ابتكار الفكرة التي يقوم عليها المقترح الذي قدّمتَه لجائزة المُصلّى. لقد كان الأمر فاتناً يسحر الألباب، لاسيما هذا الانبهار بالنور والإضاءة، وهذا الإجلال الكبير لسورة "النور" التي كانت جزءاً من قصّتك.

أريدك أن تخبرني المزيد عن كلّ ذلك. وباعتباري مهندسةً معماريّةً، فأنا دائمًا مفتونة وشغوفة بهذا النوع من الخطاب الذي يؤدّي إلى إنشاء المشاريع.

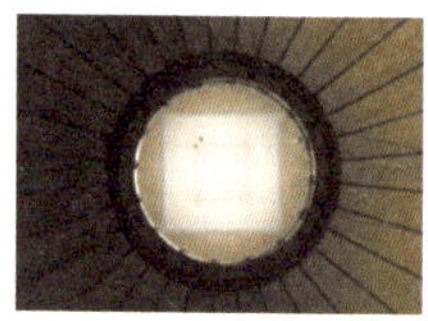

آصف خان: كان المشروع بالنسبة إليّ بمثابة لقاء جمع بين التاريخ الشخصيّ وما أنجزت من بحوث كانت مكمّلاً له. وباعتباري شخصاً وُلد في المملكة المتّحدة ويحمل هويّة فرد مسلم ينحدر من شبه القارة الهنديّة وشرق إفريقيا في آن معاً، فإنّ تراثي قد تعرّض لعمليّة الإزالة على نحو مضاعف. لذلك فعندما يقدَّم مشروع من هذا القبيل، لاسيما في هذه الفترة بالذات من حياتي الآن، وقد تجاوزتُ الأربعين وأخذت أتقدّم في السنّ، فإنّ الحاجة إلى إعادة الاتّصال بهذه الجذور وتقويتها تصبح أكثر أهميّةً كلّما ازدادت الشجرة ارتفاعاً (يشير بإصبعه إلى الأعلى). وهكذا، فعندما أتيحت لي الفرصةُ للعمل في هذا السياقِ الاستثنائيّ، القريبِ شديدَ القرب من المدن المقدّسة، وعلى هذه الطريق التي يسلكها الحجّاج في رحلة الحجّ التي لا تتكرّر إلا مرّة واحدة في حياة المرء، شعرتُ بالحاجة إلى التعمّق في أغوار نفسي، ليس في ما يتّصل بممارستي فحسب، ولكن في ما يتعلّق بماضيّ أو حمضي النوويّ أيضًا (تتدخّل ل غ بلطف: بنفسك). بالضبط. وقد استُخدم المشروع بوصفه عدسة مكبّرة لاستكشاف بعض الجوانب من ذلك. لقد كنت محظوظاً إذ إنّني تلقّيت تكويني الأساسيّ، بعد الانتهاء من دراستي، في "مؤسّسة المَلِك"، حيث قدّموا لنا تعليماً يقوم على تدريسنا الفنون التقليديّة والهندسة والتصوّر الكلاسيكيّ لعلم الجمال وفنون البناء في العالَم الإسلامي واليونان القديمة وروما القديمة. لقد كانوا يحاولون إنشاء مزيج من هذه العناصر لمساعدتنا على أن نصبح مهندسين معماريّين متميّزين. وقد أهملتُ هذا التحصيل الذي أخذته ثم وضعته جانباً لسنوات عديدة، ولكن عندما صدرت هذه المذكّرة، أخذ كلُّ ما تعلّمته قبل عشرين عاماً يظهر من جديد. بكلّ بساطة، لقد استحضرت ضرباً من التأمّل الذي أنجزه كيث كريتشلو، وهو عالِمٌ عظيم مختصّ في الهندسة المقدّسة ومعلّم للفنون الإسلاميّة، وبنى أسس تفكيره على فلسفة أفلاطون وما إلى ذلك. إنّ هذه الأنواع من الأسس العلميّة والفكريّة هي الأصول الرئيسيّة التي أستند إليها في فهمي للهندسة المعماريّة، وفي المسار الذي قطعته أثناء تنفيذ المشروع.

ل غ: ما تقوله رائع. وأعتقد أنّ هذا الارتباط بالأصل أمر يتردّد صداه كثيراً في الطريقة التي أرى بها الهندسة المعماريّة والطريقة التي نعمل بها في المنطقة. ثمّة شعور بالانتماء يظهر، وهو عميق جدّاً في داخلك، ثم يخرج فجأة، عندما تعمل في هذا السياق، لاسيما عندما تعيش في أماكن نائية. فكما تعلم، أنا أمارس مهنة الهندسة المعماريّة في باريس، وقد نشأت في بيروت، في لبنان، وهكذا فاللّغة العربيّة نفسها تعود إلى الظهور لديّ من جديد وأنا في باريس.

إنّ الروحانيّة التي يتّسم بها مقترح المصلّى الذي قدّمته، تجسّد جذورك بطريقة مّا، وتثير في النفس شيئاً يشبه السحر كثيراً. وأنا مهتمّة أيضاً بمعرفة المجهود الفنيّ الذي بذلته أثناء إعداد المشروع. فبوصفنا مهندسين معماريّين، نجد أنفسنا دائماً في موقع بين المهندسين المعماريّين والفنّانين، فنحن نصنع أو ننشئ بطريقة ما فضاءات مبنيّة تُخصَّص للسكن، ولكنّها من جهة أخرى أشكال فنيّة مأهولة وأماكن يعيش فيها الناس أيضاً، وهي قادرة على أن تبعث هذا النوعَ من المشاعر التي تنشأ داخل الفضاء. لقد شعرت أنّ هناك حسّاً فنيّاً يكمن في مشروعك. فهل اكتشفتَ ذلك خلال تنفيذك هذا المشروع؟ أم أنّه أمر موجود في كل مشروع أيضاً؟

آ خ: قطعاً هو ذاك. أعتقد أنّ هذه المسألة المتعلّقة بالتأرجح بين الفنّ والهندسة المعماريّة مسألة مهمّة. لقد أُطلق على الهندسة المعماريّة لقبُ "أمّ جميع الفنون"، وعليه فإنّ النحت... والشعر، والرقص، والمسرح، وهذه الأشكال الفنيّة، وفنّ الخط، جميع هذه الأشكال تتّحد معاً في الهندسة المعماريّة. لقد اهتدينا إلى طريقة في العمل تجعلنا نمارس مهنتنا بوصفها ممارسة فنيّة وليس مجرّد تقديم خدمة، ذلك أنّ المطلوب هو أن يكون المرء في تناغم مع نفسه وأن يجد نفسه في المشروع، وأن يتجسّد المشروع نفسه من خلالك. لذلك فأنت وسيط به يتحقّق المشروع.

أعتقد أنّني سعيت، خلال إعداد مقترحي لجائزة المُصلّى، إلى أن أجسّد ذاتي والفرصةَ التي أتاحتها لي الجائزةُ في آن واحد. فعلى سبيل المثال: ما هو المصلّى؟ وما هي العلاقة القائمة بين الإنسان وهذا الفضاء؟ ناهيك عن أنّ ما كان يسترعي اهتمامي في المقام الأوّل، هو العلاقة بين القرآن الكريم والهندسة المعماريّة. فلئن كنت قد قدِمت إلى هنا عدّة مرات من قبل، فإنّ ما تطلّعت إلى معرفته هذه المرّة هو اختبار ما إذا كان بوسعي التوصّل إلى تبيّن وجود علاقة بين القرآن الكريم، الذي تقوم عليه العقيدة الإسلاميّة، والهندسة المعماريّة التي انبثقت من تلك العقيدة.

ل غ: هذا صحيح، وهو أمر يثير الانبهار حقّاً، لأنّنا إذا رجعنا إلى كلمات القرآن الكريم، تبيّن لنا أنّها يمكن أن تكشف عن فضاء كامل، وإحساس مكثّف جدّاً بالمكان والزمان، ومن شأن ذلك أن يفتح الباب أمام عيش تجربة مكانيّة قويّة. وأشعر أنّ اهتمامك بسورة النور، قد تضمّن هذا النوع من العالَم المكانيّ الذي انفتح أمامك، وكان جميلاً جدّاً، وكان دقيقاً جدّاً أيضاً. إنّه الفضاء القائم بين العالم المحسوس والعالم غير المحسوس، وقد أثمر في مقترح المصلّى الذي قدّمته طاقةً تعبيريّةً خفيّةً، ودقيقةً جدّاً ورقيقة جدّاً. وفي الحقيقة، إنّ هذا الأمر يجسّد فكرة التواجد في الوسط؛ بين السماويّ والأرضيّ.

عندما تحدّثتَ عن علاقة الفنّ بالهندسة المعماريّة، خطر في بالي أنّ أحد القواسم المشتركة بينهما هو مسألة اليد، وكما تعلم، الصناعة اليدويّة والتصنيع. فعندما ننظر إلى جميع القطع التاريخيّة المعروضة

فضاءاتٍ عامةً وخاصةً، حيث يُستخلص جوهرُ بيئتِها مهما كان ضئيلاً عن طريقِ استخدامِ الأصواتِ والأنسجةِ والأنماطِ الزخرفيّةِ والضوءِ والروائحِ، وهي جميعُها عناصرُ أُنشئت على نحوٍ مصطنَعٍ لإحداثِ تأثيرٍ في بيئةِ الناسِ وإن كان ذلك في الحدِّ الأدنى من التأثير. وأرى أنّ هذهِ الحقيقةَ هي انعكاسٌ مهمٌّ لكيفيّةِ قيامِ التكنولوجيا، حتى في أبسطِ صورِها، بتشكيلِ الفضاءِ تشكيلاً يُؤثِر التجربةَ الإنسانيّةَ على الديمومةِ. ومع ذلك، فإنّ الممارسةَ العمليّةَ بوصفها تكنولوجيا تبدو زلقةً إلى حدٍّ بعيدٍ وواسعةً لا يُمسَك لها طرفٌ، فلا يمكن في هذه الحالِ تناولُها بالدرسِ والكتابةُ عنها ضمن هذه الملاحظاتِ القصيرةِ. فإذا ما نظرنا في مجالِ التصميمِ، بان لنا أنّ العلاقةَ مع التكنولوجيا (باعتبارها وسيلةً للإنتاجِ الابتكاريِّ أكثرَ منها مرقاةً للارتفاعِ إلى مصافِ وضعٍ شبهِ دينيٍّ) يمكن أن تتجلّى في عدّةِ وجوهٍ دقيقةٍ وضخمةٍ في آنٍ واحدٍ. ففي بعضِ الأحيانِ يكفي مجرّدُ وجودِ "الهيكل" وحدَه ليكشفَ عن البراعةِ أو التقدّمِ التكنولوجيّ - ولْنضربْ على ذلك مثلاً هو ناطحاتُ السحابِ المتناهيةُ في الارتفاعِ أو أعظمُ الجسورِ طولاً. وفي أحيانٍ أخرى، تهمس التكنولوجيا بلطفٍ عبر فضاءاتٍ لا تؤدّي صداها عن طريقِ الإنشاءاتِ العظيمةِ فحسْبُ، ولكن عن طريقِ المرونةِ والحُسنِ والانسجامِ أيضاً، مع المحافظةِ في الوقتِ نفسِهِ على طبيعةِ السياقِ المحدَّدِ والاستخدامِ المخصوصِ.

في هذا الإطارِ تحديداً أنظر إلى عملِ فضل الرحمن خان - لا باعتباره إنجازاً مفرداً، بل بوصفهِ جزءاً من سلسلةٍ متّصلةٍ من الاستكشافِ التكنولوجيّ، هي أكبرُ وأوسعُ مدىً من عملِ فردٍ واحدٍ. فإذا تناولنا بالدرسِ مثالاً مخصوصاً هو محطّةُ الحجِّ في مطارِ الملك عبد العزيز الدوليّ في جدّة، ألفينا أنّ تصميمَها يُعدّ نموذجاً نادراً، حقّق خطوةً عملاقةً نحو توظيفِ الهياكلِ النسيجيّةِ وجسّم في الوقتِ نفسه الاستمراريّةَ التاريخيّةَ والتصويرَ الفريدَ. وإذا أخذنا بالاعتبارِ مستوىً معيّناً من الريادة، فإنّ هذا التصميمَ يتوافق مع مبادئِ القدرةِ على التكيّفِ. إنّ سقفَ هذه المحطّةِ الواسعَ والقابلَ للشدِّ يعرض أمام النّاظرين ما يصفه كثيرٌ من المختصّين بأنّه نصبٌ تذكاريٌّ ناعمٌ - فهو لا يفرض نفسَه على المشاهد - متناءٍ عن الأعين، بل يبدو وكأنّه "يرتفع" إلى السماء، محاكياً "تجربة الطيران" ومردّداً أصداءً ممّا يسم الطقوسَ ورحلاتِ الحجّاجِ العابرين من خفّةٍ وعدمِ ثباتٍ. لقد صُمّمت هذه المحطّةُ لتستوعب ثمانين ألفَ مسافرٍ جوّاً، معظمُهم يأتون من دولٍ غيرِ مصنّعةٍ، ويظلّون على سفرٍ لمدّةٍ تصل إلى ستٍّ وثلاثين ساعةً. وتمثّل قاعةُ المحطّةِ مساحةً ضخمةً لا تُستخدم إلاّ على امتداد شهرين فقط طيلةَ السنة، أي قبل الحجّ وبعده.

وإذا أقمنا مقارنةً بين المُصلّياتِ، بوصفها مكاناً آخر من الأمكنةِ الصالحةِ للتجمّعِ البشريِّ المؤقّتِ، وهذه المحطّةِ، ألفينا المصلّياتِ أصغرَ بكثيرٍ، وهي تبرز عندما تَحين فريضةُ الصلاةِ. ذلك أنّها تُستخدم على نحوٍ متواترٍ لفتراتٍ قصيرةٍ من قِبل مجموعاتٍ صغيرةٍ أو عددٍ من الأفرادِ، ويمكن تجميعُها وتفكيكُها بسهولةٍ، وهي تتّخذ أشكالاً وأحجاماً عديدةً. وفي هذه الحالة، تُستخدم التكنولوجيا لتعزيزِ القدرةِ على التكيّفِ وعدمِ الثباتِ بدلاً من فرضِ أشكالٍ جامدةٍ.

إنّ التكنولوجيا التي مكّنت من إنشاءِ محطّةِ الحجِّ تكنولوجيا معقّدةٌ وعلى درجةٍ عاليةٍ من التطوّرِ. فقد قام إعدادُ التصميمِ والنمذجةُ الهيكليّةُ على عمليّاتٍ حسابيّةٍ متقدّمةٍ، ما زلنا نعتمدها إلى يومِنا هذا. ومع ذلك، فإنّ النتيجةَ المتوصَّلَ إليها بسيطةٌ. لا تصنّعَ فيها ولا لُبسَ، وهي وثيقةُ الصلةِ بسياقِها. وقد صمدت في وجهِ الزمنِ كأبهى ما يكون الصمودُ. فبعد أن أمضى خان معظمَ أوقاتِه سنةَ 1976 في دراسةِ التراثِ الإسلاميّ، أظهر كذلك قدرةً كبيرةً على التعاونِ في العملِ مع زملائِه في مكتبِ الهندسة المعماريّة «سكيدمور أوينغس ميريل»، مشرفاً على التعاملِ مع الأشكالِ الهندسيّةِ المألوفةِ التي تجمع بين الدائرةِ والكرةِ (دلالةً على عالَمِ الروح) والمربّعِ والمكعّبِ (إحالةً على عالَمِ الأرضِ والاستقرار)، وقد أُعتُمدت تلك الأشكالُ بوصفها وحدةً أساسيّةً قابلةً لأن تُدمج إلى ما لا نهايةَ له تقريبًا، وقد تضافرت جميعاً من أجلِ إنشاءِ المحطّة.

إنّ هذا المشروعَ يذكّرنا بأنّ التكنولوجيا التي نطبّقها في ميدانِ الهندسةِ المعماريّةِ ليست محايدةً أو بريئةً البتّةَ. فهو يحمل على عاتقِه أثقالَ السياقِ الذي يخدمه. وإذا تأمّلنا تجربةَ خان، بان لنا أنّ التكنولوجيا أصبحت وسيطاً بين البيئةِ والثقافةِ ومتطلّباتِ البنيةِ التحتيّةِ الحديثةِ. وما شدّني كثيراً في عمله هو غيابُ المبالغةِ وتجنّبُ الإفراطِ. فثمّة وضوحٌ نلمسه في كيفيّةِ تجسيمِ المحطّةِ لما هو أساسيٌّ - الحركة، والراحة، والمأوى - وقد قام ذلك بديلاً لمحاولةِ فرضِ سمةِ الديمومةِ التي لا فائدةَ تُرجى منها، على فضاءٍ حَدّد جوهرَ طبيعتِهِ الأصليّةِ التحوّلُ من مكانٍ إلى آخرَ، وسرعةُ انقضاءِ كلِّ تجمّعٍ يحدث بين جوانبِه، فكلُّ تلاقٍ فيه سرعانَ ما ينتهي إلى افتراقٍ.

وإنّ ما أجده مقنعاً هو الفكرةُ القائلةُ بأنّ التقدّمَ التكنولوجيَّ ينبغي أن لا يتعارض مع التقاليد، فمن شأنِ ذلك أن يسمح لنا بتخفيفِ التوتّرِ القائمِ بين الابتكارِ والتراثِ، كما لو أنّ هذين العنصرين الاثنين هما في تصادمٍ يعارِض أحدُهما الآخر. ولكنّ الأمرَ على العكس من ذلك، إذ نجد أنّ عدداً لا بأسَ به من الأشكالِ المعماريّةِ التي استمرّت قائمةً على مرِّ الزمنِ، لاسيّما في التقاليدِ الإسلاميّةِ وغيرِها من التقاليد الثقافيّة، يكشف أنّ التكنولوجيا كانت دوماً جزءاً من التاريخ. لا بوصفها قوّةً خارجيّةً، بل باعتبارها امتداداً عضويّاً للطريقة التي يسلكها البشرُ حتى يحلّوا المشاكلَ التي تعترض سبيلَهم، ويتفاعلوا مع بيئتِهم.

وبوصفي مهندساً إنشائيّاً لا يستطيع فصلَ التصميمِ والبحثِ والتصنيعِ والبناءِ والتدريسِ عن جودةِ الحياةِ، فإنّي أحرص شديدَ الحرصِ على مراعاةِ التوازنِ لدى الالتزامِ بتنفيذِ المشاريعِ والأفكارِ التي تتبنّى مبدأيْ عدمِ الثباتِ والمرونةِ، ويحرّكها إضافةً إلى ذلك الدافعُ إلى إنشاءِ هياكلَ ثابتةٍ موحّدةِ الكُتلِ. وعلى هذا النحو، تصبح إغراءاتُ تحقيقِ الأصالةِ والجِدّةِ نتيجةً متفرّعةً عن هذه الممارسة.

وأريد كذلك تجنّبَ تبنّي وجهةِ نظرٍ صلبةٍ، بسبب التأثيرِ المتسارعِ للتغييرِ المناخيّ. فالحدودُ بين الهياكلِ المؤقّتةِ والدائمةِ (سواءٌ أكانتْ جديدةً أم قائمةَ الذاتِ منذ زمنٍ) صارت تتّخذ ملامحَ جديدةً في وتيرةٍ لا سابقَ لسرعتِها، زد على ذلك أنّ "ساحة اللَّعب" بين الهياكلِ الدائمةِ والمؤقّتةِ لم تعد هي نفسَها إذ صارت في تطوّرٍ مستمرٍّ. فهذه المنطقةُ تمتلك قدرةً ساحرةً على إحداثِ المفاجأةِ وتحويلِ الاهتماماتِ الجديدةِ إلى فرصٍ جديدةٍ، تمامًا مثلما سبق لفضل عبدالرحمن خان أن فعل عندما صمّم محطّةَ الحجّ.

وممّا لا شكّ فيه أنّ ثمّةَ شيئاً يتّسم بالقوّةِ في تصميمِ الفضاءاتِ التي يمكنها التحرّكُ والتنفّس. فمن هذا المنطلقِ، لا تصير قوّةُ التكنولوجيا أداةً للتحكّمِ بل للتفاعلِ - فتكون وسيلةً تسمح للهندسةِ المعماريّةِ بالتطوّرِ جنباً إلى جنبٍ مع الحياةِ بدلاً من الوقوفِ بعيداً عنها. وعندما أقلّب النظرَ في هذا الأمرِ، يستقرّ في إدراكي أنّ ما يجذبني إلى التكنولوجيا ليس قدرتَها على العرضِ المشهديّ، بل قدرتُها على التواري في الخلفيّةِ، ومن شأن ذلك أن ينشئ ظروفاً تبدو طبيعيّةً وبديهيّةً وتتوافق مع الطريقة التي يتّبعها الناس وهم يَسكنون الفضاء. فأكثرُ الابتكاراتِ أهميّةً، في رأيي، هي تلك التي تطمس الحدودَ الفاصلةَ بين الاصطناعيِّ والطبيعيِّ، حيث تعمل الموادُّ والأنظمةُ في صمتٍ سعياً إلى خلقِ بيئاتٍ تبدو عفويّةً لم يُبذل فيها مجهودٌ كبيرٌ، لكنّها في حقيقةِ الأمرِ قد جاءت ثمرةَ دراسةٍ عميقةٍ، ولا يتسنّى ذلك إلاّ إذا اعتمدنا نهجاً متعدّدَ

الثقافة الموجودة مسبقًا أو المهيمنة هناك، وكيفيّة إدراج هذه المسألة في الحوار، أليس كذلك؟ وهنا، دائماً ما يتمحور هذا التفاوض حول الأشكال التاريخيّة. أيّ شكل منها نختار؟ فقد يكون هناك، لاسيما في الغرب، أصنافٌ كثيرةٌ من المسلمين الذين قدموا من خلفيّات متنوّعة، أليس كذلك؟ على هذا النحو، قد تجد أمامك مصريّين وربّما تجد شخصاً من آسيا الوسطى أو الصين، وجميعهم يصلّون في المسجد نفسه. لذلك، فإنّ تحديد هويّتهم فحسْب، يصطدم هو نفسه بوجود مرجعيّات تاريخيّة مختلفة يمكن الاستلهام منها. إذن إنّ هذه الأسئلة حسب رأيي مثيرة للاهتمام هي الأخرى، بمعنى: ما هو العامّ وما هو الخصوصيّ في ما يتعلّق بالمساجد، إن من الناحية الثقافيّة وإن من المنظور المحلّي؟

س ح: أعتقد أنّ ما تطرحينه مسألة شائكة، لأنّك إذا بدأت بالقول: سأقوم بتنفيذ مشروع خاصّ بثقافة الهند فقط، وهذا كلّ شيء، ويمكن إنجاز ذلك في أيّ مكان، ففي هذه الحالة ستواجهين مشكلة تحديد المرحلة الزمنيّة التي ستعتمدينها، فأيّ فترة تختارينها مصدراً لإلهامك؟ أعني أنّ ثمّة وفرةً كبيرةً من المرجعيّات التي يمكن استخدامها، لكنّني أعتقد أنّ الطريقة التي يمكن أن تتجلّى بواسطتها الهويّةُ هي طريقة أكثر عضويّة وبديهيّة. إنّها طريقة تنبع أو تنبثق من الموقع نفسه، وكأنّها ضرب من التحاور مع شعور بالانتماء. ففي التجربة التي مررت بها خلال تنفيذ هذا المشروع، كانت تقنية التقسيم المتعدّد السطوح أو فكرة المقرنصات قد فرضت نفسها بسبب السقف والأرضيّة. فلم يتعلّق الأمر بالضرورة بالإحالة إلى مرجعيّة معيّنة. وقد انبثق هذا الاختيار بصفة حدسيّة كأنّه جوهر، ولكنّه جوهرٌ يعمل في ارتباط مع السياق نفسه، جوهرٌ يحاور السياق. وأعتقد، على الأقلّ في ما يخصّ عملي، أنّ هذه هي الطريقة التي أحبّ أن أفكّر بواسطتها في التاريخ، فهو أمر ينبثق من خلال نوع من الارتباط المباشر بالسياق. بيد أنّ سؤالك مهمّ إلى حدّ بعيد، لأنّني لا أعتقد أنّ له إجابة محدَّدة. فعلى سبيل المثال، أين يمكنك رسمُ الخطّ الفاصل بين ما هو عامّ وما ليس عامّاً؟ ففي كثير من الأحيان، يخامرني الإحساسُ بأنّ حرصنا على تأكيد مرجعيّات محدّدة، يعود إلى رغبتنا في الإدلاء ببيان معيّن؛ وبذلك تصبح العمليّة تعسّفيّة جدّاً.

أأ: إذا تناولنا التصميم الذي أنجزته، ألفيناه جميلاً جدّاً إلى درجة أنّه تظهر فيه مرّة أخرى هذه الإشارةُ إلى الموقع الأثريّ. فهذا المشروع نوع من التنقيب في المناظر الطبيعيّة والتعرّف على تاريخها الذي يظهر في ثنايا التصميم. وهو يتوافق مع الموقع ويعمل باستخدام الموادّ المحلّية، ولكنّه يعمد بعد ذلك إلى أن يبتكر داخل هذا التاريخ أيضاً.

س ح: وهذا ما يفسّر وجود بعض الغموض، أليس كذلك؟ بالفعل، ثمّة غموض، لأنّ الغموض يسمح للناس بالتفسير، وإنشاء معنى خاصّ بهم، أو إسناد معنى معيّن إلى الفضاء (ترسم أأ إيماءة تعبيرا عن موافقتها). لا أريد فرض تعريف محدّد. كما تعلمين، أشعر أنّ التعريف أمر يظهر عبر الاستخدام، ومن خلال الأشخاص الذين يستخدمون الفضاء. أعني بذلك أنّ شخصاً من بلد معيّن يمكنه رؤية الأشياء بطريقة ما، ويمكن لشخص آخر تفسير الأشياء نفسها بطريقة مختلفة تمامًا، بل قد يكون التفسيران متناقضين أشدّ التناقض. وعلى هذا النحو، فإنّي أعتبر أنّ السعي إلى إيصال رسائل محدّدة وفرض معنى معيّن هو أشبه ما يكون بحشر المرء نفسه في الزاوية.

أأ: أخيراً، ما الذي تحتفظ به من هذا المشروع، وما الذي مثّل مصدر ثراء لتجربتك؟

س ح: مثلما تعلمين، فما كان مصدر ثراء إلى حدّ بعيد في السياق المحدّد لهذا المشروع، هو أنّنا لم نفكّر من قبل البتّة في إنشاء هندسة معماريّة في مساحة معماريّة في مثل هذا الحجم الكبير، في نظام ضخم، أو مأوى ضخم، وما إلى ذلك. لقد كان الأمر بالنسبة إليّ ذا دلالة شديدة الخصوصيّة، لأنّني كنت أتردّد على محطّة الحجّ عندما كانت تعمل بوصفها محطّة. لقد رأيتها مليئة بالحجّاج، فكان وقع ذلك عليّ أشبه ما يكون بالأنفاس وهي تُحبس. أما الآن فصرت أراها من زاوية مختلفة تمامًا. فعندما تكون الهندسة المعماريّة قويّة بما فيه الكفاية، وعندما تنفّذ بطريقة معيّنة قادرة على أن تعزّز استدامتها، أو ربّما عندما تكون القدرة على التحوّل متأصّلة فيها ولها معان ووظائف تتغيّر مع مرور الوقت، فحينها فقط يتجلّى للعيان مدى الأهمّية التي تكتسيها الهندسة المعماريّة.

مكتب سهل الحياري للهندسة المعمارية

تعامل مكتب سهل الحياري للهندسة المعمارية مع تصميم المُصلى على أنه تجسيد لجوهر العبادات الإسلامية، حيث تتجاوز الصلاة الحدود المادية وتتكيف مع سياقات مختلفة. تنبثق الممارسات عن محيطها، وتجسد العوالم العامة والخاصة، والداخلية والخارجية. لذلك، لا يرتبط المُصلى بالضرورة بنمط محدد له خصائص شكلية واضحة؛ بل إنه ينبثق عن فعل (صلاة) يحدث داخل مساحة ما.
إن جوهر وظيفة المُصلّى هو توفير جو مناسب للعبادة يهيئ الإنسان «للخشوع»، وهي حالة من الحضور والرهبة المتأصلة في طقوس الصلاة الإسلامية ويجب أن يعزز مكان الصلاة هذه الحالة ويفصلها تماماً عن أي مشتتات.

سعى مقترح مكتب سهل الحياري للهندسة المعمارية إلى تحديد مساحة لا نهائية داخل محطة الحج الموسعة، دون فقدان حضور أي منهما. يعبر عن مفهومهم وجود مكان الصلاة على المستوى الأرضي. يتخذ المُصلّى شكل تلة، وهي طبقة طبوغرافية من الرمال المستقرة التي تحيط بالمساحة. ويبدو المُصلى وكأنه جزء من الموقع نفسه، مما يجعله جسماً مادياً ومنظراً طبيعياً في الوقت ذاته.

تعكس الأشكال الهندسية التي تشكل التلة ارتباط الفنون والعمارة الإسلامية بالطبيعة والأجرام السماوية، من خلال التعبيرات المعدنية الجيولوجية. ويمتد ذلك إلى الترتيبات الهندسية الأكثر خصوصية للجزء الداخلي المصنوع من الطين المزجج لمُصلّى مكتب سهل الحياري. ويتصل الفضاء بالسماء من خلال فتحة تسمح للضوء بالتسلل عبر فجوات البنية الداخلية، مما يضيف بُعداً هندسياً آخر.

خاطرة: حنيف كارا

التكنولوجيا تهمس بهدوء

إنّ رصد التقاليد المعماريّة التي تُجسّد روح الإسلام لَهُو بمثابة عدسةٍ محكَمةٍ يمكننا من خلالها تبيّنُ أنّ التكنولوجيا تعايشت منذ زمنٍ طويلٍ مع فلسفاتِ التكيّفِ والتفاعلِ المعماري. ولعلّه يحسن بي أن أشير أيضاً إلى أنّ هذا الأمر قد يكون على صلةٍ وثيقةٍ بالتفسيراتِ المهمّة للإسلام، وتنوّعِ الشعوبِ الإسلاميّةِ، ومبادئِ الحياةِ الإسلاميّة. فالثنائيّةُ - القائمةُ بين المَهيبِ والمتواضِعِ - ذاتُ تأثيرٍ بليغٍ متى قلّبنا الفكرَ في الفضاءات الوظيفيّة التي شكّلت صورتَها الممارساتُ الثقافيّةُ والروحيّةُ مثلما هو الشأنُ مع فضاءِ المُصَلّى.

فاستناداً إلى تجربتي، يمكنني القولُ إنّ فضاءاتِ المصلّى، سواءٌ أكانت كبيرةَ الحجمِ أم بسيطةً، غالبًا ما تشترك في مبدأٍ أساسيٍّ واحدٍ: ألا وهو أنّها نادراً جدّاً ما تكون هياكلَ جامدةً ثابتةً بل هي في الحقيقة بيئاتٌ مرنةٌ، إن توسّعت أو ضاقت فما ذلك إلاّ استجابةً منها لاحتياجاتِ الأشخاصِ الذين يستخدمونها. ويمكن، وفقاً للسياق، أن تكون

إلى هذه المربع، قد أميل فعلاً إلى تفسيره على أنّه غياب لكائن، أو على أنّه ساحة وفناء أيضاً. زد على ذلك أنّ أوائل المساجد في الإسلام قد بنيت في الأفنية والحدائق وما إلى ذلك... في المدينة المنوّرة. لذلك يمكن أن نرى في وجود المربع تواصلاً.

أ: حدّثني عن الخطوط الزرقاء. ففي جميع أنحاء التصميم يظهر هذا الخطّ الأزرق الرائع الذي أُعدّ من الطين، وهو يذكّرنا بالعناصر الزخرفيّة الخاصّة بالأشكال الإسلاميّة التاريخيّة.

س ح: نعم بالتأكيد. الخطّ الأزرق هو إحالة مباشرة إلى الكتابات الإسلاميّة التي يمكنك العثور عليها مخطوطةً فوق المباني الإسلاميّة المنتشرة في جميع أنحاء العالَم. الدلالة المقصودة من ذلك هي إبراز أنّ الهندسة تتكرّر من خلال الخطوط، أليس كذلك؟ (أ: تومئ برأسها موافقةً) عادةً ما يكون المُقَرْنص ثقيلاً جدًا عندما تنظر إليه في شكله غير المزخرَف. لهذا فهو يُنحت نحتاً عميقاً، وإذا اشتمل على خطوط زخرفيّة فهذا يجعله يميل إلى أن يكون أكثر دقّةً ولطفاً. بناءً عليه، حاولت في اقتراحي توظيف فكرة ثقل عناصر المقرنصات عبر الخطوط الزخرفيّة. لذلك أقحمت خطّاً دقيقاً جداً، على صلة هو أيضاً برقعة السماء الزرقاء وأضلاع مظلّة المحطّة. وبفضل هذه الخطوط، قام الاتّصال المباشر بين الأرضيّة والسقف والمظلّة والسماء من وراءها.

أ: هذا التفاعل الدقيق بين الثقل والخفّة في تصميمك أمر مقنع فعلاً. فالطريقة التي يربط بها الخطّ الأزرقُ بين العناصر المكانيّة المختلفة- بدءاً من الأرض ووصولاً إلى السماء- تنشئ استمراريّة جميلة تعزّز خاصيّة المؤقّت الملازمة للمصلّى. والآن دعنا نتحدّث قليلاً عن الأجهزة. فنلاحظ في عملك وجود بعض الجوانب المبتكَرة حقّاً. إذ نرى أكياس رمل هناك، وفي ذلك إيحاءٌ بأنّ من الممكن إعادة إنتاج هذا النوع من المشاريع في أماكن أخرى، لاسيما في المناخات التي تكثر فيها الرمال.

س ح: نعم. هناك طريقتان لبناء وإنشاء الهياكل التي تتّخذ هيئة تشبه المناظر الطبيعيّة. إحداهما أبسط من الأخرى، فهي تستخدم بشكل أساسيّ أكياس الرمل لتثبيت التضاريس، وتعتمد محيطاً صلباً مع طبقة من الرمال المستقرّة في الأعلى. هذه هي الفكرة التي ننطلق منها إذن. بعد ذلك يتمّ تصنيع الجانب الداخليّ من الأجزاء نفسها بواسطة الخرسانة المسلّحة، وذلك باستخدام موادّ التربة ذاتها، مِلاط التربة، والتراب، فينشأ عن ذلك علاقة ترابط مع الرمل نفسه. إنّ الأجزاء تخلق في الأساس هذا الترابط مع الرمل. ومحطّة الحجّ نفسها تشتمل على جدران مطليّة بهذه المادّة نفسها. فقد انطلقنا كذلك من فكرة إعادة استعمال ما هو موجود بالفعل، وإعادة استنساخ تقنيات البناء الأساسيّة جداً، أو لنقل التقنيات الأوّليّة، الموجودة محلّياً، ونعني بها الخرسانة المسلّحة. بعد ذلك فرغنا من تغليف بلاط الجانب الداخلي بمربعات التيراكوتا الطينيّة (يشير س ح إلى حجم مربعات البلاط مستعيناً بالإشارة إلى المسافة بين إبهامه وسبابته)، وطُعّمت هذه المربعات بالخطوط الزرقاء على الخرسانة. لذا، فالعمل قام على الجمع بين موادّ متعدّدة تعمل معاً بشكل متناغم، على الرغم ممّا يوجد بينها من اختلاف واضح، من حيث طريقة تجهيزها وطريقة استعمالها أيضاً. وكان المقصد من ذلك أن يُعاد وضعها بيُسر في أيّ منظر طبيعي، بمجرد انتهاء البينالي.

أ: وهذا ما يتجلّى في تصميمك على نحو رائع جداً. فهو هيكل ضخم قوامه موادّ مثل الخرسانة، لكنّه مهيّأ ليفكَّك ويعاد تركيبه بالكامل في مواقع مختلفة. إنّه متنقّل ويحظى بنصيب مهمّ من خاصيّة الاستدامة، فيمكن إعادة إنتاجه في مواقع أخرى عديدة باستخدام الموادّ المتوفّرة على النطاق المحلّي.

س أ. هذا صحيح، كما إنّه لا يتطلّب الكثير من الصيانة أيضاً. إنّه في الأساس مشروع يمكن إيداعه في الهواء الطلق، وسيكون قادراً على الصمود أمام العوامل الطبيعيّة الموجودة هنا في المملكة العربية السعوديّة. (تقوم أ بإيماءة موافقة)

أ: دعنا نتحدّث إذن عن بعض الدروس الأبعد مدىً التي يمكن استخلاصها من مشروعك، ومن هذه المسابقة أيضًا، في علاقة بفكرة المصلّى والإطار المفاهيميّ المرتبط به.

ففي بحثي السابق الذي درست فيه عمارة المساجد، قمت بوضع نظريّة للمسجد ترتكز على مبادئ التصميم التوليديّ- فجوهر المسجد يتشكّل من خلال حجم الجسم، وأداء طقوس الصلاة، واتّجاهه المتأصّل، والنقاء والنظافة الطقوسيّة اللّذين يقومان تعريفاً له. وينطلق هذا المنظور من وصف النبي محمد صلّى الله عليه وسلّم للمسجد، إذ اعتبره مكاناً للسجود، مؤكّداً أنّ أيّ مكان يصلّي فيه المرء فهو مسجد. بناءً عليه، فإنّ الهندسة المعماريّة ليست ضرورة للصلاة لا تتمّ إلاّ بها: إذ يمكن أن تقام الصلاةُ في الصحراء، أو في الشارع، ويكفي بكلّ بساطة استخدامُ سجّادة الصلاة. فلماذا وكيف نستخدم إذن الهندسة المعماريّة لإنشاء مسجد؟ وما هي المعايير التي تقود المنهج الذي تسلكه لدى وضع تصميم لمصلّى أو مسجد؟ وكيف يتسنّى لك الموازنة بين فضاء مهيكل والبساطة الأساسيّة التي تتميّز بها شعيرة الصلاة، إذ يمكن أن تقام في أيّ مكان، حتى وإن أُدّيت على سجّادة داخل تجمّعٍ جماهيريّ أو في مكان مفتوح؟

س ح: هذا سؤال على غاية من الأهميّة. فما قلتِه صحيح فعلاً، ذلك أنّ الصلاة يمكن أن تقام في أيّ مكان، وسجّادة الصلاة يمكن وحدها أن تؤدّي هذه المهمّة على أحسن وجه. بيد أنّني أؤمن في المقابل بهذا المصطلح المسمّى "الخشوع"، وهو يدلّ على حالة الحضور في الصلاة قلباً وقالباً، وهي حالة تسمح لك بالحضور، وأن تكوني حاضرة في اللحظة نفسها في حضرة الله. وهذا هو الجانب الأساسيّ في الصلاة. ولهذا أتصوّر أنّ الفضاء أو الهندسة المعماريّة يمكن أن يوفّرا الإطار اللاّزم لعيش هذه اللحظة، ويتيحا الهدوء والسلام اللّذين يسمحان للمتعبّد بالانغماس في هذه الحالة. وهذا ما يجسّمه حسب رأيي، الضوءُ، والتناسبُ والأنظمةُ، بل والهندسةُ نفسها أيضاً عندما ترين المقرنص مثلاً، أو عندما ترين الأنماط الزخرفيّة الإسلاميّة المحيطة بك، فإنّ عقلك لا يركّز على جانب واحد، بل يكون مشتّتاً إلى حدّ ما. يبدو الأمر كما لو أنّ الأنا مشتّت. وهذا له تأثير نفسيّ مهمّ على العقل. وبهذا المعنى، أعتقد أنّ أماكن الصلاة أو غرف الصلاة يمكن أن تؤدّي وظيفة إضافية، تتمثل في بعث هذا الجوّ أو هذا الشعور.

أ: ولتعزيز هذه الروحانيّة.

س ح: (يقلّد حركة يد أ تعبيراً عن موافقته إياها) لتعزيز الشعور. لكنّ هذا الأمر لا يتمّ بطريقة واحدة فقط، بل يمكن أن يحدث بواسطة طرق عديدة، وهنا يكمن مبلغ جماله وتعدديّته.

أ: هذه نقطة مهمّة جداً. فمثلما تعلم، لقد أنجزت في سياق عملي الكثير من البحوث حول تمثيل الإسلام في الغرب، وكذلك بين المجتمعات والمجموعات المسلمة التي تعيش في الشتات. فتبيّن لي أنّ المسلمين الذين يعيشون في بلدان ذات أغلبيّة غير مسلمة يسعون إلى التعامل مع وسائل رسميّة يمكنهم من خلالها تصوّر هويّتهم. وفي هذا السياق، يُعتبر المصلّى هو أيضاً مسألة ترتبط بالثقافة والحضور. وفي هذه السياقات أيضاً، لاحظت أنّه من المهمّ جداً لدى هذه المجتمعات أن تستفيد من مرجعيّات تاريخيّة وثقافيّة محدّدة، تستلهمها وهي تعمل على تحديد هويّتها. ولكن بما أنّك تقوم ببناء فضاءات مخصّصة للصلاة الإسلاميّة في أماكن ذات أغلبيّة غير إسلاميّة، فإنّك تواجه مسألة التفاوض مع

حوار: أزرا أكشاميا و سهل الحياري

عن البيئة كفضاء، وعن البيئة كمادة

أزرا أكشاميا: أنا معجبة بعملك منذ مدّة طويلة، ومن الجميل حقّاً أن نرى الابتكارات التي تجلّت في المقترح الذي قدّمته لجائزة المُصلّى 2025. فهلاّ توسعتَ قليلاً في بسط الأفكار الأوّليّة التي قادتك إلى هذا المفهوم؟

سهل الحياري: حسناً، في البداية، اهتممت بدراسة وظيفة المصلّى وهو فضاء يخصّص للصلاة، ونظرت كذلك في طبيعة الصلاة في الإسلام، وأهمّ سماتها أنّها لا ترتبط بالضرورة بمكان مقدّس بعينه. وهكذا ارتكز المقترح على فكرة صناعة فضاء أو إنشاء فضاء يكون بمثابة تقاطع بين: الأرض، والكائن، ومساحة المصلّى. ويعود تفسير ذلك إلى أنّ المصلّى يمكن أن يظهر في أيّ مكان. فقد يكون على جانب طريق من الطرقات، أو في الصحراء، أو في غرفة داخل أحد المباني. فثمّة إذن هذا الغموض الذي انعكس على المفهوم الذي انبنى عليه المقترح: إنشاء كائن يكون منظراً طبيعيّاً في جزء منه، وكائناً في جزء ثان، ويحتوي في داخله على هذه التجربة المكانيّة المتميّزة إلى أبعد حدّ.

أ أ: أجل، فغالبًا ما يستمدّ عملك تميّزه من ارتباطه القويّ جدّاً بالموقع، وها نحن نقف هنا في هذا الهيكل المذهل ذي السقف القائم على الأعمدة، وهو موجود في محطّة الحجّ. فأين يكمن التوافق بين مشروعك وهذا الموقع؟ وكيف كان ملائماً له؟ فهل يتعلّق الأمر بقابليّة التكرار (تستخدم يدها اليمنى راسمة حركة دائريّة متكرّرة) وفكرة التوسّع داخل المشهد الطبيعي (تفصل بين يديها للتأكيد على فكرة التوسّع)؟

س ح: إذا نظرت إلى هيكل قاعة الأعمدة وحجمها، سيتبيّن لك أنّها تنحو إلى أن تشرف على الأفق، تقريبًا مثل الجوّ الذي يحيط بالأفق. لذلك فالمشروع اتّخذ بعداً يضاهي مستوى منظر طبيعيّ (يميل إلى الأمام قليلاً للتأكيد على كلمة منظر طبيعيّ)، وليس مستوى كائن، أو مبنى، أو مجرّد فضاء مّا. وهكذا، يصبح المشهد نفسه عنصراً تركيبيّاً مهمّاً، ويغدو المُصلّى إيماءة، وتتحوّل الأرض تحوّلاً حقيقيّاً من حيث التضاريس. فترتفع إلى أعلى، زد على ذلك أنّه يوجد تحوّل آخر أيضاً: وهو جسم المصلّى نفسه. إذا راق لك أن تترجميه إلى مصطلحات موسيقيّة، فهو تقريبًا مثل النغمات المتقطّعة حيث يكون لديك حركة موسيقيّة واحدة تتحوّل إلى حركة أخرى. ولا تتميّز الحركات كلّياً بعضها عن بعض، إذ إنّ كلّ حركة هي تحوّل هندسيّ نتج عن حركة أخرى.

باختصار، إنّ الرمل في اقتراحي قد شرع يتّخذ تعبيراً هندسيّاً. فنسيج المصلّى ولون جسمه متماثلان، لكنّ له مظهرين مختلفين. فقد تحوّل من طبيعته التضاريسيّة إلى مُقَرْنَص ذي أوجه تتّخذ شكل مشكاة. إنّ المقرنص عادةً ما يكون منطقة انتقاليّة زخرفيّة بين الجدار والقبّة. فإذا اعتبرنا أنّ لدينا قبّة هنا (يلقي نظرة سريعة إلى الخلف للإشارة إلى خيمة المحطّة أعلاه)، يصبح المصلّى نفسه هو المُقَرْنَص، أي المساحة الانتقاليّة التي تربطك بالسماء، بالكوّة.

أ أ: هذا الجانب مثير للاهتمام حقّاً. فثمّة كذلك ابتكار معماريّ يتّصل بالمقرنصات نفسها، إذ ليس من المفترض أن تكون بالضرورة جزءاً هيكلياً من المبنى، أليس كذلك؟ لقد استعرتَ هنا شيئاً من عالم الديكور والحرف اليدويّة وحوّلته إلى زخرفة هيكليّة.

س ح: بالضبط تماماً. لقد كانت الطريقة التي يتمّ بها إعدادُ المقرنصات على شكل أجزاء مفردة، مصدرَ إلهام لنا في ما يتعلّق بإنشاء قطع يمكن تجميعُها وربطُها بعضها إلى بعض ومن ثَمّ تفكيكها، لأنّ هذا الإجراء كان جزءاً من كرّاس الشروط التي التزمنا بها.

أ أ: إذن في هذه الحالة، يصحّ أن نقول إنّه نظام معياري.
س ح: نعم، إنّه نظام معياريّ، والمقرنصات نفسها هي نظام معياريّ، ولكن في ما يتعلّق بتجربتنا: أصبح هذا النظام هيكليّاً ومكانياً أيضًا. فالفضاء بأكمله أصبح مُقَرْنصاً.

أ أ: رائع. بهذا المعنى، يمكنك مضاعفة النماذج إلى ما لا حدّ له.
س ح: بالفعل، يمكنك ذلك.

أ أ: أفقيّاً، وربما عموديّاً أيضاً؟

س ح: نعم بالتأكيد. فيمكننا، عن طريق إضافة قطع أخرى، إنشاءُ قسم أو ارتفاع، بل يمكننا حتى استعمال مقياس مختلف تماماً. للمقرنص هذه القدرة.

أ أ: أعتقد أنّ هذا يجعله معاصراً على نحو مخصوص، ولكنّه عنصر زخرفيّ إسلاميّ بأتمّ معنى الكلمة أيضًا. فيمكننا القول إنّ المقرنصات هي عنصر فريد من نوعه في العمارة الإسلاميّة. في حين أنّ سائر العناصر الأخرى تطوّرت في سياق الحوار الذي أقيم مع الأشكال المعماريّة الموجودة من قبل.

س ح: بالضبط. أعتقد أنّ الالتزام بالهندسة في العمارة الإسلاميّة كان أمراً مميّزاً من الناحية التاريخيّة. وأقصد بذلك هندسة هذه العناصر، كيف تظهر وكيف تبدأ في إنشاء الفضاء ونحته، أليس كذلك؟ يوجد إذن هذا الرابط مع المشروع، وبالطبع، أمكن ذلك لأنّ هيكل المصلّى حُدّد موقعه تحت الكوّة. ثم لديك مظلّة المحطّة الحاليّة (يحدّد خاصيّة المقطعيّة الشاملة للمحطّة باستخدام يديه)، وأخيراً هناك الكوّة التي ترى من خلالها رقعةً من السماء الزرقاء.

أ أ: يوجد داخل الهيكل مربّع مجوّف. إنّ الأمر يشبه إلى حدّ طابعاً مميّزاً للكعبة. فهذا المربع ذكّرني بحضور ما للكعبة، أو بغيابها. هل كانت هذه إشارة مقصودة؟

س ح: لم يكن في ذلك إحالة مرجعيّة مقصودة حقّاً. ولكن عندما أنظر

المقترح الذي تقدّمتما به لجائزة المصلّى، وقصة الأطوار التي مرّ بها عملكما بصفة أعمّ.

مكتب الهندسة AAU أنسطاس

فسّر مكتب الهندسة AAU أنسطاس مشروع المُصلّى الخاص به على أنه سلسلة من التشابك بين المقاييس والعتبات، بدءاً من دخول البوابات ومروراً بالبنية التحتية الضخمة لمحطة الحج، وأخيراً وصولاً إلى المُصلّى الأصغر حجماً، وفي ذلك إشارة إلى دور جدة كعتبة انتقالية يجتازها الحجاج للوصول إلى مكة المكرمة.

تتجلى هذه المقاييس والأبعاد المتغيرة لمُصلّى مكتب الهندسة AAU أنسطاس عندما ينظر الزوار إليها من وجهات نظر متعددة. يتحول هذا البناء المحلي الصغير إلى مبنى حجري، وتتكشف تفاصيل هندسته المعمارية بتأمل شكله وتصميمه يوماً بعد يوم. فخلال النهار والليل وعبر الفصول المختلفة، تختلف ظروف الإضاءة وتظهر تباعاً تحولات في طبقات الحجر، مما يجعل مظهر المصلى دائم التغير. ولا تعتمد العتبات على المكان فحسب، بل يجري تحديدها أيضاً من خلال الضوء والوقت. وبذلك، تصبح هندسة المُصلّى شاهداً و كاسراً على محيطه المباشر.

كان نهج مكتب الهندسة AAU أنسطاس في بناء المُصلّى راسخاً ومنبسطاً في تقنيات البناء الحجرية التقليدية العالمية والمحلية. جمع الفريق بين مبدأ أساسي في بناء الحجارة، وهو الطنف - طريقة توزيع حمل لهيكل البناء - وممارسة معمارية شائعة في جدة، وهي «التاكليل» - حيث يتم استخدام الخشب لتوزيع الأحمال. ومن خلال هذا النهج، تتحرر الهياكل الحجرية الثقيلة وتصبح متعددة الاستخدامات. وتعزيزاً لفكرة «عدم الثبات» هذه، يمكن أن يكفي 476 حجراً من الحجر المرجاني محلي المصدر، ليُشكل المُصلّى عربة تحميل واحدة.
وعند الدخول إلى المُصلّى عبر ستارة من القماش الشفاف، يظهر فناء مزروع بأشجار الرمان والليمون والزيتون وقاعة صلاة. ينشئ التباين الجلي بين صخب البينالي والحجر الخام للتصميم الخارجي وبين الهندسة الناعمة والمنحنية للتصميم الداخلي والإضاءة المنتشرة أجواءً تجعل المسجد أشبه بملجأ للسكينة والهدوء والتأمل.

خاطرة: وسام العسلي
تراكيب باب المردوم: تجارب في المصلّى

«بسم الله الرحمن الرحيم، أقام هذا المسجد أحمد بن حديدي من ماله ابتغاء ثواب الله، فتم بعون الله على يد موسى بن علي البناء وسعادة فتم في المحرم سنة تسعة وثلث مائة»

على مدخل باب مسجد باب المردوم، احتاج للحظات سريعة لتأمل وإدراك المكان: غابة مصغرة من الأعمدة والنقوش، والقليل من الضوء لتستأنس العين المشهد. في تلك اللحظات التي تعاير فيها العين نفسها، أفكر بالضوء مرة أخرى ، ثم أعود لتأمل مجازات المسجد المقطعة بالحجارة والطوب. للمسجد مقاربة فريدة، ثلاثة تراكيب تكثفت في ظروف هذا المسجد الصغير بمساحته التي لا تتجاوز ستة وثلاثين متراً مربّعاً.

تركيبة الأرض

تحضر التركيبة الأولى في نمط هذا المسجد بمسقطه الأفقي: مربع من تسعة مربعات تحمل تسع قباب. ثلاثة أروقة متداخلة بتكرار عذب ومكثف يحبه أكثر المعماريين حتى الحداثيين منهم. ظهرت طفرة هذا النموذج على خريطة العالم الإسلامي بين القرنين الثامن والعاشر، من الموصل إلى طليطلة ومن أسوان إلى القيروان. وسمّى مؤرخو العمارة الإسلامية هذا التشكيل غير السائد بنمط "التسع قباب"، على اسم مسجد الحاج بيدا بالكرخ، أول مسجد تسع-قباب نعرفه. أتذكر كيف عزاه كروزيل لعمارة المدافن، وأويرت للعمارة الإسلامية المبكّرة في قصر خربة المفجر، وغيرهم لعمارة الخزانات البيزنطية. هذا الأصل المفتوح لنمط عمارة مسجد باب المردوم هو أول تركيبة لاقتراح عمارة دينية غير صرحية، تجريبية ومتنوعة في موادها وتطبيقاتها، وكأنها وصفة هندسية قابلة للتطبيق في سياقات دينية ودنيوية.

تركيبة الحياة اليومية

أقرأ في الدليل المكتوب أن مسجد باب المردوم واحد من مساجد أخرى ذات تسع قباب انتشرت في الحي وبقي منها القليل، بناها حكام وشخصيات بارزون في المجتمع الأندلسي، وحار بها المؤرخون عمّا إذا كانت مساجد خاصّة لعائلات هذه الشخصيات أو مفتوحة للعموم. أفكر في جدران المسجد المصمتة وأتخيلها كما كانت، أقواس مفتوحة تعلوها مشربيات قرميدية، وأميل مع هذا التخيل للقول إن منشأة باب المردوم هي مصلّى مديني بمفهومنا للمصليّات اليوم. وهي واحد من مصليّات طليطلة التي طرزت نسيج المدينة بعمارة دينية متخلخلة تشتبك بالحياة اليومية، مغايرة تماماً لعمارة المساجد الكبيرة التي تشتبك بالسياسة والحكم. فمصلى باب المردوم واحة معمارية بمربع طول ضلعه ستة أمتار فقط، يستخدم العمارة بكثافة ليختلف عما حوله من المدينة، والدنيا، وأحوالهما.

تركيبة السماء

في المصلّى المديني عمل إنشائي ممتع، إذ تختلف كل قبة من القباب التسع عن غيرها، على عكس أكثر مساجد التسع قباب. يبدو المشهد ككولاج ثلاثي الأبعاد من تشكيلات مختلفة للأقواس المتقاطعة تحت القباب. أقرأ في غرفة الفندق عن الأقواس المتقاطعة في العمارة الأندلسية، لأعرف أن أول ظهور كان في توسعة جامع قرطبة الكبير على يد الخليفة الحكم الثاني، قبل ثلاثين عاماً فقط من بناء مصلى باب المردوم. أتخيّل كيف لهذه التقنية الفنيّة أن تفتن بنّاء ومعمار المصلّى (موسى بن علي) [illegible] موسى غارقاً في سبر تكويناتها العديدة المحتملة. يدير الأقواس بزوايا مختلفة، مربعة وثمانية وست عشرية، ليبتكر تشكيلات جديدة. يعود ليكتشف أن بعض هذه التشكلات هي نسخ فراكتاليّة من قباب مسجد قرطبة، كالقبة المركزية المرتفعة عن غيرها في المصلى. تبدو القباب مساحة لتجريب سريع لتقنيات الإنشاء على مقياس صغير، فهي ليست بإتقان قباب مسجد قرطبة المزخرفة لكنها أكثر منها غنىً بالحلول المختلفة. كأنها مزّاجة تكوينية لحلول تركت أثراً على عمارة القباب المتقاطعة في الأندلس، من عمارة ملوك الطوائف مروراً بالعمارة القوطية وحتى حداثة إسبانيا.

في لقاء تركيبات عمارة باب المردوم دروس لكيف يمكن استخدام المصلّى كمساحات تجريب معمارية وعمرانية واجتماعية، حيث يسمح المقياس بالتجريب، والمساحة بالتكثيف. كأني أرى بهذا المصلى المبني في القرن العاشر تجربة تشبه المسابقة والسبق في عمارة المصلّيات وهو امتداد تاريخي لما فعله المعماريون في هذا الكتاب من دفع العمارة الدينية، فكرياً وتطبيقياً، نحو آفاق أكثر تعقيداً وحرية.

هو حسّ المادّيّة وطريقة البناء. وهذا يقودني إلى مفهوم آخر وظّفتماه أيضاً في مقترحكما، وأقصد به ما أطلقتما عليه تسمية ثنائيّة الفناء وفضاء الصلاة. فهل يمكنكما تعريفنا بأهميّة هذه الثنائيّة في تطوير مفهوم المصلّى؟

إ أ: أحد الأشياء التي حرصنا على الترويج لها حقّاً هي فكرة العتبة، وهي شكل من أشكال الهندسة المعماريّة التي تربط العديد من الأماكن في الجنوب العالمي، حيث ما فتئت الهندسة المعماريّة تزداد نفاذيّةً أكثر فأكثر. على هذا النحو، فقد أردنا لدى إنجازنا مقترح المصلّى، أن نتعمّق في دراسة أشكال فضاءات الصلاة وأنماطها التقليديّة جدّاً، ومن ثَمّ حاولنا إضفاء طابع رسميّ على تفسير جديد، علاوةً على مناقشة حجم البنية التحتيّة لمظلّات محطّة الحج، والسعي إلى إيجاد طريقة تخوّل لها أن تكوّن فضاءً منغلقاً يرتفع على مدى أكبر بكثير من حجم الإنسان. وقد توصّلنا إلى تجسيم ذلك من خلال توظيف ازدواجيّة الفضاء: فلدينا قسم يركّز على الضوء الذي يخترقه، وآخر يجسّد فكرة الطبيعة، فيجد الزوّار في ذلك عاملاً يدفعهم إلى عزل أنفسهم وإعادة الاتّصال بروحانيّتهم الخاصّة.

ع م: يبدو لي إذن أنّ للحديقة أهميّة كبيرة في المصلّى. فهل لكما أن تشرحا كيف ساهمت في التجربة المكانيّة التي أشرتما إليها، والجوّ الروحاني الذي أوجدته الطبيعة، والتأمل داخل مكان الصلاة؟

ي أ: أتصوّر أنّ المشروع هو عبارة عن سلسلة من العتبات، مثلما قال إلياس. فإذا نظرت إليه من مسافة بعيدة، أمكنك أن تطلق عليه تسمية: شكل عضويّ. ولكن مع اقترابك منه، تبدأ بعض التفاصيل في الانكشاف. وهكذا تبرز إذن العتبة الأولى للمشروع. وبمجرّد أن يقترب منه المرء أكثر، يدخل فضاءً ومن ثَمّ يجد نفسه في فناء أو حديقة. ثم نجتاز عتبة أخرى تفضي إلى مكان الصلاة. إنّ هذه السلسلة من العتبات تربط العمارة الهندسيّة الخاصّة بالمقترح، بالنمط الذي يُعدّ مكوّناً أساسياً في العمارة الإسلاميّة. وقد تساءلنا بطريقة استفزازيّة إلى حدّ ما ونحن في بداية هذا المشروع، عمّا إذا كانت العمارة الإسلاميّة موجودة فعلاً أم لا. ذلك أنّ ما يوجد في واقع الأمر، هو أنماط مرتبطة بالعمارة في الإسلام، يمكن تحويلها وتكييفها. ولهذا الأمر صلةٌ ما بالعمل الذي نقوم به في فلسطين، فإذا أمعنتَ النظر في المدينة الفلسطينيّة التاريخيّة ستكتشف أنّه لا وجود لهندسة معماريّة ذات خصائص مميّزة هناك. فالعمارة تستمدّ خصوصيّتها هنا من ارتباطها بالنمط والمناخ، وطريقة العيش التي تتأثر بأبعاد المكان والنوافذ والعتبات؛ لذلك أنشئت فضاءات مشتركة بين الخارج والداخل، فضاءات ليست عامّة ولا خاصّة. إنّها ليست فضاءات عامّة بأتمّ معنى الكلمة حقّاً. وهي ليست فضاءات خاصّة بأتمّ معنى الكلمة كذلك. وكان من شأن ذلك أن أعطانا هندسة معماريّة غنيّة، لكنّها من جهة أخرى مرنة لها قابليّة كبيرة للتكيّف.

ع م: يبدو لي أنّ العلاقة بين النمط والقضايا البيئيّة أمر أساسيّ في المشروع. والعتبة هي نتيجة لهذا الأمر، فهي مرتبطة ارتباطاً وثيقاً بمفهوم الطبقات، وطبقات البناء، وكذلك بتصميم الفضاء في شكل طبقات متعدّدة على أساس أنّها تمثّل انتقالاً من مكان إلى آخر. وهكذا، فعلى الرغم من أنّ بين يديك حجراً ثابتاً، فإنّك تحاول أن تجد توازناً بين الحجر وأنواع أخرى من موادّ البناء التي من شأنها أن تسمح بالانتقال من الخارج إلى الداخل، بفضل توظيف عنصرَيْ الضوء والحديقة. وبذلك أنت تجمع أشياء كثيرة بعضها مع بعض، بدءاً من البناء وصولاً إلى المعنى، مروراً بالتقاليد والإحساس بالفضاء والمكان. وهذا ما يقودني إلى سؤالكما عن المبادئ الأساسيّة التي التزمتما بها، لاسيما في ما يخصّ مشروعكما الأكبر الحامل عنوان "مسائل الحجر"، الذي يسعى إلى تطوير استخدام حجر البناء في الهندسة المعماريّة المعاصرة. فكيف يساهم الحجر في تعميق الخطاب حول القضايا البيئيّة المتعلّقة بتأثير الكربون ومقاومة الضغط واستغلال المحاجر بشكل مسؤول؟ وإذا تناولنا استعمال الحجر على نطاق أوسع، فكيف تريان دوره في تطوير ممارسات معماريّة أكثر استدامة؟

إ أ: هذا سؤال خطير جدّاً (يبتسم)، ولكن ربما كان من المهمّ أن نتّبع تاريخ مشروع "مسائل الحجر". فقد ولدنا في عائلة من المهندسين المعماريّين وكان جدّنا مهندساً معماريّاً، وبنى عدّة جسور باستعمال الحجارة الضخمة. وقد ورثنا في فلسطين قانوناً أصدرته الدولة العثمانيّة قبل ما يزيد على مائة عام، يقضي باستخدام الحجر في المباني. ثم شهد استخدام الحجر تطوّراً خلال القرن الماضي، فابتعد شيئاً فشيئاً عن القيام بدور المكوّن الهيكليّ والمعدِّل الحراري، ليقتصر استخدامه على اتّخاذه غطاءً زخرفيّاً للهياكل الخرسانيّة فقط، وقد ازداد هذا التوجّه انتشاراً بعد خمسينيّات القرن الماضي وستينيّاته، عندما ساد نزوع عالميّ وإقبال متعاظم على استخدام الخرسانة المسلّحة.

وقد أدّى استعمال الحجر في فلسطين، إلى تحوّل في التشكّلات الحضريّة، ارتبط بطريقة استخراج الحجارة، ذلك أنّ كل بناء كان له محجر في الفناء الخلفيّ، فنتج عن ذلك أنّ البصمة الكربونيّة كانت منخفضة إلى حدّ بعيد. بناءً عليه، أردنا - في ظلّ أزمة المناخ والتحوّل الذي طرأ على مدننا، وبمساعدة التكنولوجيا وما يملكه قاطعو الحجارة في فلسطين من معرفة غنيّة جدّاً- أن نستكشف الطريقة التي تخوّلنا إيلاء استخدام الحجر منزلة جديدة ضمن لغة معاصرة، مع العمل في الوقت نفسه على معالجة القضايا البيئيّة.
في بادئ الأمر، انطلق المشروع في صورة مقاربة تجريبيّة لاستخدام الحجر، وشرعنا في تطوير عناصر معماريّة مختلفة مثل الأقبية والأسقف المسطّحة، والأعمدة، والألواح الحجريّة، والسواكف وغيرها من الموادّ التي استُعملت بوصفها عناصر مستقلّة. وفي سياق هذا المشروع، أنجزنا إلى حدّ اليوم، نحو عشرة تكرارات تصميميّة مختلفة في مستويات متعدّدة، وقد بلغنا الآن مرحلة صار بإمكاننا فيها تجميع الهياكل والمباني على أساس هذه المبادئ.

ع م: إنّه لمن الرائع حقّاً أن يستمع المرءُ إلى تفاصيل تخصّ المقاربة متعدّدة الطبقات التي انبنى عليها تفكيركما في الحجر، باعتباره مادّة بناء يمكن أن تكون معاصرة لنا، ولكنها ترتبط في الوقت نفسه بالإحساس بالفضاء والمكان. شكراً لكما لتفضّلكما بسرد قصّة

على الحجر بوصفه مادّة بناء، وسعينا إلى تبيّن كيف اضطلع الحجر بدور مركزيّ في بناء المدن الفلسطينيّة خلال أوائل القرن العشرين. ومن ثَمّ الانتهاء إلى دراسة كيف تغيّر تطوّر مادّة البناء على مدى المائة عام الماضية تغيّراً تامّاً. إنّ أحد العناصر الرئيسيّة في البناء الحجريّ الذي أثار اهتمامنا، هو دراسة الكيفيّة التي أزيل بها طابع القداسة عن استخدامِ الحجر، وتيسير الوصول إليه بوصفه مادّةَ بناء متاحة للجميع. وعلى هذا المنوال، لم يعد استعمال الحجر يقتصر على الأنماط النبيلة فحسب، بل صار له تأثير في الظروف المناخيّة والاجتماعيّة التي نمرّ بها هنا، وفي جميع أنحاء العالم. وقد قمنا في هذا السياق، بدراسة التصنيفِ التاريخيّ للمصلّى، والاستخدامِ المعاصر للهياكل الحجريّة الضخمة، لاسيما من خلال فنّ قطع الحجارة- الطريقة التي تُقطع بها الحجارة من أجل إنشاء هياكل قائمة بذاتها- باعتباره وسيلة لإعادة إدراج الحجر ضمن معجم أو مفردات خاصّة بالإنتاج المعماريّ، أكثر ديمقراطيّةً وانفتاحاً. وهكذا نستنتج أنّ المصلّى يُعتبر شكلاً مقدّساً ونبيلاً جدّاً من أشكال الهندسة المعماريّة، ولكنّه في الوقت نفسه شكل هندسيّ معماريّ يُفترض أن يكون متاحاً لأكبر شريحة من السكان. وإنّ محاولة تحقيق التوازن بين هذين البعدين هي وسيلة لإلغاء طابع القداسة عن الحجر.

ع م: لذا، اسمحا لي أن أتابع في هذا الاتّجاه، وأضيف سؤالاً آخر يتعلّق بالحجر. ففي المقترح الذي تقدّمتما به لجائزة المصلّى، وفي عملكما بشكل عام، تطرحان مسألة خفّة الحجر. فهل بوسعكما أن تخبرانا كيف أدرجتما مسألة خفّة الحجر في صلب تصميمكما، وكيف أدّت إلى إعادة النظر في التصوّر التقليديّ الذي يتعامل مع الحجر باعتباره مادّةً صلبة وثقيلة؟ وما هو الدور الذي اضطلعت به خفّة الحجر في تحديد خصائص مشروعكما المكانيّة والمناخيّة؟

يوسف أنسطاس: ربما يحسن للإجابة عن هذا السؤال أن نبدأ بشيء بالغ الدلالة، فالحجر بشكل عامّ له كثافة مماثلة لكثافة الزجاج.

وهكذا، فإذا أخذت كتلة من الزجاج مساوية لكتلة من الحجر، فسيكون لهما وزن مماثل. ولكن عادةً ما تعتبر هاتان المادّتان متضادّتين، إذ إنّ إحداهما شفيفة، والأخرى معتّمة تعتيماً كاملاً. فإذا عدنا القهقرى في الزمن ورجعنا إلى روبرت هوك، وهو مهندس معروف عاش في القرن السابع عشر، ألفيناه قد عمل على حلّ لغز الشكل المثاليّ للقوس، وقد توصّل إلى ذلك فعلاً لكنّه ضمّن الحلّ في وصيّته، فلم يُكشف عن السرّ إلاّ بعد وفاته. وقد استمدّ هذا الحلّ الخاصّ بالشكل المثاليّ للقوس، من شكل خطّيّ مرن مقلوب، منحنى السلسلة (يرسم بيديه شكل قوس مقلوب). وقد أثمر هذا الحلّ إنتاج هيكل للضغط فقط، حيث لا يوجد شدّ، ومنذ ذلك الحين اعتُبر الحجر مادّة قابلة للضغط فقط. لكنّ هذا التصوّر لم يكن صحيحاً تمام الصحّة، وعلى الرغم من أنّ نظريّته حقّقت كثيراً من التقدّم والتطوّر في مجال البناء الحجريّ، فإنّها قلّلت في الوقت نفسه من حجم إمكانات البناء الحجريّ. فلو تأمّلنا بناءً حجرياً يعود تاريخ إنشائه إلى ما يزيد على خمسة آلاف سنة، للاحظنا استخدام السواكف الحجريّة والألواح الحجريّة كذلك، وهي مثبّتة بواسطة الشدّ أيضاً. فقد كان لدينا في القديم معجمٌ خاصّ بالعناصر المعماريّة الحجريّة التي تعمل بواسطة الشدّ والضغط معاً. فعندما يبدأ الحجر في مقاومة الشدّ، تظهر خفّة وزنه ويترتّب على ذلك ظهورُ العديد من الإمكانات فجأة.

ع م: بالإضافة إلى عنصر الماديّة نفسها، تلفت الانتباهَ كذلك طريقةُ البناء التي استخدمتماها، وهي تقنيةُ التطنيف أو الوصلة الحاملة. فهل لكما أن تشرحا كيف وُظّف القوس المزخرف في مقترحكما من حيث صلته بالحجر والخفّة والروحانيّة؟

ي أ: خلال أوّل زيارة قمنا بها إلى المدينة القديمة في جدّة، رأينا هياكل مبنيّة من الحجارة المرجانيّة. وبإمكان المرء أن يرى داخل هذه الهياكل على طول الجدران، أجزاء خشبيّة أفقيّة مشدودة إلى دعامات مؤقّتة يتمّ تركيبها خلال فترات الصيانة. ففي بعض الأحيان يحتاجون إلى استبدال أو إصلاح الحجر المرجانيّ، وهذا لا يمكن أن يتمّ عندما يكون حوامل، لذلك يقومون بتثبيت دعامات تسند الأجزاء الخشبيّة الأفقيّة، ما يعطي بعض الراحة للحجر المرجاني. ثم يقومون بإزالة الحجر التالف وإصلاحه واستبداله. وفور إزالة الدعامات، يشرعون في تحميل الجدران بالكامل مرّة أخرى.

لقد اعتبرنا أنّ هذه الطريقة تدعو إلى التشكيك في جدوى قوالب البناء والهياكل الحجريّة. إنّ البصمة الكربونيّة للهياكل الحجريّة أشدّ انخفاضاً بكثير من نظيرتها الموجودة في الهياكل الخرسانيّة والفولاذيّة بل وحتى الخشبيّة أيضاً، لاسيما إذا كان المصدر الذي نحصل منه على الحجر قريباً منّا. ومع ذلك، شرعنا في البحث عن أمثلة مرجعيّة اعتمدت البناء بالحجر مع الحدّ الأدنى من قوالب البناء، مثل قبّة كنيسة "سانتا ماريا ديل فيوري" في فلورنسا، التي بُنيت بدون قوالب بناء، عن طريق استخدام هيكل حلزوني. ويمكن العثور على أمثلة أخرى في الهياكل المملوكيّة، التي دمجت بين القبو التقليديّ والطَّنَف.

إنّ إنشاء هيكل ذي قوس مزخرف يقتضي تثبيت كلّ طبقة من الحجر بعيداً في الفضاء عن الطبقة الموجودة تحتها (يرسم بيديه حلقات ذات أحجام تتدرّج تنازليّاً)، ولا يتطلّب أيّ قوالب بناء لأنّ كل طبقة مثبّتة في موضعها. لقد استخدمنا مبادئ تطنيف مماثلة لدى إنجازنا مقترح المصلّى الذي تقدّمنا به للجائزة، وقد تأثّرنا في الوقت نفسه بما رأيناه في جدّة، إذ أخذنا في الاعتبار أنّ المشروع سيُجمَّع ويُفكَّك عدّة مرّات.

إ أ: سأضيف أمراً واحدًا فقط له علاقة مباشرة بعملك يا دكتور علي. والسؤال الذي يواجهنا باستمرار في الإستوديو هو تقرير ما إذا كان ينبغي علينا الاستمرار في بناء المباني، أو تركيز جهودنا أكثر في الحفاظ عليها من خلال استكشاف صيغ ترميم جديدة. لذلك، وهذا ما واجهناه نحن أيضاً في هذه التجربة، فقد اندرج تفكيرنا في المصلّى ضمن منهجيّة حاولنا فيها تصميم مبنى سيعمّر مدّة طويلة من الزمن، مع الحرص في الوقت نفسه على وضع تصوّر يجعله قابلاً ليُفكّك ويُحمل إلى الطبيعة ليصبح قطعة أثريّة أو موقعاً أثرياً. لذلك اعتمدت طريقة البناء إلى حدّ كبير على هذه الاعتبارات، وعلى فكرة الدعامة أيضاً.

ع م: يتبيّن لي أنّ المفهوم البيئيّ مهمّ جدًا بالنسبة إليكما، في ما يتعلّق باستخدام مادّة البناء نفسها، من حيث دقّتها واستدامتها ودورة حياة الكربون المتجسّد فيها، وكذلك من حيث تجديد المبنى. ويبدو لي كذلك أنّ مبدأً آخر احتفظتما به إضافة إلى كل هذه المبادئ الأساسيّة،

ما مجالها، فإنّه لا يزال محافظًا في الأساس على صورتها في زمن النبي محمّد (صلّى الله عليه وسلّم) بوصفها: كياناً سماويّاً وُضع في حرم أرضيّ. لقد كانت الكعبة قائمة دائمًا بمفردها وسط فضاء مفتوح يحيط به ما نعتبره المُصلّى الرئيسيّ والأكثر أهمّيّةً ويسمّى "الصحن"، وهو يمتدّ في جوهره عبر العالَم بأكمله، بوصفه فضاءً متّصلاً لا حدود له، يجد فيه المسلمون، أينما كانوا، مكاناً لهم للتواصل أثناء الصلاة.

من هنا، يمكننا أن نشرع في إدراك كيف تجد مجموعة متنوّعة من الفضاءات المخصّصة للصلاة سياقَها في عالمنا. ويخبرنا الرسول (صلّى الله عليه وسلّم) أنّ الدنيا قاطبةً قد خلقت لتكون مسجداً تؤدّى فيه الصلاة: «جُعلت لي الأرض مسجداً وطَهوراً، فأيّما رجل من أمّتي أدركته الصلاةُ فليُصلِّ». فهذا الحديث النبويّ الشريف يؤكّد بشكل أو بآخر مبدأ امتداد المصلّى حول الكعبة الشريفة ليغطّي العالَم بأكمله. ومن الجدير بالتبيين أيضاً أن نذكر أنّ مصطلح المسجد في القرآن يشير إلى المسجد الحرام في مكّة والمسجد الأقصى في القدس، وهو لا يعيّن مبنًى أو هيكلاً ملموساً، بل يحيل على فضاء حَرَم مبارَك في هذا العالم - ﴿ سُبْحَانَ الَّذِي أَسْرَى بِعَبْدِهِ لَيْلاً مِّنَ الْمَسْجِدِ الْحَرَامِ إِلَى الْمَسْجِدِ الأَقْصَى الَّذِي بَارَكْنَا حَوْلَهُ لِنُرِيَهُ مِنْ آيَاتِنَا إِنَّهُ هُوَ السَّمِيعُ الْبَصِيرُ﴾ (سورة الإسراء، الآية 1).

استناداً إلى ذلك، ندرك أنّ العالَم الطبيعيّ هو انعكاس السماء على الأرض، وبذلك فهو يشكّل البيئة الأكثر بدائيّةً التي نعاين من خلالها تجلّي المقدّس - فالطبيعة هي المصلّى الأوّلي. وبناءً عليه، لن يكون من الضروريّ إقامةُ مسجد، يخصَّص فضاءً للصلاة، وسط الطبيعة البكر الطَّهور. فلا تنشأ الحاجة إلى بناء هياكل المساجد إلاّ عندما يتوجّب علينا إنشاءُ فضاء للصلاة الخاشعة في بيئة مجزّأة، فقدت الجمال الأصليّ المميّز للعالم الطبيعي.

إنّ الصلاة تقتضي الدخول في حالة تأمّليّة تستلزم الابتعاد عن سياق حياتنا اليوميّة القائم على التجزّؤ والتشتّت، والتوجّه نحو عالَم جوهرنا الروحيّ. ومنطلق ذلك أن تنعقد النيّةُ في نفس المصلّي، ويبدأ ذلك ويتعزّز من خلال وضع أنفسنا في البيئة الواقعيّة الملائمة لأداء الصلاة في خشوع- أي فضاء تأمليّ يساعد على استعادة السكينة الروحيّة، ويضبط الإيقاع الحقيقيّ الذي سيسير قلبنا على هديه.

فإذا أردنا أن نبني مساجد تُعتمد فضاءات لأداء الصلاة الجماعيّة، وجب علينا حينها أن نقيم مبانيَ تعيد إنشاء تجربة السكينة الملهِمة التي يمنحنا إياها العالمُ الطبيعيّ. ذلك أنّه غالباً ما يُساء فهمُ عمليّة زخرفة المساجد وأماكن الصلاة الأخرى باستعمال أنماط زخرفيّة هندسيّة وأشكال حيويّة - أصبحت طابعاً مميّزاً للعمارة الإسلاميّة - فيُنظر إليها خطأً على أنّها تمرين تجميليّ يركّز على مجرّد زخرفة السطح. بيد أنّ الأمر أعمق من ذلك بكثير في الحقيقة، فلئن كانت العمليّة تجميليّة فليس ذلك إلاّ وفق المعنى الأصليّ للجذر اللغويّ في العبارة الإنجليزيّة (cosmetic) أي: جعل الزخرفة شبيهة بالكون، وتفسير الأشكال الواقعيّة الملموسة في العالم الطبيعيّ والنظام الإبداعيّ الكامن وراءها، ومن ثَمّ تثبيتها على المباني المخصّصة للصلاة. وعلى هذا النحو، تمكّن هذه الطريقة في الزخرفة المصلّين من أن يشعروا بالتناغم مع أشكال وإيقاعات النظام الإلهيّ المسيّر للعالم الطبيعي، القائم في جوهر كياننا نحن أيضاً، ذلك الذي نختبره غريزيّاً من خلال فطرتنا التي جُبلنا عليها، وبفضله أُلهمنا الإقرار بوحدانيّة الله.

أمّا المُصلّى فيمثّل ببساطة فضاءً يخصَّص للصلاة وسط المجال الطبيعي. ذلك أنّه متّصل مباشرةً بالأرض، بوصفها فضاءً أعلن النبي محمّد (صلّى الله عليه وسلّم) بأنّه مكان مقدّس بأكمله، يصلح لأن يقيم فيه المرء الصلاة حيثما وُجد فيه. وقد يكون المصلّى في أصل طبيعته مكاناً سريع الزوال، فهو يمثّل ببساطة المكان الذي قرّر فرد أو مجموعة ما إقامةَ الصلاة فيه. ولا يتطلّب هذا الفضاء توسيع نطاق النظام الطبيعيّ ليشمل مكان الصلاة من خلال تجسيم ذلك النظام معماريّاً، لأنّ المصلّى يرتبط بالطبيعة ارتباطاً مباشراً.

إنّ هذه الأفكار التي عرضتُها الآن، قد تيقّنت من صحّتها مباشرةً، من خلال تجربة شخصيّة مررت بها أثناء رحلة قمت بها في جبال الأطلس، خارج مدينة فاس. فقد كنت في زيارة إلى قرية صغيرة دُفن فيها رجل تقيّ ألهمتني كتاباته فكرة القيام بهذه الرحلة. وأثناء وجودي هناك، ارتفع صوت الأذان معلنا حلول وقت الصلاة، ولم أكن أعرف إلى أين أذهب، لذلك اتّبعت بكل بساطة أفواج الناس الذين كانوا يسرعون قاصدين اتّجاهاً معيّناً قدّرت باديَ الأمر أنّه مسجد القرية. ووصلنا في نهاية المطاف إلى فضاء كبير مفتوح، حيث اصطفّ السكّان المحلّيون جنباً إلى جنب استعداداً لإقامة الصلاة. فاتّخذنا أماكننا في صفوف امتدّت في الهواء الطلق نطلّ على الجبال والوديان، محاطين بأشجار البلّوط والفلّين، وقد أُخذت منها طبقةٌ من الفلين فُرشت أرضاً لتكون سطحاً مريحاً للصلاة. حينها أدركتُ أنّه ما من حاجة في هذه البيئة الجميلة، إلى بناء مسجد. فيكفي فقط تحديد رقعة من الأرض لتكون فضاءً يخصَّص للصلاة. لقد كان العالَم الطبيعيّ هو مصلّانا، وقد استقمنا نؤدّي الصلاة مدفوعين بطبيعتنا الأصليّة التي جبلنا عليها، بفطرتنا، في كنف النظام الطبيعيّ الذي خلقه الله.

كانت تجربة بسيطة لكنّها عميقة جعلتنا ندرك أنّ الطبيعة البِكر هي البيت الحقيقي الذي تسكن إليه أرواحنا. فنحن في تآلف مع جوهرها الذي هو جوهرنا الحقيقيّ أيضاً، وليس ثمّة أيُّ انفصال أو ثنائيّة بين طبيعتنا الأوّليّة والعالم الطبيعيّ - فكلاهما خلق جزءاً لا يتجزّأ من النظام الإلهيّ الذي يسيّر الوجود، ومن خلالهما يتجلّى العالَم السماوي في المجال البشريّ.

فعندما نعقد النيّة على الصلاة في مكان معيّن، فإنّنا نبادر إلى تثبيت أنفسنا في هذا السياق الروحيّ ونتفاعل مع مركزنا - وهو في الأساس مركز الوجود بأكمله. وما ييسّر علينا الوفاء بهذا الالتزام متى عقدت النيّة، هو المصلّى الذي لا شكل له، إنّه العزم المبارك الذي نحمله في دواخلنا ويجعلنا متأهّبين لأداء الصلاة أينما كنّا. ومن خلال ربطنا هذا المركز بمكان ما، عن طريق فعل الصلاة، نتيح للمصلّى أن يتّخذ شكلاً ملموساً. وعلى هذا النحو، يصبح هذا المصلّى المخصوص امتداداً شخصيّاً للمصلّى الأصليّ، أي للصّحن المحيط بالكعبة الشريفة، ونقطةَ اتّصال في الوقت نفسه أيضًا بالكعبة ذاتها بوصفها رمزاً لمركز وجودنا ولتوجّهنا الروحيّ نحو الأبديّة.

حوار: علي ملكاوي مع إلياس ويوسف أنسطاس

علي ملكاوي: يستكشف هذا المعرض وهذا الكتاب المُصلّى باعتباره صنفاً مرناً وقابلاً للتكيّف، وهو ينشأ بشكل عضويّ تلبيةً للحاجة إلى فضاء تقام فيه الصلاة سواء أكانت فرديّة أم جماعيّة. وعلى هذا النحو، فإنّ هذه الفضاءات تجسّد مبادئ التصميم ذات الصدى الثقافي، فهي تدمج الروحانيّة في التعبير الهندسيّ المعماريّ إدماجاً متناغماً. سؤالي هو الآتي: كيف تريان قدرة المُصلّى على أن يساهم أو يتماشى مع رؤيتكما الأوسع القائمة على إنشاء هندسة معماريّة مستدامة وذات أهمّيّة ثقافيّة على حدّ سواء، والحال أنّ المصلّى هو فضاء مرن موجّه نحو الصلاة؟

إلياس أنسطاس: إحدى الطرق المناسبة للإجابة عن هذا السؤال هي تفحّص العمل الذي ارتكزت عليه ممارستُنا، على مدى السنوات الاثنتيْ عشرة أو الثلاث عشرة الماضية، ولاسيما البحوث التي أجريناها

والتقنيات الجديدة، والموادّ الجديدة التي يجدها الناس جذّابة. لكنّنا صرنا الآن أكثر ثقة في أنفسنا، وأصبحنا نستخدم مواردنا، كما قلت، لنروي قصّتنا. ومن المهمّ أن نتعلّم من كلّ هذه العمليّات والتقنيات، ذلك أنّنا عندما نتأمّل التاريخ، يتبيّن لنا في الحقيقة أنّ العالم لم يكن في يوم ما منعزلاً بعضه عن بعض البتّة. ربما كانت وسائل التواصل أقلّ وأبسط، لكنّها كانت مترابطة دائماً بشكل من الأشكال. ويتأكّد ذلك خاصّةً إذا تأمّلنا مثال جدّة، فهي مكان استقرّ فيه منذ سنوات طويلة، أشخاصٌ ينحدرون من مناطق مختلفة، حاملين أفكارهم، وقد توصّلنا معاً إلى خلق هويّة للمكان (يضع راحتيه إحداهما فوق الأخرى).

س د: إنّ هذا التعدّد الثقافيّ - كما تراه في الطعام هنا - له تأثير حقيقيّ في كلّ هؤلاء الحجّاج الذين استقرّوا هنا على مرّ السنين. فمن شأن ذلك أن يخلق مزيجاً فريداً. لقد تحدّثت مؤخّراً مع أحد الأشخاص فأخبرني أنّ الكلمة التي تعبّر لديه عن جدّة هي "اليخنة" (ابتسمت ابتسامة عريضة)، وهي مزيج من موادّ مختلفة، لكنّها تشكّل خليطاً لذيذاً جدّاً (انفجر كلاهما بالضحك)، وليس بوسعنا تحديد أصل اليخنة بالضبط.

ف د: لنعد إلى فكرة الشرق والغرب. فطريقة التفكير الغربيّة تقوم على تقسيم كلّ مشكلة إلى أجزاء فرعيّة، لذا فإنّ الفنّ والهندسة المعماريّة والرسم، وغير ذلك، ولنقل الطعام، جميعها مختلفة جدّاً بعضها عن بعض، أما في تقاليدنا نحن فجميعها متماثلة، تمامًا كما سبق وقلتِ بالضبط، فعليكِ أن تشمّي رائحة المبنى وتتنفّسيه. والأمر لا يتعلّق برائحة المبنى فحسب، بل رائحة السماء أيضاً، إنّها كلّها معاً مرّةً واحدةً. وهذا ما يبعث الشعور بالمكان، والشعور بالمكان هو الشعور بالانتماء. والأهمّ في ذلك كلّه، أنّ توفّقَ المهندس المعماريّ في الإحساس بشعور الانتماء، سيوصل هذا الإحساس نفسه إلى المستخدمين فيشعرون هم أيضاً بالانتماء.

س د: وتلك هي رسالتنا مدى الحياة.

الدباغ للهندسة المعمارية

يتصل تصميم الدباغ للهندسة المعمارية اتصالاً وثيقاً بموقع محطة الحج «ميقات» - وهي المحطة التي يمر عليها الحجاج والمعتمرون من أجل «الإحرام». سعى تصميم المُصَلى إلى تسخير ذاكرة مئات الآلاف من الحجاج والمعتمرين بهذه المساحة المعينة على مدى سنوات عديدة، في تلك اللحظة المهمة من رحلتهم الروحية لممارستهم شعائر دينهم.
إن «الإحرام» هو نية الدخول في النسك لأداء فريضة الحج - وهو إعلان داخلي وخارجي عن الالتزام بالطهارة والبعد عن أي مشتتات مادية. ويجب التجرد من أي مظاهر تنم عن الثروة أو المكانة الاجتماعية، مع تغطية الجسم بقطعة قماش بيضاء بسيطة وغير مخيطة.

وقد جلب فريق الدباغ للهندسة المعمارية بعداً مقدساً روحانياً لتصميم المُصَلى من خلال الإشارة إلى قطعة القماش البيضاء التي يرتديها الحجاج والمعتمرون عند «الإحرام». وكان تصميم المُصَلى الخاص عبارة عن أسطوانة مركزية مكونة من جدران ترابية منخفضة وشاشات خصوصية شبكية منسوجة من خيوط الألياف الزجاجية، تعلوها مظلة دائرية هندسية شراعية شبكية من الفولاذ والنسيج المستدام. يمكن خفض ورفع الألواح الشبكية الخارجية شديدة المرونة لتوفير تكوينات ونقاط دخول متعددة. بما في ذلك مساحة مركزية مفتوحة لاستقبال العامة، مثل المعارض. إن التكيف المعاصر للهندسة الإسلامية عبر مظلة المُصَلى من شأنه أن يمد جسراً للتواصل بين الماضي والحاضر، تكريماً لتاريخ المكان واحتفاءً بذكراه. على مر التاريخ، كان الحجاج والمعتمرون المسافرون برّاً وبحراً يشرعون في أداء طقوس «الإحرام» عند وصولهم إلى جدة، جنوب المدينة عند الميناء بالقرب من حيّ البلد. وهو المحل الدائم المناسب لمُصلّى فريق الدباغ للهندسة المعمارية للهندسة المعمارية، فهو يعيد ذكرى نقطة دخول الحجاج إلى جدة إلى موقعها الأصلي.

خاطرة: خالد عزام

المُصلّى الأوّل

توجد الحالة الإنسانيّة بين بعدين أساسيّين. أحدهما هو حالتنا الجسديّة الفعليّة التي نلامسها من خلال أجسادنا، وهي تتحدّد انطلاقاً من ارتباطها بزمان ومكان معيّنين. أمّا البعد الثاني فهو روحنا الأبديّة التي تسعى إلى أن تحقّق اكتمالها في عالَم الأبد. إنّ أداء الصلاة هو جمع بين هذين البُعدَين.

فعندما نصلّي، نولّي وجوهنا نحو الأبديّة ونتواصل معها رمزيّاً من خلال ما نحمل في أرواحنا من شوق إليها. ومع ذلك، فإنّنا ننقل هذا الشوق من خلال العالَم الحسيّ الذي يشغله جسمنا ولا يمكنه التعالي فوقه. وما إن نعقد النيّة على الصلاة، حتى نثبّت أنفسنا في مكان مخصوص، مبتعدين عن عالَم اللّهو والتشتّت الذي يحكم حياتنا اليوميّة. ثم يبدأ فعل الصلاة، فنرسّخ هذا التثبت في صميم وعينا سعياً للاهتداء إلى مركز ذاتنا. إنّ هذا المركز قائم الذات بوصفه وحدة للوجود، تقع بعيداً عن عالم اللّهو والتشتّت والتعدّد الذي يسيطر على حياتنا اليوميّة. وبفضل أداء الصلاة، يتحقّق لنا التواصل مع مركزنا، ويغدو هذا المركزُ المحورَ الرأسيَّ للعالَم السماويّ، وبدءاً منه تنطلق رحلة الروح إلى الأبديّة. فاتّصالنا بمركزنا، عن طريق الصلاة، هو الذي يمنحنا نعمة استكناه روحنا الأبديّة.

وكما أنّ كلّ مسلم يولّي وجهه نحو مركزه منتوياً القيام برحلته الروحيّة، فكذلك تتّجه المجموعة المجتمعيّة نحو مركزها المشترَك. والكعبة الشريفة هي مركز العالَم لدى المجتمعات المسلمة، ولكنّها كذلك نقطة التقاء السماء والأرض، وقد جسّم هذا الالتقاءَ نزولُ الحجر الأسود من السماء إلى مكّة المكرّمة. وعلى هذا النحو، تمثّل الكعبةُ بداية المحور الرأسيّ الذي يصل بين السماء والأرض، ومن ثَمّ فإنّ المجتمع المسلم لا يتوجّه نحو موقع جغرافيّ فحسب حين يتوجّه نحو مكّة المكرّمة، بل نحو المحور الروحيّ المرتبط بالسماء أيضاً.

ولا تقع الكعبة الشريفة داخل مسجد بالمعنى المحدّد لمصطلح مسجد، بل هي في قلب مكان مقدّس مفتوح يسمّى "الحرم". فعلى الرغم من أنّ عددًا من الهياكل قد بُني حول الكعبة واقتحم إلى حدّ

بسيط جداً إلى درجة أنك لا تحتاج إلى جميع العناصر الإضافيّة التي قد تحتاجها في المسجد. إنّها طريقة أخرى للامتثال حقّاً لجوهر الإسلام، ونعني به التجرّد من البهرج، والابتعاد عن العالم الماديّ. فكما تعلم، يمكنك أن تحدّد أيّ منطقة تريد وتقرّر الصلاة فيها، وبمجرّد عقدك نيّة الصلاة تصبح تلك المنطقة مكاناً للعبادة. الأمر على غاية من البساطة. أتصوّر أنّ المسألة المهمّة حقّاً في هذه المسابقة وفي بينالي الفنون الإسلاميّة بصفة عامّة، هي طرح السؤال الآتي: ما هو الفنّ والهندسة المعماريّة الإسلاميّان المعاصران؟ وقد قام تفسيرنا على أنّ البساطة هي قيمة أساسيّة حقيقيّة، وأنّ وجودها في مكان مخصّص للعبادة يساهم في بعث الشعور بالمقدّس. بيد أنّ ذلك لا يمنعنا من أن نستخدم الموادّ المعاصرة. فإحدى الموادّ التي عاينّاها كانت عبارة عن شبكة من ألياف الكربون، تمّ نسجها بغية الإشارة إلى رداء الإحرام. ومن المعروف تاريخيّاً، أنّ العمارة الإسلاميّة كانت كثيرة الميل إلى الابتكار، والدلالة التي نستنتجها من ذلك أنّه لا ينبغي علينا أن نلتفت إلى الماضي فقط، بل يمكننا بالمثل أن نتطلّع إلى المستقبل، ونقوم بأعمال ملائمة لنا في عصرنا الحاليّ.

ف د: يُعدّ معيار الملاءمة جانباً مهمّاً جدّاً، لا يكترث الكثيرون به. ففي مقترحك حقّقتِ ملاءمة المساحة من خلال تثبيت غطاء تحت غطاء آخر (يرسم شكل قبّة بيديه). إنّه أمر فريد من نوعه تماماً أن يكون المرء قادراً على تخيّل مساحة محشورة داخل مساحة مقفلة أخرى. فكيف ترين هذه الطبقات؟

س د: رغم أنّنا نقف الآن تحت إحدى هذه المظلّات (نتوقّف لبرهة من الزمن وننظر إلى مظلّة محطّة الحجّ)، فإنّ الفتحة الموجودة في الخيمة تنشئ اتّصالاً بين المحطّة والسماء. لذلك، فلئن كانت المحطّة مغطّاة - ما يخلق نوعيّة جميلة من الضوء ويجعلها أكثر برودةً بفضل مناخها الموضعيّ الخاصّ بها - فإنّ الاتّصال بالسماء قائم بصفة دائمة. لقد أمكننا طرح هذا الأمر للنقاش، من خلال وضع مقترحنا تحت الكوّة الموجودة في الوسط.

ف د: بالعودة إلى المسألة التي أثرتها قبل قليل والمتعلّقة بالابتكار من ناحية الموادّ المستعملة ودور المهندس المعماريّ في مسار هذه الابتكارات؛ أشير إلى أنّ ثمّة وظائف معيّنة لا تتغيّر، أمّا قدرتنا على التفسير والابتكار وإنشاء هيكل ملائم لعصرنا الحاليّ، فهذا أمر مهمّ جدّاً.

س د: إنّنا في مرحلة مثيرة حقّاً في ما يتّصل بالموادّ. فكثير من الموادّ التي تشهد عمليّات تطوير، على ارتباط وثيق بخصائص المواقع المحليّة. وأتصوّر أنّ من المهمّ بالنسبة إلينا استخدامُ تلك الموادّ لالتقاط ذاكرة المكان. فالجانب المتعلّق بالموادّ يمكنه أن ينشئ فعلاً شعوراً بالانتماء، ويبرز تاريخ المكان وتراثه. تأمّل على سبيل المثال خشب النخيل الرقائقي الملصَق وعلاقته بجدّة.

ف د: تطرّقت قبل قليل إلى فكرة البساطة، وهذا ينطبق أيضاً على بساطة الموادّ والتقنيات. أنت تحيلين على نحو ما، إلى مفهوم "الظاهر والباطن"، إلى السطح الخارجيّ وتوظيف الموادّ في المجال الداخلي. وها أنت تشيرين الآن إلى خشب النخيل الذي يتّصف بأنّه بسيط من ناحية سطحه، لكنّه في الوقت نفسه ذو طبيعة مركّبة جدّاً في المستوى الموضعيّ الأصغر. فثمّة دائماً إذن حركة تنقّل بين البساطة والتعقيد.

س د: نعم، يمكننا أن نختبر كيف يعزّز الملموسُ التجربةَ غير الملموسة، وللقيام بذلك، يجب أن يكون الملموس مرتبطاً بالمكان، سواء أكان ذلك في الطريقة التي اعتُمدت في صنعه، أم في المادة الخام نفسها. بيد أنّ هذه التجربة غير الملموسة التي نحاول تحفيزها بعيدة المنال إلى حدّ ما.

ف د: قمتِ في مسيرتك المهنيّة، بتصميم عدد من المساجد الدائمة. والآن ها أنت تواجهين تحدّياً يتمثّل في تصميم فضاء مؤقّت للصلاة. فكيف تنقّلت بين هاتين المرحلتين؟

س د

إذا كنتَ تنتهج تطبيق البساطة بوصفها مبدأ توجيهيّاً عامّاً، فيمكن لمنهج المقاربة أن يكون متماهياً إلى حدّ بعيد في المرحلتين معاً، ذلك أنّ التجربتين الاثنتين تسعيان للعودة إلى جوهر الأشياء. ما لا ريب فيه أنّ أهدافهما مختلفة، لكنّ نهجهما مشترك.

ف د

أحد الملامح المميّزة للمهندسين المعماريّين أنّهم دائمًا ما يستخلصون الدروس، من مشروع إلى آخر. إنّهم يصنعون شيئاً ما، ولكنّهم لا يلبثون بعد ذلك أن ينظروا من جديد إلى ما صنعوا، ويفكّروا إن لم يكن بوسعهم أن ينجزوا شيئاً آخر مختلفًا. فهل عشت لحظة من هذا القبيل؟

س د: ما قلته يذكّرني بعمل جياكوميتي الذي رأيته ذات مرة في باريس. فلا ترى سوى أشكال متعدّدة، متعدّدة، طويلة ومتعدّدة (ترسم بيدها حركات عموديّة إشارةً إلى منحوتات جياكوميتي النحيلة). يبدو الأمر كما لو كان يبحث عن شيء ما، حسْبُه أن يحاول ويحاول ويحاول ويحاول. إنّ الهندسة المعماريّة، في رأيي، أمر مماثل لما قام به جياكوميتي. فهي لا تكفّ عن البحث عن هذه الجودة غير الملموسة. فأنت تتوصّل إليها، لكنّك في كل مرّة تعمل فيها تودّ لو يتاح لك أن تحسّن أكثر، وتتعمّق أكثر وتكتشف شيئاً آخر. حقّاً أن تكون مهندساً معمارياً فذلك يعني استكشافاً لا ينتهي البتّة. ذلك أنه دائماً ما يخامرنا الشعور بأنّ بوسعنا تحقيق المزيد، وأنّ ثمّة دائمًا شيئاً إضافيّاً لا بدّ من القيام به، وأنّ ثمّة دائمًا ما يستوجب مزيداً من التعمّق فيه، ولكن (تتوقّف برهةً وتميل بنظرها مفكّرةً)، إنّه أمر رائع ومُجز إلى أبعد حدّ. علاوةً على ذلك، فهو مهمّ بالنسبة إلى المنطقة، لأنّ ما نسعى إلى القيام به من خلال عملنا هو استعادة تراثنا. وأعتقد أنّ منطقتنا ظلّت لفترة طويلة تستورد الكثير والكثير، استوردنا الموادّ، واستوردنا الهندسة المعماريّة. وقد حان الوقت - وها إنّ النهضة قد انطلقت بالفعل- لنتوقّف ونقول: نريد أن نروي قصّتنا للعالَم (يومئ ف د موافقاً، ويكرّر قائلاً : قصّتنا)، بدلاً من الذهاب بعيداً خارج منطقتنا من أجل سماع قصّتنا. هكذا وبهذه الطريقة نفسها، نريد بعث هذا الشعور بالانتماء من خلال الهندسة المعماريّة. نريد بعث هذا الشعور بالارتباط مع تراثنا من أجل صياغته في لغة معاصرة. لا أقول إنّنا نريد العودة إلى الوراء سعياً إلى إعادة ابتعاث الماضي، ولكنّنا نريد حقّاً خلق شيء ملائم ومعاصر ومبتكر. لقد بدأ هذا يحدث فعلاً، ولكنّنا نودّ أن نرى المزيد في المنطقة.

ف د: أنت تثيرين مسألة مهمّة جداً في ما يتعلّق بالاستمراريّة. فبعضهم ينظرون إلى الاستمراريّة بوصفها تكراراً للماضي بدلاً من استلهام الماضي. للأسف، وكما قلتِ، قد يكون هذا ردّ فعل على التطوّر السريع

وقابليّته للتنقّل من مكان إلى آخر هو سجّادة الصلاة: فهي سطح في حجم الإنسان، قابل للطيّ ويُحمل في اليد، وهكذا يتسنّى للمرء بسطُها متى وجب عليه أداء الصلاة ومن ثَمّ يطويها ويخبّئها بعيداً. هذه البساطة في استخدام السجّادة يمكن جعلها أضعافاً مضاعفةً عندما يقوم أشخاص كثيرون ببسط سجّاداتهم الخاصّة بهم بعضها إلى جانب بعض لأداء صلاة جماعيّة، وبذلك يتحوّل أيُّ موضع يكونون فيه إلى مصلّى. وقد يستمرّ هذا التحوّل مدّةَ صلاة واحدة، كما قد يتواصل طيلة الوقت الذي تستغرقه صلواتٌ عديدة. فلا عجب إذن أن تتحوّل سجّادة الصلاة إلى لوحة مُنمنَمة تجسّم مسجداً مصغّراً، يتصدّر وسطَه محرابٌ مزخرَف أو مقوّس أو مفصّص، يحيط به شريطٌ من الأنماط الزخرفيّة الهندسيّة أو الزهريّة. وعلى هذا النحو، تستكنه سجّادةُ الصلاة دلالةَ الصلاة، إلى حدّ الإحاطة بجوهرها.

حوار: فاروخ درخشاني و سميّة الدبّاغ

فاروخ درخشاني: مرحباً سميّة، إنّه لمن الرائع أن أكون هنا معك. إنّ معرفتي بكِ وبعملك، وعلمي بأنّك أصيلة مدينة جدّة، حيث يقع هذا المشروع، جعلاني أمتلئ فضولاً لأطّلع على ما شعرتِ به عندما طُلب منك تقديم مقترح، وازددت شوقاً إلى ذلك عندما عرفتُ أنّ هذا المكان مخصّص لتبادل الآراء.

سميّة الدبّاغ: لقد تملّكني شعور قويّ بالافتخار عندما تمّت دعوتي. فكما تعلم، إنّ نشأة المرء هنا في مدينة جدّة تجعله يكتسب فهماً جوهريّاً لهذه المدينة. وقد اشتُهرت تاريخيّاً بحصنها وعبور الحجّاج منها؛ فكان الناس يتدفّقون عليها دوماً. لكنّ هذا الموقع (تتطلّع بنظرها إلى الأعلى، إلى مظلّة محطّة الحجّ، في حين أنّ راحة يدها اليسرى تتّجه نحو الأسفل، مفتوحةً وثابتةً) مميّز إلى أبعد حدّ. عندما قدمت لزيارة هذه المحطّة، استشعرت في نفسي الإحساس بالطاقة الكبيرة التي امتلأت بها نفوس آلاف الحجّاج الذين مرّوا من هنا. لقد أحسست أنّه من المهمّ حقّاً التقاط هذا الشعور بالفضاء، خاصّةً إذا تعلّق الأمر بمشروع مثل المُصلّى. لقد كانت رحلة ممتعة.

ف د: هذا هو لبّ التصوّر الذي بموجبه تُعتبر جدّة فضاءَ عبورٍ، فضاءَ عبورٍ نحو حالة ذهنيّة أخرى. إنّ فكرة وجود فضاء مؤقّت، مثل المصلّى، هي بطريقة ما، أمر مميّز جدّاً لهذا الموقع. فكيف يمكننا العودة إلى تصوّر مبنى يُهيّأ ليكون مؤقّتاً والحالُ أنّ المباني تُبنى عادةً لتكون دائمة؟

س د: ما قلتَه صحيح تماماً، فالصلاة هى حالة ذهنيّة. إنّها تحوّلك من حياتك اليوميّة إلى حالة بديلة، حالة عبادة، مكان تغمره السكينة لفترة قصيرة من الزمن، إلى أن تعود إلى حياتك اليوميّة. وكذلك الشأنُ بالنسبة إلى الحاج، فثمّة "الميقات" وهو الحدّ الفاصل الذي تعبره وتدخل في إحرامك (هو حالة ذهنيّة تُعقد خلالها نيّةُ الحجّ مقرونةً بارتداء ملابس الإحرام وفق ما تقرّه مناسك الحجّ، والاغتسال والتطهّر). إنّه لحظة التحوّل من حالة المشاغل الدنيويّة إلى حالة التعبّد والسكينة والتخلّي عن جميع المشاغل والاهتمامات المادّيّة. وهو فعل رمزيّ، إذ من خلال قيامك بالإحرام تخبر جميع الناس وتقول إنّني دخلت في هذه الحالة الذهنيّة وعقدت النيّة، وإنّني أستعدّ للحجّ، لا عمليّاً فحسب ولكن ذهنيّاً وروحيّاً أيضاً،

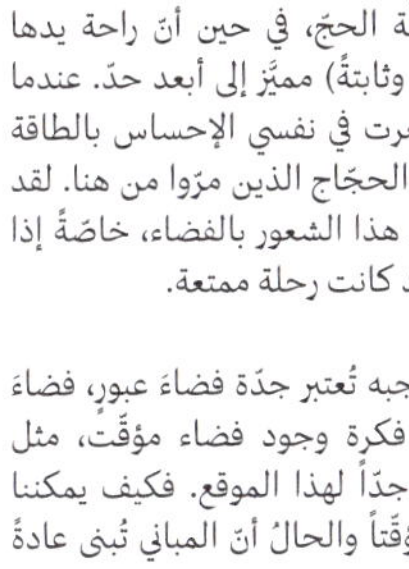

وهذا ما تعلنه لنفسك. ولذلك يستقرّ في أذهاننا انطباعٌ بوجود توافق بين فكرة الميقات، أي الإحرام بالملابس، وتصميم المُصلّى.

ف د: ما تقولينه عن الإحرام مهمّ جدّاً، لأنه هو الذي يجعل الناس متساوين بعضهم أمام بعض. وما عاينتُه في مشروعك كان بشكل ما، بمثابة عبور إلى حرم داخلي، كأنّ الأمر أشبه ما يكون بغطاء داخل غطاء (يشكّل يديه في حركة تشبه الشرنقة). فهل يمكنك التوسع قليلاً في عرض حضور مفهوم الميقات في الأفكار التي قام عليها مشروعك؟

س د: توجد في جدّة عدّةُ نقاط يجوز للحجّاج أن يبدؤوا فيها إحرامَهم. إنّها حدود حسيّة، وتذكير ملموس بهذا التحوّل. وهذا وجه من وجوه التناظر أردنا تسليط الضوء عليه في شكل المصلّى، من خلال تثبيت سلسلة من الدوائر المتّحدة المركز (تستخدم كلتا يديها مشيرةً بهذه الحركة إلى الدوائر التي تندغم بعضها في بعض). إنّه مخطّط كلّما تحرّكتَ فيه نحو المنتصف، وجدت نفسك تقترب من الفضاء المقدّس وتركت الوظائف الأخرى في الخارج. أضف إلى ذلك، أنّنا عندما أمعنّا النظر في إرث المشروع أو مصيره في قادم الأيّام، فكّرنا أنّه سيكون من المناسب حقّاً نقلُه إلى جدّة القديمة، حيث يقع الميناء القديم، وكان محطّة وصول أخرى للحجّاج، حين كان الناس يأتون عن طريق البحر.

ف د: لذلك كان اختيار شكل الدائرة وسيلة لوصف فضاء ملائم للعيش المشترَك، أينما كان. وفي سياق الحديث عن المؤقّت والسريع الزوال، أتذكّر أنّ المملكة العربيّة السعوديّة قد عرفت في ثمانينيّات القرن العشرين موجةً من عمليّات تطوير قطاع البناء والبنية التحتيّة. فكان بإمكانك العثور على هذه الإعلانات في مجلّات البناء التي كانت تقوم بالإشهار للحاويات وتبشّر بأنّها قادرة على أن تصبح مكاتب، وأماكن للنوم، وما إلى ذلك، وكانت تشتمل أيضًا على مكوّن هو بمثابة مكان مخصّص للصلاة، أي مصلّى. كانت بمثابة هيكل مدمج، كان يُستخدم حسب ما تمليه الحاجة، ثم يقومون بإزالته ويلقونه جانباً. مفهوم المؤقّت وسريع الزوال هذا عاد إلى الظهور في مقترحك أيضاً، من خلال فكرة المجموعة التي يمكنك أخذُها معك حيثما توجّهت. فهل يمكنك التوسّع في تحليل هذا المعطى؟

س د: إنّ وجود مصلّى في موضع مثل هذا وفي إطار تظاهرة مثل بينالي الفنون الإسلاميّة لمدّة أربعة أشهر، يجعل من المهمّ أن نمعن التفكير في خاصيّة سرعة الزوال التي تحدّد طبيعته. فالتعامل معه يقوم على استخدامه، وتعبئته في حاوية، ثم نقله إلى مكان آخر لإعادة تركيبه من جديد، بغيةَ اتّخاذه مصلّى في المستقبل، لخدمة تجمّعات أخرى في حالة تنقّل. فالإرث الذي بقي من هذا النوع من المصلّيات هو أنّها تنتقل من مكان إلى آخر.

ف د: لقد تطرّقتِ إلى مسألة مهمّة جداً. فيحقّ لنا القولُ إنّ فضاءات الصلاة في الإسلام تختلف عن نظيراتها في الأديان الأخرى، لأنّها فضاء للتجمّع، والتداول في شؤون الحياة المجتمعيّة. والناظر في مقترحك يتّضح له أنّك أخذت هذا العامل في الاعتبار، وأقصد أنّ المصلّى فضاء يمكن استخدامه للصلاة، ولكن يجوز خارج أوقات الصلاة، استخدامُه لأداء وظائف أخرى أيضاً، فهو فضاء متعدّد الوظائف.

س د: هذا ما مثّل عنصر تميّز في الملفّ: العمل على أن يكون للفضاء وظيفتان أو أكثر. وهذا يجلب بعداً آخر، يتعلّق بوضع تصميم لسيناريوات متعدّدة. ولكن مرّة أخرى تظهر ميزة أخرى خاصّة بالمصلّى، وهي أنّه

والزمانيّ الذي يمثّله الميقات - فهو بمثابة عتبة تمثّل بداية طقوس الإحرام والحجّ، إذ قدّم هذا المقترح إعادة تفسير معاصرة للخيام الخفيفة التي شوهدت قديماً عند بوّابات مكة المكرّمة. أمّا مكتب سهل الحياري للهندسة المعماريّة فقد تناول المشروع بطريقة معدنيّة، من خلال إدخال تشويش يطمس الحدود الفاصلة بين الأرض والفضاء والسماء. ونذكر أخيرًا، المقترح الفائز بالجائزة، «عن النسيج»، الذي أنجزه إستوديو إيست للعمارة الهندسيّة، وريان تابت وكريستوفر بلست من وكالة أكت II فقد عالج مسائل التصنيف المكانيّ للفناء، وتوظيف النسيج بوصفه حرفةً وبنيةً، وإعادة استخدام الموادّ المستعادة من المهملات. وبفضل اعتماد الفريق لهذه المقاربة، احتضن مشروعهم السجلات التاريخيّة والماديّة والمعاصرة التي تمّ من خلالها وضع تصوّر لتصميم المعرض.

وإلى جانب هذه القطع والرسومات، توجد سلسلة من الصور والوثائق الأرشيفيّة التي ترسّخ إنتاج الموادّ المعاصرة في قصّة المصلّى المتواصلة.

يُظهر هذا المنظر الطبيعيّ محطّة الحجّ بمزدلفة، الواقعة بين مُنى وعرفة. حقوق الصورة: السيّد عبد الغفّار، المكتبة البريطانيّة: الفنون البصريّة، 13/X463، مكتبة قطر الرقميّة

التطلّعات

من خلال الكشف عن أهمّية فضاءات المصلّى في عصرنا الحاليّ، يضع مشروع «عابرٌ متجذِّر» ثلاثة أفكار رئيسيّة مسبقة داخل هذا التخصّص، موضعَ المساءلة والتشكيك. فهو يتحدّى في المقام الأوّل منظور الديمومة الذي يُعتمد أساساً يقوم عليه تصميم جزء كبير من البيئة المبنيّة، وبدلاً من ذلك يقترح هذا الكتاب أفكاراً جذريّة تتّصل بالعمارة القابلة للتحويل. ثانياً، يسلّم الكتاب بأنّه ما يزال ثمّة وفرة من الممارسات المكانيّة والماديّة التي لم تُستكشف إلى حدّ الآن في تاريخ العمارة الإسلاميّة. ففي حين ركّز هذا التاريخ على الأماكن العامّة والأثريّة، فإنّ المصلّى يوجّه انتباهنا نحو جانبيْ الحميميّة والحياة اليوميّة في العمارة الإسلاميّة، ومن شأن ذلك أن يُثري معجم الباحثين والممارسين في المستقبل. وأخيرًا، دعّم هذا المشروع الأصوات الداعية إلى عصرنة العمارة الإسلاميّة . إنّ هذه الاستفزازات الثلاثة تشير إلى أنّ الممارسات العمليّة والمكانيّة البديلة المتجذّرة في الزوال يمكن أن تحوّل البيئات المبنيّة المعاصرة. ومن خلال تقصّي مختلف الطرق التي تظهر بها هذه الفضاءات وتؤدّي وظيفتها وتتحلّل، يدعونا مشروع «عابرٌ متجذِّر» إلى التفكير في طبيعة المصلّى القابلة للتكيّف والزمنيّة. ونرجو بإنجازنا لهذا العمل، أن نكون قد كشفنا عن البراعة والجمال الخفيّ الكامنين في هذه الفضاءات الانتقاليّة، واحتفينا بالممارسة الخالدة المتمثّلة في إنشاء التجمّعات المقدّسة حيثما وكلّما وجب القيام بذلك.

خاطرة: ناصر الرباط

المصلّى: الخاصيّة المكانيّة لمصطلح صوتيّ

المُصلّى (جمعه مصلّيات) مصطلح ذو تاريخ (معماريّ) طويل. وقد عبَرَ العديد من الأطر المفاهيميّة، بدءاً ممّا هو عفوي، وشخصيٌّ وحميميٌّ، وصولاً إلى ما هو ضخم ومَهيب. إضافةً إلى ذلك، فهو مصطلح يحاور مصطلحات عربيّة أخرى تدل على الأماكن المخصّصة للعبادة، مثل "مسجد" و"محراب" (دلّ هذا اللّفظ في أصل معناه على غرفة الصلاة، قبل أن يتحوّل إلى الدلالة على محراب الصلاة وهو نتوء في منتصف الجدار المواجه للقبلة يُستدلّ به على اتّجاهها) و"معبد". كلّ اسم من هذه الأسماء مشتقّ من فعل تعبّديّ مخصوص، ولكن لكلّ واحد منها في الوقت نفسه، امتداد في المجال الدلاليّ الخاصّ بالمصطلحات الأخرى. فمصطلح المصلّى، على سبيل المثال، يأتي من الجذر الثلاثيّ ص-ل-ى ، ويعني "الصلاة"، في حين أنّ اسم المسجد ينحدر من جذر س-ج-د، ومعناه على وجه التحديد "السجود"، وأما مصطلح "المعبد" فمشتقّ من جذر ع-ب-د ويدلُ على معنى العبادة. ومع ذلك، فإنّ مصطلح المسجد هو الذي أصبح التسمية الأساسيّة المعتمدة للدلالة على أماكن العبادة الإسلاميّة، ولعلّ السبب في ذلك عائد إلى أنّ هذه العبارة تشير إلى حركة تعبّديّة يختصّ بها الدين الإسلاميّ حصرياً، إذ إنّ الصلوات الرسميّة في الديانات الأخرى لا تشتمل في طقوسها على فعل السجود.

يجسّد مصطلح المصلّى في هذا التقسيم الدلالي البعدَ الصوتيَّ للصلاة، وهو يتراوح في الإسلام بين الصلاة الخافتة التي يُسِرّ بها المرء لنفسه، وقد وُصفت على نحو رائع بأنّها "تشكيل الكلمات في الفم دون صوت"، إلى الصلاة الجهريّة. وقد تُرجم هذا التسلسل من الأصوات تاريخيّاً إلى مساحات للصلاة متدرّجة في الحجم، بدءًا من المصلّى الشخصيّ الحميم والمؤقت، حيث تؤدّى الصلاة سرّاً في أغلب الأحيان، وصولاً إلى مصلّى العيد الكبير حيث تُتلى الصلاة جهراً أمام جمع غفير، وغالبًا ما يتمّ تضخيمُ صدى الصوت بواسطة تكرار التكبير للصلاة من قبل مردّدين يتوزّعون على مواضع مدروسة، فيتسنّى بذلك سماعُ تكبيرات الصلاة لجميع السكّان الذكور البالغين في بلدة أو مدينة مّا، عندما يجتمعون معاً لأداء أوّل صلاة في العيد. كانت هذه المصلّيات في الأيام الأولى من الإسلام، عبارة عن مساحات كبيرة مفتوحة في الهواء الطلق خارج المدينة، مع وضع علامة تشير إلى القبلة في اتّجاه مكة المكرّمة، أحياناً تتّخذ شكل محراب وأحياناً تكون مجرّد جدار لا سقف له. وقد انتشرت تلك المصلّيات في جميع المدن تقريباً، قبل أن تظهر المساجد الجماعيّة الضخمة الحجم، التي استحوذت على وظيفة المصلّيات في بعض الأحيان مما أدى إلى اختفائها. ومع ذلك ما تزال المصلّيات المفتوحة منتشرة في عدد من المناطق التي يتمسّك فيها الناس باتّباع السنّة النبويّة، الداعية إلى إقامة صلاة العيد في الهواء الطلق.إنّ المرونة المكانيّة، بل قل اللّدونة، التي يتّسم بها مصلّى العيد التاريخيّ تتجلّى في تصميمه المفتوح وبساطة علاماته البصريّة. هذا الفضاء المفتوح كان يحفل بحركة المصلّين مرّتين في السنة، إذ يتجمّع سكان المدينة من الذكور البالغين هناك في اليومين الأوّلين من عيد الفطر وعيد الأضحى. أما في سائر الأيّام، فيعامَل مصلّى العيد بوصفه مساحة عامّة مفتوحة على مدار العام، ويرى عدد كبير من الفقهاء أنّه لا وجود لأيّ قيود دينيّة تحدّد طبيعة استخدام هذا الفضاء خارج أيام العيد. إنّ هذه البراغماتيّة الوظيفيّة نابعة من المبدأ الدينيّ الأعلى المتمثّل في قاعدة تحقيق "المنفعة" (المنفعة العامّة)، وهو المبدأ الذي يقوم عليه النهجُ الإسلاميّ المشترَك في المناطق الحضريّة. ومع ذلك، قد يكون تعدّد أشكال استخدام مصلّى العيد أحد العوامل التي أدّت إلى زواله من أغلب المدن، حين حُكرت الضواحي وانتشر البنيان فيها بفعل توسّع المدن وارتفاع قيمة الأراضي في ظلّ ضغط التنمية والتوسع. أمّا المصلّيات الأصغر حجماً التي تشمل المصلّى الشخصيّ والفضاء الخاصّ بمجموعة صغيرة من المصلّين، فقد وُظّفت على نحو مختلف. ذلك أنّها تستجيب للتغيير من خلال قابليّتها للإزالة، سواء أُهيّئت لأداء صلاة واحدة، أم امتدّ استعمالُها فترةً من الزمن تشمل فترة توقّف مجموعة من المسافرين في مكان ما خلال ترحالهم. بيد أنّ سرعة زوال هذا النوع من المصلّيات لم يكن سمة اكتسبتها على مرّ الأيام. بل إنّه خاصيّة متأصّلة فيها، فمنذ بداية الإسلام كانت قابليّتها للإزالة عنصراً أساسيّاً في مكوّنات الفضاء الشخصيّ الذي يتّخذه المرء ليؤدّي الصلاة منفرداً، وكان يحكمها إيقاعُ الصلوات الخمس المفروضة على المسلم كلّ يوم، من الصباح إلى المساء. فكلّما حان وقت الصلاة، جاز للمسلم أن يحوّل أيَّ مكان -يصلح لأن يتلو فيه صلاته ويسجد على أرضيّته في اتّجاه الكعبة- إلى مصلّى شخصيّ، يُزال فور الفراغ من الصلاة ليستأنف وظيفته المعتادة. إنّ أفضل مثال يجسّد حركيّة المصلّى الشخصيّ

عبور جسر معان – وهو أحد الجسور الأربعة التي تمّ بناؤها خصّيصاً على طول الطريق لتجنّب السيول - وصولاً إلى تبوك في يوم افتتاح المحطّة.

عربة الصلاة في سكّة حديد الحجاز، 1907

ونظراً للسرعة التي صرنا نتنقّل بها اليومَ بين الأماكن المتنائية في البعد، فقد عرفت عربة الصلاة تحوّلاً هي نفسها، فأصبحت أكثر ديمومةً، إذ غدت تستقلّ بفضاءات خاصّة بها لا تُطمس وهي مغلقة، من قبيل الحجرات التي نراها في محطّات القطار، ومراكز التسوّق، وغيرها من المؤسّسات. ومن خلال الآثار الثلاثة التي عرّفتُ بها، يمكننا أن نلاحظ الروابط القائمة بين الخيوط التاريخيّة التي يحيلنا عليها المصلّى، وانتقاله إلى فضاء معاصر فريد، يتأثّر بالتحوّلات الاجتماعيّة والاقتصاديّة والتكنولوجيّة والماديّة.

على هذا النحو، فإنّ الإجابة على السؤال الذي طرحته على نفسي والمتعلّق بالمكان الذي يجب أن نتوجّه إليه للعثور على آثار قصّة المصلّى، هي في الحقيقة إجابة بسيطة نسبياً: فآثار المصلّى موجودة في كلّ مكان؛ فلم يكن مطلوباً منّي بكلّ بساطة إلاّ أن أتخلّى عن بعض أساليبي المكتسَبة، وأبحث عن تلك الآثار عبر الضباب. وهذه دعوة لك أيّها القارئ لتفعل الشيء نفسه.

التشابكات

لقد نُشر هذا الكتاب الموسوم بعنوان «عابرٌ متجذِّر»، كجزء من جائزة المصلّى في نسختها الأولى (2025)، وتنتظم هذه الجائزة نفسها في بينالي الفنون الإسلاميّة، وقد منحت لفريق مميّز متعدّد التخصّصات، يتكون من إيست للهندسة المعماريّة، وريان تابت، و أكت .II. وتزامن إصدار هذا الكتاب مع تنظيم معرض يحمل العنوان نفسه، في دير سان غريغوريو، بالتوازي مع بينالي البندقيّة للعمارة 2025.

فمن خلال الكتاب والمعرض، يسلّط مشروع «عابرٌ متجذِّر» الضوء على خاصيّة العبور المميِّزة لطبيعة فضاءات المصلّى، بوصفها مواقع مرنة صالحة للتجمّع والاجتماعات التي غالبا ما تتحوّل وتختفي بمرور الوقت. وكان هدفنا، من الاستعانة بهذين الوسيطين (الكتاب والمعرض)، هو استكشاف العلاقات المتشابكة عميق التشابك بين السجلّات الثلاثة التالية: الخيوط التاريخيّة، والسرديّات الماديّة، والتاريخ المعاصر.

لقد كان التصميم تعاونيّاً وانعكاسيّاً، ونادرا ما نجح تصميم دون هذين الشرطين. على هذا النحو، ارتأيت أنا وشريكي في التحرير نوّاف بن عيّاف، أن يكون هذا الكتاب في شكل مجموعة مركّبة من المحادثات، والتأمّلات، والسرود البصريّة التي تعمّق النظر في قصّة المصلّى.
وسعياً إلى جمع الأفكار المضمّنة هنا، تواصلنا مع الأشخاص الذين يمكنهم تقديم رؤىً متنوّعة وثاقبة في ما يتّصل بالمصلّى، وحفّزناهم في رفق ودون إلحاح، على سبر أغوار المصلّى انطلاقاً من خيوطه التاريخيّة، وسرديّاته الماديّة، وتاريخه المعاصر. فتساءل ناصر رباط في مقاله الافتتاحيّ عن الأصول المكانيّة لمصطلح المصلّى. بعد ذلك، استذكر خالد عزّام أداءه الصلاة ذات مرّة في العراء، وشرح كيف يمكن للمصلّى أن يرسّخ أقدامنا في الأرض ويحرّرنا في الوقت ذاته. أما حنيف كارا فناشدنا من جهته أن ننحني إلى الأمام ونستمع في عناية إلى التكنولوجيا عندما تهمس. ووصف وسام العسلي كيف تدعونا فضاءات المصلّى إلى أن نقلّب نظرنا متنقّلين بين الأرض والسماء. وسلّط زياد جمال الدين الضوء على إمكانات الممارسات العمليّة والمكانيّة، في إشارة إلى الأرشيف المعماريّ. وأخيراً، وصفت نورا السايح الخصائص الصوتيّة لأماكن الصلاة داخل المباني المعاصرة.

ولتبيين الطرائق التي اعتمدها كثير من المشاركين في تعاملهم مع المصلّى، جمعنا بين أحد أعضاء لجنة تحكيم جائزة المصلّى وأحد المصمّمين الذي نختاره مسبقاً (أو فريق من المصمّمين)، في محادثة عفويّة إلى حدّ مّا، تجري بينهما تحت مظلّات محطّة الحجّ التي وضع تصميمها فضل الرحمن خان. وقد عمدنا إلى تدوين هذه المحادثات، سعياً منّا إلى تقريب القارئ قدر الإمكان من التفاعلات الإنسانيّة التي عاشها المشاركون. وهكذا، ستجد أيّها القارئ الكريم في النصّ، لحظات رئيسيّة تدخّلنا خلالها لوصف الإيماءات وردود الفعل التي طرأت بشكل عابر أثناء المحادثات. وستلتقي في هذه الصفحات أزرا أكشامية وسهل الحياري وهما يناقشان ضبابيّة الرؤية بين المناظر الطبيعية والكيان والفضاء؛ وستقرأ المحادثة التي دارت بين لينا غطمة وآصف خان وتبادلا خلالها الأفكار حول العلاقة بين القصص الشخصيّة، والتراث وإنتاج الأعمال المعاصرة والراسخة في الأصالة أيضاً؛ وستطّلع على ما دار بين أنسطاس AAU وعلي ملكاوي وهما يتأمّلان فضاء المصلّى من خلال خفّة الحجر؛ وستنصت إلى فاروخ درخشاني وسميّة الدباغ اللّذين استكشفا مدينة جدّة بوصفها مكاناً اختصّ بالعتبات التي يمكن أن تنبثق منها الهندسة المعماريّة المعاصرة. ونذكر في خاتمة المطاف، الحوار الذي جرى بين نوّاف بن عيّاف وفريق إستوديو إيست للعمارة الهندسيّة، وريان تابت وكريستوفر بلست من وكالة أكت II للكشف عن الأفكار والعمليّات المركّبة التي سمحت لمشروعهم بأن يتشكّل ويأخذ صيغته النهائيّة، في إطار تعاونيّ متعدّد التخصّصات.

أما المعرض فيقدّم هذه السجلّات المتشابكة من خلال تجميع عدد من التدخّلات في شكل عيّنات صغيرة من الاقتراح الفائز، بالإضافة إلى نماذج لتصاميم معماريّة مصغّرة، وصور ورسومات، أخذناها من جميع فرق التصميم الخمسة المشاركة في المسابقة. ومن محاسن الصدف، أنّ جميع المقترحات وإن كانت قد تناولت مشروع المصلّى من زوايا مختلفة، مع التركيز على مرونة المصلّى، فإنّها قد أقامت في الوقت نفسه حواراً في ما بينها أيضاً. ففي حين تمحور اقتراح AAU أنسطاس على سبيل المثال، حول فكرة «إنشاء نسخ نمطيّة» عن طريق قطع الحجارة وتجميعها، فتنحصّل على عدد كبير من النسخ المتشابهة التي تتضافر بعضها مع بعض لإنشاء مجموع كلّيّ أكبر وأثقل وأكثر مساميةً، اشتغل إستوديو آصف خان على الطرف الآخر من الطيف التكتوني، فبسط خطّاً معمارياً خفيفاً، ممتدّاً إلى «ما لا نهاية له»، لإنشاء بناء طيفيّ للصلاة. وعلى الرغم من هذا الاختلاف، فإنّ كلا المشروعين يحيل إلى الطبيعة التأمليّة للتكرار.

هذا الانقسام بين المواقف العمليّة المتناقضة التي تتقاسم خيطاً مفاهيمياً مشترَكاً، نعثر عليه كذلك في مقترحيْ شركة الدبّاغ للهندسة المعماريّة، ومكتب سهل الحياري للهندسة المعماريّة. فكلاهما يمتلك حسّاً أثريّاً: سريع الزوال عند أوّلهما، أمّا الثاني فيعرض آثاراً مرئيّة على الأرض. فقد اعتمد مهندسو شركة الدبّاغ على فكرة الفضاء المكانيّ

↑ البحرين: المدافن، 1918، تصوير إدوين أوبري ستورز-فوكس. مصدر الصورة: [-15ب] (1/1)، المكتبة البريطانيّة: سجلّات مكتب الهند والأوراق الخاصة، صورة عدد 30/6/496، في مكتبة قطر الرقميّة.

↖ البحرين: المدافن، 1918، تصوير إدوين أوبري ستورز-فوكس. مصدر الصورة: [-16أ] (1/1)، المكتبة البريطانيّة: سجلّات مكتب الهند والأوراق الخاصة، صورة عدد 496/6/31، في مكتبة قطر الرقميّة.

لقد عثرت على الآثار الأولى في كتابِ صورٍ مجلّد، وهو عبارة عن مجموعة تتكوّن من ثمان وأربعين صورة فوتوغرافيّة بالأبيض والأسود، بتقنية الجيلاتين الفضيّ، التقطها القسّ إدوين أوبري ستورز- فوكس. فهذه المجموعة من الصور توثّق رحلاته في شبه الجزيرة العربيّة بين عاميْ 1916 و1918، ومن المرجّح أن تكون رحلته قد انطلقت من مدينة كراتشي. إنّ اللّوحة المزدوجة العرضيّة التي أشاركها هنا، والتي من المحتمل أنّها التُقطت في اليوم نفسه من شهر فبراير 1918، تجسّم منظراً يقع في تلال مدافن دلمون في البحرين، وهي تُعتبر الآن أحد مواقع التراث العالمي حسب تصنيف منظّمة الأمم المتّحدة للتربية والعلم والتثقافة، اليونسكو. ففي الصورة الأولى، الملتقَطة من نقطة مراقبة عالية نسبيّاً، قد تكون من أعلى أحد التلال، تظهر مساحة من تلال المدافن تمتدّ عبر الأفق. وعلى يسار الصورة، يظهر في منطقة مسطّحة بين التلال، ثلاثة رجال وثلاثة حمير (وإن كانت تدوينة ستورز-فوكس تشير إلى وجود حمارين فقط). ورغم أنّه من الصعب تبيّن محتوى المشهد بوضوح، نظرا لبعد المسافة التي التُقطت منها الصورة، فإنّ أحد الرجال يبدو وهو يرتدي ما يسمّى بالملابس الأوروبيّة.
أما في الصورة الثانية الملتقَطة من موقع آخر وفي اتجاه آخر، فنرى على مسافة أبعد شريطاً كثيفاً من بساتين النخيل، وربما كان الأمر متعلّقاً بمستوطنة بشريّة على يسار الصورة. فهنا تبدو التلال أقربَ بعضها إلى بعض، وهذا ما يسمح بإيجاد مجموعة من الفضاءات الحميميّة التي يمكن لرجلين وثلاثة حمير أن يقيموا فيها. ولا يظهر الرجل الذي يرتدي البدلة في أيّ موضع داخل المشهد العام، لكنّ ستورز-فوكس يخبرنا بأنّ «في المنتصف، يوجد رجل جاثٍ على ركبتيه، وربما كان بصدد أداء الصلاة[3]».

فإذا افترضنا أنّ ستورز فوكس كان دقيقاً في وصفه، فإنّه يكون قد وثّق أحد مظاهر المصلّى، ونعني بذلك وجود فضاء واسع وحميميّ في الوقت نفسه، يظهر فور الحاجة إليه، ولا يترك بعد إزالته أيّ دليل أثريّ داخل موقع أثريّ عريق.

→ «بائع السكاكر»
المصوّر: كريستيان سنوك هرخرونيه، المكتبة البريطانيّة: سجلّات مكتب الهند والأوراق الخاصّة، 1781.ب.55/6، في مكتبة قطر الرقميّة.

في بعض الأحيان كان عليّ أن ألتقط آثار المصلّى في القطع المرتبطة بالصلاة، كما لو أنّها تريد أن تذكّرنا بمعناها. فعلى سبيل المثال، يملك المستشرق الهولندي كريستيان سنوك هرخرونيه (1857-1936)، مجموعة كبيرة من الصور ذات اللّون البنيّ الداكن التي التقطها خلال إقامته لمدّة عام في جدّة ومكّة المكرّمة بين عاميْ 1884 و1885، وفي صورة تعليميّة له نرى صورة شخصيّة كاملة لبائع متجوّل في جدّة، وقد أُرفقت الصورة بتعليق توضيحيّ وردت فيه عبارة "Süssigkeitskrämer" ومعناها «بائع السكاكر». ففي هذه الصورة، نرى رجلاً يتّكئ على صينيّة مستطيلة، موضوعة على حامل أعدّ بواسطة تجميع عشوائيّ لما يبدو أنّه أغصان أشجار، مثلّثة الشكل ومربوطة بعضها إلى بعض بحبل، فنشأ عن ذلك هيكلٌ يُفترض بديهيّاً أنّه هيكل صلب. ويخبرنا سنوك هرخرونيه أنّه رأى في الصينيّة «العديد من العصيّ التي تعلوها أشكال تشبه الطيور وأشكال أخرى متعامدة مع الصينيّة. وتظهر على يسار الصينيّة كومة أخرى من سيقان أعرض من الأولى». ويبدو أنّ هذا التشابك من «السيقان الأعرض من الأولى» هو المسواك، وهذا ما ذكره هرخرونيه نفسه وإن لم يكن على يقين تامّ بأنّ الأمر يتعلّق بالمسواك. والمسواك هو فرع من شجرة الأراك وتسميتها العلميّة هي «سلفادورا بيرسيكا»، ويمكن أن نسمّيها شجرة فرشاة الأسنان، وهي شجرة دائمة الخضرة موطنُها شبه الجزيرة العربيّة وشبه القارة الهنديّة وإفريقيا، وتستعمل أعوادها لتنظيف الأسنان. واستخدام المسواك سنّة في الإسلام ، يقوم بها المرء عادةً أثناء الوضوء الذي يسبق أداء الصلاة. إنّ تفاصيل كثيرة في الصورة تجسّد جوهرَ فضاءِ المصلّى نفسه، وإن لم يكن للمصلّى حضور ماديّ فعليّ. فعلى مستوى الموادّ المستعملة، نرى أنّ الحامل نفسه الذي تمّ تجميعه بشكل مرتجل من موادّ استُعيدت من الطبيعة لأداء وظيفة معيّنة، يحاكي المظهر الخارجيّ للمصلّيات القائم على تجميع موادّ متنوّعة، يُضمّ بعضها إلى بعض. وأمّا على مستوى التصوّرات، فإنّ وجود المسواك لدى بائع متجوّل يثبت انتشار أماكن الصلاة في كلّ مكان، وسرعة زوالها في هذا المشهد الحضريّ. والتقطتُ خيوط الأثر الثالث من مقطع فيديو يعود إلى عام 1964، تظهر فيه عربة قطار تحوّلت إلى مكان للصلاة يقصده عمّال السكك الحديديّة في مدينة هيلمشتيت الألمانيّة[4]. ففي هذا الفيديو القصير، الذي لا تتجاوز مدّته 90 ثانية، نرى مجموعة تتكوّن من ستّة عمّال في السكك الحديديّة، يؤدّون الصلاة داخل عربة قطار أثناء فترة استراحتهم من العمل. ويظهرون في المقطع وقد تقاسموا سجّادة صلاة واحدة، واتّخذوا مكانهم خلف رجل يؤمّهم في الصلاة. إنّ هذه العربة المعدّة بصفة مرتجلة لتكون فضاء للصلاة، قد سبقتها في أداء هذه الوظيفة عربةُ قطار أخرى فريدةٌ من نوعها، ونعني بها: العربة التي خُصّصت لتكون مصلّى، في قطار واحد على الأقلّ من قطارات سكّة حديد الحجاز[5].

وكانت هذه السكّة مشروعاً عثمانيّاً بدأ إنشاؤه سنة 1900، وقامت بالربط بين دمشق والمدينة المنوّرة، إلى أن توقّفت عن العمل خلال الحرب العالميّة الأولى. وكان أحد أهدافها تيسير القيام برحلة الحجّ بين إسطنبول ومكّة خلال موسم الحجّ السنويّ. وقد وصف المؤرّخ ريتشارد توريت عربة الصلاة في هذا القطار على النحو الآتي:
«إنّ العربة رقم 13، عربة الصلاة الشهيرة التي أُنشئت خصّيصاً في ترسانة القسطنطينيّة وجُهّزت بمئذنة قابلة للفك بارتفاع 1.93 متراً (!)، تحتوي على فضاء كبير مفتوح تؤدّى فيه الصلاة، وعلى دورة مياه كذلك»[6]. ثمّة أمر آخر يبرّر جعل عربة المصلّى موضوعاً للنقاش في سياق دراستنا هذه، وهو غيابها. فنادراً ما تظهر عربة المصلّى في الصور التي التُقطت لقطارات الحجاز، عبر مختلف المناظر الطبيعيّة والعصور، بدءاً من الدخول في النفق الرابط بين عَمّان والقصير، إلى

[3] Rev. Edwin Aubrey Storrs-Fox, "Bahrein: The Tombs, 1916-1918," QDL, February 8, 2025. https://www.qdl.qa/en/archive/81055/vdc_100023814039.0x000026.

[4] AP Archive, "Can 99 Mobile Mosque," YouTube video, 1:30:00, https://www.youtube.com/watch?v=vwnN1EupM_o&ab_channel=APArchive

[5] يستخدم ريتشارد توريه مصطلح «عربة المسجد»، لكنّني اخترتُ عربة المصلّى الأنسب نظرا للتمييز الذي يهدف هذا الكتاب إلى إبرازه بين هذين النوعين من الفضاءات؛ للاطّلاع على وصف مفصل لعربة الصلاة والسياق الذي ظهرت فيه، انظر: David Simonowitz, "The Mobile Matrix: The Hijaz Railway as Ritual Space and Generator of Space" in Islamic Architecture on the Move: Motion and Modernity, ed. Christiane Gruber (Chicago, IL: Intellect, The University of Chicago Press, 2016): 61-100.

[6] Richard Tourret, Hedjaz Railway (Abingdon: Tourret Publishing, 1989), 55.

[7] "First Train to Medina," Kent Ve Demiryolu, accessed February 2, 2025, https://kentvedemiryolu.com/medineye-ilk-tren-mo-1908/

كما كُلفت اللجنة بالنظر في كيفية تبني المقترحات واستخدام التقنيات المتطورة أو تقنيات الحرف اليدوية لدعم أساليب البناء السريع. وكانت الاستدامة من بين العوامل المهمة واللازمة في التصميم، والتي يجري على أساسها تقييم المتسابقين من حيث قدرتهم على تهيئة المبنى ليكون له أثر إيجابي وقابلية إعادة استخدام المبنى بعد انتهاء المعرض. ومن هذا المنطلق، حرص المتسابقون على أن يكون المُصلّى بمثابة هدية للمجتمعات التي تحتاج إلى مسجد أو لتركيب متجول.

انعقدت لجنة التحكيم في يونيو 2024 في مبنى «وايت كولار فاكتوري»، الحائز على جوائز، في لندن لمقابلة المتنافسين المدرجين في القائمة القصيرة. وبعد عروض تقديمية قدمتها الفرق المشارِكة، ناقشت لجنة التحكيم جودة المقترحات الخمسة. وقام أعضاؤها بفحص ومناقشة كل من المزايا والمخاوف بمقارنتها مع معايير التقييم: إبراز الهوية المعمارية للمُصلّى، وإسهامه في الفن والعمارة الإسلامية، والدقة الفنية، والاستدامة والأثر.

وبعد مناقشة مفعمة بالحماس، ظهر إجماع حول مقترح استوديو إيست للهندسة المعمارية، بعنوان «عن النسيج». فقد قدم الاستوديو تصميماً تصويرياً نموذجياً لإعادة استخدام مستدامة لأشجار النخيل كمادة لصنع هيكل المُصلّى والكسوة النسيجية.

وافق أعضاء لجنة التحكيم بالإجماع على التوصية بمقترح استوديو إيست للهندسة المعمارية باعتباره الفائز بـ«جائزة المُصلّى» (2025)، مع منح التزكية لصاحب المركز الثاني، إستوديو آصف خان.

استهلال: فيصَل طبَارة

تذبذبات، وآثار، وتشابكات، وتطلّعات

التذبذبات

إنّ التفكير في المُصلّى[1] ، لاسيما من خلال منظور البيئة المبنيّة، هو رحلة ممتعة تشبه المتاهة. فهل نعتبر المصلّى فضاءً مادياً، أم كائناً، أم ظاهرةً؟ فإذا ما كانت الإجابة أنّه فضاء ماديّ، فهل ننظر إليه على أنّه فضاء منفرد مخصّص لشخص واحد، أم بوصفه فضاءً احتفالياً قادراً على أن يضمّ تجمّعاً لكثير من الأشخاص؟ وهل هو فضاء وصول واستقرار، أم فضاء انتقاليّ، أم هو منطلق للمغادرة؟ وأما إذا كانت الإجابة أنّ المصلّى كائن، فهل ندرسه بوصفه تجميعاً لعدد من الموادّ، أم ندرس التجمّعات المجتمعيّة التي يتيح القيام بها؟ ونبحث إن كان قد تمّ بناؤه، أم وقع تحويله، أم تصميمه؟ وإذا ما اعتبرنا المصلّى ظاهرةً، فهل نتتبّع ماضيه، أم ندرسه في حاضره، أم نتخيّل كيف تكون صورته في المستقبل؟ إنّ المصلّى يتأرجح بين هذه الحوافّ البعيدة بعضها عن بعض أقصى البعد، محافظاً بذلك على امتناعه عن أن يُحجز في مكان بعينه، فيُظهر لنا بذلك عوالم جديدة يمكن استكشافها، معلناً عن حضوره في الآثار الدقيقة التي يتركها في الأفراد الذين يشغلونه بوصفه فضاءً، وكائناً، وظاهرةً.

لقد ورد في الحديث الشريف أنّ النبيّ محمد (صلى الله عليه وسلم): قال «جُعلت لي الأرض مسجدًا وطهوراً. وأيُّما رجل من أمّتي أدركته الصلاة فلْيصلّ« (سنن النسائي 736). ففضاءات المصلّى تنبثق كلّما دعت الحاجة إلى إقامة الصلاة، سواء أكانت صلاة فرديّة أم جماعيّة. إنّ تكيّف محدّدات الفضاء في المصلّى مع محيطها الماديّ والزمنيّ الفوريّ، وإعادة تصميم المباني التي تتلاشى تلاشياً تامّاً بأتمّ معنى الكلمة، يدفع إلى إعادة النظر في الممارسات المكانيّة والماديّة الثابتة التي تُعتبر الأساس الذي تقوم عليه قواعد الهندسة المعماريّة. فقد أدّت هذه الممارسات ماضياً وحاضراً، إلى ظهور مجموعة واسعة من الأشياء والفضاءات، بدءاً من الخُمرة، وهي سجّادة منسوجة من سعف النخيل يضعها المسافر على الأرض حين يتوقف برهة من الزمن طلباً للراحة، إلى الظروف الحضريّة التي يُعاد استخدامها كفضاءات مؤقّتة يخصّصها عدد قليل من الأشخاص للصلاة ، وصولاً إلى المساحات المفتوحة في العراء والأكثر اتّساعاً، مثل تلك التي تُستخدَم خلال إقامة صلاة العيدين، فهي عادةً ما تكون على مشارف التجمّعات الحضريّة. ومهما تكن الطريقة التي يقع عليها اختيارنا لدى تناولنا موضوع المصلّى، فإنّه يسمح لنا كيفما تطرّقنا إليه، بتصوّر بيئات مبنيّة بشكل بديل، من خلال إعادة توجيهنا نحو الممارسات المكانيّة والماديّة الراسخة في الزوال.

الآثار

أين يمكن أن نكتشف آثار قصّة المصلّى، ليتسنّى لنا تصوّر العوالم المحتمَلة العديدة التي تريدنا أن نكتشفها؟ لقد تبيّن لي وأنا أواصل السير في طريقي المتاهة الضبابيّ، أنّ الأمر أكثر غموضاً والتباساً ممّا كنت أتوقع في البداية. فعندما بدأت في وضع تصوّر لهذا الكتاب، انكببت أنجز ما أقوم به عادةً كلّما تصدّيت لإنجاز مشروع متجذّر عميقَ التجذّر في التاريخ والثقافات الماديّة، وأعني بذلك: البحث في الأرشيف عن قرائن تدلّنا على طبيعة ذلك المشروع. وما كدت أبدأ في التفكير حتى انتبهت على الفور تقريباً إلى حقيقة أذهلتني: فكيف يمكنني العثور على سجلّ لشيء عابر في أصل طبعه؟ ولئن أدركت حدسيّاً أنّ فضاءات المصلّى هي فضاءات عابرة ومتغيّرة ومتحرّكة، فإنّ الأرشيف هو الذي أرشدني إلى الحضور اليوميّ للمصلّى في كل مكان. على هذا النحو، وجدت نفسي لا أبحث، أثناء محاولتي قراءة قصّته، عن كيانات أو فضاءات يمكن التعرّف عليها، بل وجّهت بحثي إلى تقصّي صور الحياة اليوميّة.

يذكّرني ذلك بكيفيّة سعي علماء الآثار إلى فهم الطريقة التي توسّلتها المجتمعات الرعويّة البدويّة في العصر البرونزيّ، لتتّخذ من مناظرها الطبيعيّة فضاءات للسكن والتفاعل. ونضرب مثالاً على ذلك، الفرق بين الآثار التي تشير إلى وجود بيوت شبه جوفيّة في الماضي من جهة، والآثار التي تكشف عن وجود هياكل مؤقّتة سريعة الزوال من جهة أخرى. ففي حين يتمّ التعرّف على الهياكل الأولى من خلال ما يُعثر عليه من بقايا أساساتها الحجريّة، تحدَّد الهياكل السريعه الزوال من خلال أصغر الآثار التي تتركها وراءها، من قبيل البقع البيضاويّة الشكل التي تنتشر في العشب ودلائل أخرى قليلة جدّاً لا تكاد تذكر، ولا يمكن إثبات وجود هذهع القرائن الثانية إلاّ عن طريق التحليل الكيميائيّ[2].

ومن خلال الربط بين الحضور اليوميّ للمصلّى - الذي ينشأ عن طريق الاستخدام أو التأصيل - وبين طابعه الزائل، يمكننا أن نتخيّل عوالم جديدة تتعارض مع قواعد الهندسة المعماريّة، سواء أكان ذلك على الصعيد النظريّ أو الصعيد العمليّ. بناءً عليه سأحاول قراءة هذه العوالم الجديدة المحتملة اعتماداً على ثلاثة آثار تمكّنت من استخلاصها في آخر المطاف.

[1] تعني عبارة المصلّى وجمعها مصلّيات المكان الذي تقام فيه الصلاة في الإسلام.

[2] Michael D. Frachetti, "Variability and Dynamic Landscapes of Mobile Pastoralism in Ethnography and Prehistory," in The Archaeology of Mobility: Old World and New World Nomadism, ed. Hans Barnard (Los Angeles: Cotsen Institute of Archaeology, 2008), 366–396; First found in Christiane Gruber, "Islamic Architecture on the Move," in Islamic Architecture on the Move: Motion and Modernity, ed. Christiane Gruber (Chicago, IL: Intellect, The University of Chicago Press, 2016): 1–24.

المياه والمصارف وخدمات السفر واستلام الأمتعة. وقع الاختيار على شركة الهندسة المعمارية «سكيدمور أوينغز آند مريل» (SOM) الأمريكية بقيادة غوردون بانشافت و فضل الرحمن خان، المهندس الرئيسي لدى الشركة، لتصميم هذا الصرح المعماري. كان التحدي فريداً بسبب خلو هذه الصالة من الزوار معظم أيام العام، وفي نفس الوقت كان من الضروري أن تستوعب الصالة عدداً هائلاً من الحجاج في ميقات الحج سنوياً وأن توفر لهم ما يحتاجون إليه من الخدمات على أكمل وجه. كان المقترح حلاً مبتكراً ورائداً، يتمثل بـ 210 وحدات سقف شبه مخروطية مصنوعة من الألياف الزجاجية ومطلية بالتفلون ويبلغ عرض الواحدة منها 45 متراً، وقد تم تصميمها لتشبه مجموعة من الخيام. وخلافاً للخيام التقليدية، جرى تعليق هذه الأسقف على ارتفاع 20 متراً عن سطح الأرض. أدرك المهندس خان الدور الفريد الذي تلعبه صالة المطار بصفتها بوابة إلى مكة المكرمة، وقد حرص على تصميمها بذكاء بارع، واضعاً في الاعتبار دورها المميز ومركزاً على توفير بيئة ترحيبية ترقى بالرحلة الروحانية للحجاج. امتاز التصميم بإعطاء الأولوية للمساحات التي توفر الاستظلال للحجاج والمساحات المجتمعية وفضلها على المساحات المغلقة والمكيفة اصطناعياً، مستلهماً هذا التصميم البارع من أشكال المأوى التقليدية العربية. وعام 1981، أُفتتحت صالة استقبال الحجاج التي تُعد جزءاً من مطار الملك عبدالعزيز الدولي الذي يغطي مساحة واسعة تبلغ 450 ألف متر مربع، ويُعد سقفه الأكبر من نوعه في العالم. وبعد مرور عامين، حاز هذا الصرح المعماري جائزة الآغا خان للتصاميم المعمارية، تقديراً لتصميم خان الأنيق الراقي. ولكن لسوء الحظ، رحل المهندس المعماري بعد فترة وجيزة من افتتاح صالة المطار، دون أن يشهد تقدير العالم لعمله الرائد.

من خلال مشروع لمشروع صالة الحجاج يطرح فضل الرحمن خان ممارسات فراغية ومادية تعكس روح جائزة المصلى، بالإضافة إلى الأبحاث والخواطر والحوارات التي جُمعت في هذا الكتاب. على الرغم من التعقيدات التقنية الكثيرة لمشروع صالة الحجاج، إلا أن حل خان تطور من مقاربة مفاهيمية بسيطة متجذرة بعمق في سياقها الثقافي. يُحوّل حل خان صالة الحجاج إلى نقطة وصول، والخطوة الأولى في الحج، تُمكّن من التحول الروحي الذين يحتمون تحت مظلاتها. كما أنها مكانٌ للصلاة، وسوق، وقاعة طعام جماعية، ومكان انتظار. إنها كل هذه الأشياء في آنٍ واحد، مُحوّلةً لتلبية احتياجات الأشخاص الذين تؤويهم. ومن أوجه التشابك الأخرى التي شوهدت طوال مسيرة خان المهنية بشكل عام، وفي صالة الحجاج بشكل خاص، التشابك المُعقد بين المعماري والمهندس والمكان. بتجسيد كل هذه التشابكات، تصبح صالة الحجاج نقطة انطلاق مثالية للتفكير في دور مساحات المصلى في واقعنا المعاصر.

ملاحظة تحريرية عن جائزة المُصلّى

تقام «جائزة المُصلّى» الدولية للمرة الأولى في سنة 2025، وهي تُقدَّم لتصميم مُصلّى ذي مساحة نموذجية للصلاة ولاستقبال جميع الزوار دون تمييز. تتضافر الأطروحات التصميمية للمُصلّى بين جوانب الإيمان والفن والعمارة، ويُقدَّم ضمن فعاليات النسخة الثانية من بينالي الفنون الإسلامية؛ وهو بينالي عالمي يحتفي بالفنون الإسلامية.

مستلهماً من موقع البينالي الفريد، أي صالة الحجاج في مطار الملك عبدالعزيز في جدة والتي صُممت من قِبل شركة «سكيدمور أوينغز آند مريل» وحازت جائزة الآغا خان للتصاميم المعمارية الإسلامية، تعكس وتمكِّن الجائزة القيمة التاريخية والثقافية للمبنى بمبادرة «أفكار وإبداعات معمارية» التي تجود بها مختلف ثقافات العالم العربي والإسلامي. وسيكون هذا المعلَم العريق هو الشاهد على لحظة إهداء «جائزة المُصلّى» للفريق الفائز.

فُوِّضت وكُلِّفت المؤسسة لإعداد قائمة طويلة تضم مواهب متنوعة من المهندسين المعماريين والمصممين الذين تلهمهم الصناعة اليدوية أو ممارسات التصنيع الرقمي أو يهتمون بها. كما سعت إلى استقطاب المهندسين المعماريين الذين يتمتعون بالحس الثقافي الذي يمكّنهم من الإسهام بمواهبهم وأفكارهم في تصميم نوع المُصلّى الذي تنشده المسابقة، وهو مبنى له غرضان؛ الأول هو أن يكون مساحة روحانية للتعبد وممارسة الشعائر والطقوس الدينية، والثاني هو أن يصبح مكاناً رحباً للتفاعل الثقافي والاجتماعي بعيداً عن العالم الافتراضي.

وعلى وجه الخصوص، حرصت المؤسسة على إرساء مبدأ التنوع والشمولية بين المشتركين، مما شجع مزيداً من استوديوهات التصميم الناشئة والقائمة بالفعل على الانضمام للمسابقة، وتجدر الإشارة هنا إلى أن ثلث قائمة الاستوديوهات المشاركة مقرها العالم العربي، و38% منها تديرها نساء أو بقيادة مشتركة مع النساء.

وأثمر ذلك إنشاء قائمة تضم أكثر من 100 استوديو من ست قارات، وُجهت إليها الدعوة للمشاركة في المسابقة. وقد أعرب 83 استوديو عن اهتمامها بالمشاركة، فيما قدَّم ستة وخمسون استوديو أخرى طلبات بالانضمام. حدد كل منها مقترحه للمشاركة فيما يجمع المعماري والفنان والمهندس تحت سقف واحد، ويقدِّم دراسات عن حالات ذات صلة بالمشروع، ويعرض مقالة فكرية مخصصة حول موضوع الفن والعمارة الإسلامية. وبعد مراجعة ومفاوضة ونقاش لهذه الطلبات الأولية، حدد رئيس لجنة التحكيم ومؤسسة بينالي الدرعية خمسة استوديوهات للتقدم إلى مرحلة التصميم.

حصلت الاستوديوهات الخمسة على ملخص مفصَّل من المؤسسة، والذي يلخص الرؤية الإستراتيجية ومتطلبات برنامج المؤسسة، كما أُتيحت لها الفرصة للقيام بجولة في جدة ومحطة استقبال الحجاج بالمطار في وقت مبكر من عملية التصميم التي استمرت تسعة أسابيع. تناول الملخص أربعة موضوعات، وهي: التداخل بين الفن والعمارة؛ والانفتاح على التعبير الثقافي والفني المتنوع؛ ودمج الحرف اليدوية التقليدية مع الصناعة والتعبير المعاصرين؛ وضمان استدامة المُصلّى على المدى الطويل بعد انتهاء معرض البينالي.

قامت اللجنة بتكليف المتسابقين بالاستعانة بتصميم مسجد تقليدي وإعادة تصميمه بعدسة معاصرة، وذلك لإنشاء تصميم تصوري مبتكر من الناحيتين الإنشائية والمعمارية، وذلك مع استخدام التقنيات المتطورة واستراتيجية البناء السريع.

حدد الملخص الفني للمسابقة مجموعة أولويات من ضمنها الاستدامة، وبالتالي تطبيقها على تصميم المُصلّى وأثره على البيئة في المستقبل. ركز الملخص أيضاً على المعايير المعاصرة للبناء مثل إعادة الاستخدام التحويلي لمواد البناء والوعي عن كثافة البصمة الكربونية المصاحبة لعمليات البناء. أُرفقَت مقترحات التصميم بإستراتيجية عمل ليجري استخدامها بعد انتهاء البينالي، سواء كان ذلك انتقالاً دائماً الى موقع آخر، أو معرضاً متجولاً أو استخداماً مختلفاً تماماً.

اختيار الفائز

نجحت لجنة تحكيم المسابقة في جمع نخبة من أبرز المصممين المحليين والعالميين، وهم: الأمير نواف بن عياف (رئيس لجنة التحكيم)، وأزرا أكشاميا، وفاروخ درخشاني، ولينا غطمة، وعلي ملكاوي. وكان دور اللجنة اختيار فريق نموذجي متعدد التخصصات لتصميم المُصلّى - مبنى معماري يدمج الجانب الإيماني مع جوانب الفن والعمارة لإتاحة مساحة روحانية مشتركة تتجسد فيها روح الوحدة والعبادة.

مقدمة: معالي الأستاذ راكان الطوق

مساعد وزير الثقافة ونائب رئيس مجلس أمناء مؤسسة بينالي الدرعية

يكمن جمال فن العمارة في الجمع بين إبداع تصميم المباني العمرانية وما يحمله ويشير إليه من المعاني الإنسانية الكامنة في تفاصيله. فمنذ فجر الحضارة الإسلامية، امتدّت روائع العمارة من أرض الجزيرة إلى آفاق الأندلس، مستلهمةً من تعاليم الإسلام وقِيَمه الإيمانية. تلك المساحات لم تكن مجرّد أبنية، بل آفاقاً رحبةً تتشكّل منها المجتمعات، تفتح باب التأمل وتربط الماضي بالحاضر، والتراث بالمعاصرة، والحس بالمعنى. وتأتي صالة الحجاج الغربية، التي تحتضن بينالي الفنون الإسلامية بتنظيم مؤسسة بينالي الدرعية، شاهداً على هذا التناغم البديع بين الشكل والمضمون؛ لتصوغ فضاءً للإبداع يرتقي بالأذواق ويُروي شَغَفنا بالجمال.

وبوصفها بوابةً إلى أطهر بقاع الأرض ومهد الإسلام، مكة المكرمة، تستمدّ هذه المساحة المصمَّمة بعنايةٍ من مركزيّة الموقع ورمزيّته لتمنح الحجّاج والزوّار موضعاً للتجمّع والصلاة والتفكّر في المعاني الإيمانية السامية. وفي هذا التفاعل المتناغم بين الإنسان والبنيان، وبين الحس والمعنى، يتّضح سرّ اختيار صالة الحجّاج لتكون حاضنةً نموذجيّة لبينالي الفنون الإسلامية.

وتحقيقاً لهذه الرؤية؛ أطلقنا "جائزة المُصلَّى المعمارية"؛ لتكون دعوةً للفنانين والمعماريين لإعادة تشكيل فضاء الصلاة، حيث تستلهم هذه المسابقة من مَعين القِيَم الإسلامية، وترنو نحو الابتكار والإبداع، مُجسّدةً رسالة بينالي الفنون الإسلامية وأهدافه السامية؛ المتمثّلة في الاحتفاء بالفنون الإسلامية بأكثر أشكاله شمولاً وتنوّعاً، وتهيئة فضاءات تفتح آفاقاً وفرصاً جديدة للابتكار والإبداع.

إنّ للعمارة قدرةً على صياغة تفاعلاتنا، وتشكيل ملامح مجتمعاتنا، فهي تمنحنا فضاءً نعبِّر فيه عن ذواتنا ونتواصل من خلاله مع الآخر. ومن يزور صالة الحجّاج تأمل تلك المظلات التي تحتضن الأفق بلا نهاية لا يملك إلا أن يشعر بطمأنينةٍ وسلام يغمران شعوره؛ بما تحمله أرجاء المكان من معاني ارتباطه بالبقاع المقدّسة. وإنني لآمل أن تمضي جائزة المُصلَّى قُدُماً في استكشاف آفاق جديدة، لتُعيد صياغة توظيفنا للأمكنة في استلهام مظاهر الجمال واستنزال السكينة والرحمة من السماء.

ويطيب لي أن أهنّئ الفائزين في المسابقة بدورتها الأولى: استوديو إيست للهندسة المعمارية، وريان تابت، وشركة إيه كيه تي II الهندسية. كما أتوجّه بخالص الشكر والامتنان لأعضاء لجنة التحكيم الموقَّرة: فاروخ درخشاني، ولينا غطمة، وأزرا أكشاميا، وعلي ملكاوي، برئاسة الأمير نواف بن عياف، على تفانيهم وجهودهم القيِّمة.

وختاماً، آمل أن تستمتع بالقراءة عن الجائزة الفريدة، ونتطلّع إلى نسختنا القادمة التي ستصدر في عام 2027

مقدمة: آية البكري

الرئيس التنفيذي لمؤسسة بينالي الدرعية

يهدف بينالي الفنون الإسلامية منذ تأسيسه إلى إبراز جماليات حضارتنا الإسلامية، بما تزخر به من روائع الفنون الإسلامية بأشكالها ووسائلها المختلفة، ومزجها بثقافتنا الأصيلة وقِيَمنا الإيمانية. وكان الحرص على توفير فضاءٍ يجتمع فيه الزوّار للصلاة والتأمُّل في المعاني الإيمانية السامية ركيزةً أساسيةً في رؤيتنا، كما هو الشأن في عرض البينالي للأعمال الفنية المعاصرة والتحف التاريخية في أقسامه المختلفة.

في هذه النسخة الثانية من البينالي، وبقيادة معالي الأستاذ راكان الطوق، نائب رئيس مجلس أمناء مؤسسة بينالي الدرعية ومساعد وزير الثقافة في المملكة العربية السعودية، أطلقنا مسابقة معمارية دولية بعنوان "جائزة المُصلَّى"؛ لتصبح جزءاً دائماً من برامج البينالي. تهدف هذه الجائزة إلى إبراز العمارة كركنٍ أصيلٍ من الفنون الإسلامية، وشكلٍ حيٍّ من أشكال التعبير الثقافي الذي نسعى إلى الاحتفاء به وتعزيزه.
وقد دعونا الاستوديوهات المعمارية المتنافسة في هذه الجائزة إلى التعاون مع المهندسين والفنانين؛ لتطوير مساحة عملية للصلاة تمتاز بجاذبية تصميمية فريدة، نظراً لما يحمله موقع المُصلَّى من أهمية خاصة ضمن سياق البينالي وتصميمه.

ونظراً لطبيعة بينالي الفنون الإسلامية الذي يجمع ما بين الحِرَف التقليدية وأشكال التعبير الفني المعاصرة؛ وجب أن يراعي تصميم المُصلَّى الدمج بين هذه الحِرَف وأساليب التصنيع الحديثة، مع إضافة لمسة من الابتكار في الإنتاج لتشييد جناح مستدام وقابل لإعادة الاستخدام.

يسرُّني أن أعبِّر عن جزيل الشكر لرئيس لجنة التحكيم الأمير نواف بن عيّاف، وأعضائها: أزرا أكشاميا، والبروفيسور علي ملكاوي، وفاروخ درخشاني، ولينا غطمة؛ على جهودهم الثمينة وتفانيهم في العمل.
فاز بجائزة المُصلَّى لعام 2025 استوديو إيست للهندسة المعمارية، بالتعاون مع الفنان ريّان تابت وشركة إيه كيه تي II الهندسية، من خلال تصميمٍ حاز على إعجاب لجنة التحكيم؛ بتميُّزه في اعتماده على مواد طبيعية محلّية لإبداع مكوِّنات تتناغم مع مساحة عصرية، تجمع بين جمال العمران وروحانية المكان، وتحاكي المساحات التي أُنشئت لأول مرة منذ قرون من موارد طبيعية مماثلة.
يقدّم هذا الكتاب الذي شارك في تحريره نواف بن عيّاف وفيصل طبّارة، فكرة عن الحوارات، والمفاهيم، والرؤى التي ساهمت في إعداد الطبعة الأولى لهذه الجائزة. فآمل أن يخلب هذا الكتاب خيالك، ويحفِّزك على القدوم شخصيّاً ورؤية المبنى الفائز في مدينة جدّة.

ملاحظة تحريرية عن صالة الحجاج

﴿وَأَذِّن فِي النَّاسِ بِالْحَجِّ يَأْتُوكَ رِجَالًا وَعَلَىٰ كُلِّ ضَامِرٍ يَأْتِينَ مِن كُلِّ فَجٍّ عَمِيقٍ﴾– سورة الحج: الآية 27

تجاوز عدد الحجاج والمعتمرين الذين سافروا عبر مطار الملك عبد العزيز الدولي لأداء العمرة أو فريضة الحج أكثر من 12 مليون زائر عام 2022. وأثناء انتظار الحجاج لوصول حافلاتهم، أثارت الأسقف المائلة للمبنى الشبيهة بالخيام إعجاب الكثيرين منهم، إذ تذكرهم بخيام مِنَى. ولكن قلة منهم كانوا على دراية بالقصة الملهمة وراء بناء هذا الصرح المعماري الفريد من نوعه.
بحلول عام 1970، استمر عدد الحجاج الوافدين إلى المملكة العربية السعودية في الازدياد بشكل كبير، مما دفع الحكومة إلى البحث عن سبل لاستيعاب مئات الآلاف من الحجاج الوافدين جوّاً كل عام وتوفير وسائل نقل مريحة لهم، إذ خص الله سبحانه وتعالى فريضة الحج بزمان معين ومكان محدد. ونظراً لتدفق عدد هائل من الحجاج في هذا الوقت المحدد من العام، فقد فرض ذلك تحديات لوجستية فريدة.
كان صاحب السمو الأمير سلطان بن عبد العزيز آل سعود، وزير الدفاع والطيران آنذاك، قد وكَّل بتطوير صالة المطار وتزويدها بكل ما يلزم من المرافق ووسائل الراحة لخدمة الحجاج. أسندت مهمة الإشراف على هذا المشروع إلى الجنرال سعيد أمين، مدير مشروع المطارات الدولية. وقد كان من الضروري أن يمتاز التصميم بقدرة فائقة على حماية الحجاج من قسوة المناخ والحرارة الصحراوية والرطوبة العالية، وأن يوفر الخدمات الأساسية مثل الطعام ودورات

مؤسّسة بينالي الدرعيّة 2025

عابرٌ متجذِّر

يصدر هذا الكتاب بمناسبة معرض «*عابرٌ متجذِّر*» الذي ينظّم في دير سان غريغوريو، وهو فعاليّة تقام بالتوازي مع الدورة التاسعة عشرة من بينالي البندقيّة الدولي للعمارة، الموسوم بعنوان «ذكاء. طبيعي. اصطناعي. جماعي.» ، وذلك من 7 مايو إلى 26 نوفمبر.2025

التحرير: نوّاف بن عيّاف وفيصَل طبّارة

مساعد باحث: عمر درويش
تدقيق ومراجعة اللّغة الإنجليزيّة: زينة عسّاف
الترجمة العربية: د. محمد آيت ميهوب
تدقيق اللّغة العربية: محمد حمدان
طباعة فصل الألوان الأربعة: نديم زبليط، -سكوب أتلير

التصميم: باي تو
الناشر: كاف للنشر

التوزيع في أوروبا:

ليه بيرس دي رييل (Les Presses du Réel)
35 شارع كولسون
21000 ديجون
فرنسا
www.lespressesdureel.com

إيديا بوكس (Idea Books)
نيو هيمويغ R 6
BG 1013 أمستردام
هولندا
www.ideabooks.nl

التوزيع في الشرق الأوسط:

سيبال لتوزيع الكتب (CIEL)
التقاطع الثالث، منطقة القوز الصناعيّة 1
ص.ب 282005
دبي، الإمارات العربيّة المتحدة
www.ciel.me

شركة متاجر المتاحف/ الهال
طريق الأمير تركي بن عبد العزيز الأول،
المحمديّة، ساحة الباب، الطابق الأول
الرياض، المملكة العربيّة السعوديّة

التوزيع في أمريكا وآسيا
وأستراليا:

آرت بوك/ D.A.P., 75 برود ستريت
جناح 630
نيويورك، نيويورك 10004
www.artbook.com

طبع هذا الكتاب في مطبعة إيديتوريال بورتولازي-ستاي، فيرونا، إيطاليا.

الإيداع القانوني: ISBN: 978-614-8035-75-3

جائزة المصلّى 2025

عابرٌ متجذّر

المحرران نوّاف بن عيّاف وفيصَل طبّارة